2nd Clinical Natural Language Processing Workshop (ClinicalNLP 2019)

Minneapolis, Minnesota, USA
7 June 2019

ISBN: 978-1-5108-8773-2

NAACL HLT 2019

The 2nd Clinical Natural Language Processing Workshop

Proceedings of the Workshop

June 7, 2019
Minneapolis, Minnesota, USA

Sponsored by:

PHILIPS

Preface

This volume contains papers from the 2nd Workshop on Clinical Natural Language Processing (ClinicalNLP), held at NAACL 2019.

Clinical text offers unique challenges that differentiate it not only from open-domain data, but from other types of text in the biomedical domain as well. Notably, clinical text contains a significant number of abbreviations, medical terms, and other clinical jargon. Clinical narratives are characterized by non-standard document structures that are often critical to overall understanding. Narrative provider notes are designed to communicate with other experts while at the same time serving as a legal record. Finally, clinical notes contain sensitive patient-specific information that raise privacy and security concerns that present special challenges for natural language systems. This workshop focuses on the work that develops methods to address the above challenges, with the goal to advance state-of-the-art in clinical NLP.

This year, we received the total of 28 submissions, out of which 10 were accepted as oral presentations and 10 as posters.

Organizers:

Anna Rumshisky, UMass Lowell
Kirk Roberts, University of Texas Health Science Center at Houston
Steven Bethard, University of Arizona
Tristan Naumann, Microsoft Research

Program Committee:

Sabine Bergler, Concordia University
Parminder Bhatia, Amazon
Vivek Datla, Philips Research North America
Dina Demner-Fushman, National Library of Medicine
Dmitriy Dligach, Loyola University
Jungwei Fan, Mayo Clinic
Sadid Hasan, Philips North America
Lynette Hirschman, The MITRE Corporation
Yoshinobu Kano, Shizuoka University
Kathy Lee, Philips Research North America
Stephane Meystre, University of Utah School of Medicine
Timothy Miller, Boston Children's Hospital
Martha Palmer, UC Boulder
Hoifung Poon, Microsoft Research
Ashequl Qadir, Philips Research North America
Chaitanya Shivade, IBM
Weiyi Sun, Nuance
Sumithra Velupillai, KTH Royal Institute of Technology
Karin Verspoor, The University of Melbourne
Byron Wallace, Northeastern University
Ben Wellner, The MITRE Corporation
Jenna Wiens, University of Michigan
Stephen Wu, University of Texas Health Science Center at Houston

Invited Speaker:

Heng Ji, University of Illinois at Urbana-Champaign

Invited Panelists:

Hongfang Liu, Mayo Clinic
Piet de Groen, University of Minnesota
Elmer Bernstam, University of Texas Health Science Center at Houston

Table of Contents

Conference Program

Friday, June 7, 2019

09:00–09:15 *Opening remarks*

09:15–10:30 *Invited speaker: Heng Ji*

10:30–11:20 *Coffee break*

11:20–12:30 Oral session 1

11:20–11:40 *Effective Feature Representation for Clinical Text Concept Extraction*
Yifeng Tao, Bruno Godefroy, Guillaume Genthial and Christopher Potts

11:40–11:55 *An Analysis of Attention over Clinical Notes for Predictive Tasks*
Sarthak Jain, Ramin Mohammadi and Byron C. Wallace

11:55–12:10 *Extracting Adverse Drug Event Information with Minimal Engineering*
Timothy Miller, Alon Geva and Dmitriy Dligach

12:10–12:25 *Hierarchical Nested Named Entity Recognition*
Zita Marinho, Afonso Mendes, Sebastião Miranda and David Nogueira

12:30–14:00 *Lunch*

14:00–15:30 *Oral session 2*

14:00–14:20 *Towards Automatic Generation of Shareable Synthetic Clinical Notes Using Neural Language Models*
Oren Melamud and Chaitanya Shivade

14:20–14:40 *A Novel System for Extractive Clinical Note Summarization using EHR Data*
Jennifer Liang and Ching-Huei Tsou

14:40–14:55   *Study of lexical aspect in the French medical language. Development of a lexical resource*
Agathe Pierson and Cédrick Fairon

14:55–15:10   *A BERT-based Universal Model for Both Within- and Cross-sentence Clinical Temporal Relation Extraction*
Chen Lin, Timothy Miller, Dmitriy Dligach, Steven Bethard and Guergana Savova

15:10–15:25   *Publicly Available Clinical BERT Embeddings*
Emily Alsentzer, John Murphy, William Boag, Wei-Hung Weng, Di Jindi, Tristan Naumann and Matthew McDermott

15:30–16:00   *Coffee break*

16:00–16:45   ***Poster session***

A General-Purpose Annotation Model for Knowledge Discovery: Case Study in Spanish Clinical Text
Alejandro Piad-Morffis, Yoan Guitérrez, Suilan Estevez-Velarde and Rafael Muñoz

Predicting ICU transfers using text messages between nurses and doctors
Faiza Khan Khattak, Chloe Pou-Prom, Robert Wu and Frank Rudzicz

Medical Entity Linking using Triplet Network
Ishani Mondal, Sukannya Purkayastha, Sudeshna Sarkar, Pawan Goyal, Jitesh Pillai, Amitava Bhattacharyya and Mahanandeeshwar Gattu

Annotating and Characterizing Clinical Sentences with Explicit Why-QA Cues
Jungwei Fan

Extracting Factual Min/Max Age Information from Clinical Trial Studies
Yufang Hou, Debasis Ganguly, Lea Deleris and Francesca Bonin

Distinguishing Clinical Sentiment: The Importance of Domain Adaptation in Psychiatric Patient Health Records
Eben Holderness, Philip Cawkwell, Kirsten Bolton, James Pustejovsky and Mei-Hua Hall

Medical Word Embeddings for Spanish: Development and Evaluation
Felipe Soares, Marta Villegas, Aitor Gonzalez-Agirre, Martin Krallinger and Jordi Armengol-Estapé

Attention Neural Model for Temporal Relation Extraction
Sijia Liu, Liwei Wang, Vipin Chaudhary and Hongfang Liu

Automatically Generating Psychiatric Case Notes From Digital Transcripts of Doctor-Patient Conversations
Nazmul Kazi and Indika Kahanda

Clinical Data Classification using Conditional Random Fields and Neural Parsing for Morphologically Rich Languages
Razieh Ehsani, Tyko Niemi, Gaurav Khullar and Tiina Leivo

16:45–17:30   *Panel discussion: NLP vs. structured data in the clinical domain (with panelists: Hongfang Liu, Piet de Groen, Elmer Bernstam)*

17:30–17:45   *Closing remarks*

Effective Feature Representation for Clinical Text Concept Extraction

Yifeng Tao
Roam Analytics
Carnegie Mellon University

Bruno Godefroy
Roam Analytics

Guillaume Genthial
Roam Analytics

Christopher Potts
Roam Analytics
Stanford University

Abstract

Crucial information about the practice of healthcare is recorded only in free-form text, which creates an enormous opportunity for high-impact NLP. However, annotated healthcare datasets tend to be small and expensive to obtain, which raises the question of how to make maximally efficient uses of the available data. To this end, we develop an LSTM-CRF model for combining unsupervised word representations and hand-built feature representations derived from publicly available healthcare ontologies. We show that this combined model yields superior performance on five datasets of diverse kinds of healthcare text (clinical, social, scientific, commercial). Each involves the labeling of complex, multi-word spans that pick out different healthcare concepts. We also introduce a new labeled dataset for identifying the treatment relations between drugs and diseases.

1 Introduction

The healthcare system generates enormous quantities of data, but its tools for analytics and decision-making rely overwhelmingly on a narrow subset of structured fields, especially billing codes for procedures, diagnoses, and tests. The textual fields in medical records are generally under-utilized or completely ignored. However, these clinical texts are our only consistent source of information on a wide variety of crucial factors – hypotheses considered and rejected, treatment rationales, obstacles to care, brand recognition, descriptions of uncertainty, social and lifestyle factors, and so forth. Such information is essential to gaining an accu-

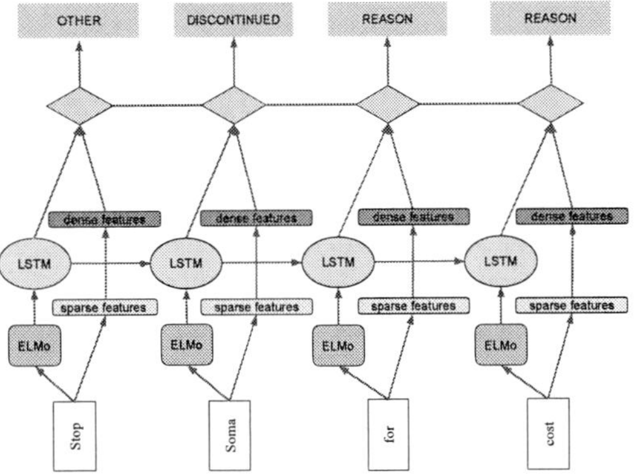

Figure 1: Model diagram. In our full model, words are represented by pretrained ELMo embeddings, which feed into LSTM cells, and by sparse ontology-derived feature representations, which are fed to a dense layer with dropout to produce a lower-dimensional representation that is concatenated with the hidden states of the LSTM. The resulting mixed feature representation is fed into a CRF layer that forms the basis for token-level label predictions. We assess this full model against variants without the LSTM or hand-built features to motivate the full version.

rate picture of the healthcare system and the experiences of individual patients, creating an enormous opportunity for high-impact NLP.

However, annotated clinical text datasets are scarce and tend to be small, for two reasons. First, data access is usually highly limited because of privacy considerations; the inherent richness of language data means that de-identification is hard or impossible (Uzuner et al., 2007). Second, because healthcare concepts are complex, the needed annotations generally must be provided by domain

1

Proceedings of the 2nd Clinical Natural Language Processing Workshop, pages 1–14
Minneapolis, Minnesota, June 7, 2019. ©2019 Association for Computational Linguistics

specialists who are trained both in the practice of healthcare and in the interpretation of healthcare records. Such experts are in high demand, and the annotation work they do is intellectually challenging, so the annotated datasets they produce are, by any measure, very expensive. The result is that even the largest annotated clinical text datasets are small by comparison with those from other areas of NLP, and this has profound consequences for the kinds of models that are viable in this space.

In this paper, we define a hybrid LSTM-CRF model that is effective for real-world clinical text datasets. The architecture is sketched in figure 1. Its crucial property is that it synthesizes two kinds of feature representation: dense representations that can be trained on any large text corpus (not necessarily using clinical text) and sparse, high-dimensional feature representations based on hand-built feature functions. Hand-built feature functions are especially powerful in healthcare because they can leverage the numerous high-quality medical lexicons and ontologies that are publicly available. As a result, such features can achieve impressive coverage with relatively little additional effort.

We show that this combined model yields superior performance on five datasets of diverse kinds of healthcare text: two clinical, one social media, one scientific, and one commercial/regulatory (official drug labels). Each task involves the labeling of complex, multi-word spans that pick out diverse healthcare concepts: the Chemical–Disease Relation dataset (CDR; Wei et al. 2015); the Penn Adverse Drug Reaction Twitter dataset (ADR; Nikfarjam et al. 2015); a new disease diagnosis dataset; a new prescription reasons dataset that involves identifying complex REASON spans for drug–prescription actions; and a new dataset of 10K drug–disease treatment descriptions, which we release with this paper.

2   Models

Our full model is depicted schematically in figure 1. Its modular structure defines a number of variations that allow us to quantify the value of including dense and sparse feature representations obtained from diverse sources.

Individual words are represented in two ways in the full model: with dense, pretrained vectors and with sparse, high-dimensional feature representations derived from hand-built feature func-

tions. If the dense representations are removed, the LSTM cells are also removed, resulting in a standard CRF (Lafferty et al., 2001; Sutton and McCallum, 2011). If the sparse representations are removed, the result is a standard LSTM-based RNN (Hochreiter and Schmidhuber, 1997).

We explore two ways of initializing the dense representations: random initialization according to the method of Glorot and Bengio (2010) and the ELMo embeddings released by Peters et al. (2018). The ELMo embeddings were trained on the 1 billion word benchmark of Chelba et al. (2013) – general newswire text not specialized to the healthcare space. What is special about ELMo embeddings, as compared to more standard word representation learning, is that they are obtained from the parameters of a full language model, so that each word's representation varies by, and is sensitive to, its linguistic context; see also McCann et al. 2017; Radford et al. 2018.

The nature of the hand-built feature representations varies by task, so we leave most of the details to section 3. All the models featurize each word in part using the word and part-of-speech tag of the current word and the preceding and following four words. They also include features that seek to characterize the nature of the semantic environment: markers of negation, uncertainty, hedging, and other core task-specific contextual cues. Finally, the feature functions make extensive use of drug and disease lexicons to identify the types of words. The drug lexicons are RxNorm, the National Drug Code (NDC), FDA Drug Labels, FDA Orange Book, and the OpenFDA fields found in a number of public FDA datasets (e.g., Drug Adverse Events). The disease lexicons are derived from historical ICD-9 and ICD-10 code sets, SNOMED-CT (Spackman et al., 1997), the Disease Ontology (Schriml et al., 2011; Kibbe et al., 2014), and the Wikidata graph (Vrandečić and Krötzsch, 2014). The wealth and diversity of these sources is typical of healthcare and highlights the potential for taking advantage of such resources to help overcome the challenges of small datasets. Table A1 shows an example of hand-built features.

In the full model, we include a dense layer that transforms the sparse feature representations, and we apply dropout (Hinton et al., 2012) to this layer. These transformed representations are concatenated with the hidden states of the LSTM to produce the full representations for each word.

Dataset	Example
Diagnosis Detection	Asymptomatic/POSITIVE bacteriuria/POSITIVE , could be neurogenic/CONCERN bladder/CONCERN disorder/CONCERN .
Prescription Reasons	I will go ahead and place him on Clarinex/PRESCRIBED for/REASON his/REASON seasonal/REASON allergic/REASON rhinitis/REASON .
Penn Adverse Drug Reactions (ADR)	#TwoThingsThatDontMixWell venlafaxine and alcohol- you'll cry/ADR and throw/ADR chairs/ADR at your mom's BBQ.
Chemical–Disease Relations (CDR)	Ocular/DISEASE and/DISEASE auditory/DISEASE toxicity/DISEASE in hemodialyzed patients receiving desferrioxamine/DRUG .
Drug–Disease Relations	Indicated for the management of active/TREATS rheumatoid/TREATS arthritis/TREATS and should not be used for rheumatoid/CONTRA arthritis/CONTRA in/CONTRA pregnant/CONTRA women/CONTRA .

Table 1: Short illustrative examples from each of our five datasets, with some modifications for reasons of space. CDR examples are typically much longer, encompassing an entire scientific title and abstract. Section 3 more fully explicates the labels. All unlabeled tokens are labeled with OTHER.

Where the hand-built representations are left out, the word representations are simply the hidden states of the RNN; where the dense representations are left out, the word representations are simply the sparse representations, resulting in a standard linear-chain CRF.

There is a natural variant of the model depicted in figure 1 in which the CRF layer is replaced by a softmax layer. In our experiments, this was always strictly worse than the CRF layer. Another variant feeds the compressed hand-built features together with ELMo embeddings into the LSTM. This too led to inferior or comparable performance. Finally, we evaluated a version that used a bidirectional LSTM, but found that it did not yield improvements. Therefore, we do not include those experimental results, to simplify the discussion.

3 Experiments

We report experiments on five different datasets: two from transcribed clinical narratives, one from social media, one from scientific publications, and one from official FDA Drug Labels texts. For each, the task is to label spans of text that identify particular healthcare concepts. We are particularly interested in the capacity of our models to identify multi-word expressions in a way that is sensitive to the semantics of the environment – for example, to distinguish between a drug prescribed and a drug discontinued, or to distinguish disease mentions as diagnoses, diagnostic concerns, or ruled-out diagnoses. Table 1 gives a short illustrative example from each dataset. Table A2 gives detailed statistics for each dataset.

Three of the datasets are already partitioned into training and test sets. For these, we tune the hyperparameters using 5-fold cross-validation on the training set, train the model with tuned hyperparameters on the training set, and then evaluate the performance of the trained model on the test set.

The other two datasets do not have predefined splits. For these, we divide them equally into five parts. For each fold, the hyperparameters are tuned on the training data (also using 5-fold cross-validation), and the best model is then applied to the test data for the evaluation. These experiments are repeated three times to smooth out variation deriving from the random initialization of the model parameters, though we use the hyperparameters selected for each fold in the first run in the subsequent two experiments to save computational resources.

We use the Adam optimizer (Kingma and Ba, 2014), with $\beta_1 = 0.9$ and $\beta_2 = 0.999$, the training batch size set to 16, and the dropout rate set to 0.5 for all the experiments. The step size η and the coefficients of the ℓ_1 and ℓ_2 regularizers c_1 and c_2 are tuned. The step size is first tuned by setting both $c_1 = c_2 = 0$, and then c_1 and c_2 are tuned using random search (Bergstra and Bengio, 2012) for ten settings. Table A3 provides additional details on our hyperparameters and evaluation protocol.

The source code for our experiments and models is available.[1]

3.1 Diagnosis Detection

Our Diagnosis Detection dataset is drawn from a larger collection clinical narratives – de-identified transcriptions of the reports healthcare professionals record about their interactions with patients. The corpus was provided to us by a healthcare start-up. We sampled and labeled 6,042 sentences for information about disease diagnoses. The labels are POSITIVE DIAGNOSIS, CONCERN, RULED-OUT, and OTHER. The labeling was done by a team of domain experts. The challenging aspects of this task are capturing the complex, multiword disease names and distinguishing the semantic sense of those mentions (as summarized by our label set) based on their sentential context.

For the hand-built parts of our representations, we extend the basic feature set described in section 2 with cue words that help identify whether a description is about a patient's history or current condition, as well as cue words for causal language, measurements, and dates. The power these features bring to the model, beyond what is captured in the ELMo-LSTM representations, is evident in table 2, column 1.

3.2 Prescription Reasons

Our Prescription Reasons dataset is drawn from the same corpus of clinical narratives as our Disease Diagnosis dataset and was annotated by the same team of domain experts. This dataset contains 5,179 sentences, with labels PRESCRIBED, DISCONTINUED, REASON, and OTHER. For the first two labels, the majority are unigrams naming drugs. Of special interest is the REASON category, which captures long, highly diverse reasons for actions taken concerning prescription drugs. (The relations are captured with additional edge annotations connecting spans, but we do not model them in this paper.) This information about the rationale for prescription decisions is the sort of thing that appears only in text, and it has clear value when it comes to understanding these decisions, making this an especially interesting task.

Our hand-built feature representations are similar to those used for Diagnosis Detection, but they additionally contain features based in large drug lexicons, as discussed in section 2, as well as features based on cue-words for different prescription actions: switching, discontinuing, increasing, decreasing, and so forth. The results in table 2, column 2, clearly favor the combined model that uses both these features and the ELMo-LSTM.

3.3 Penn Adverse Drug Reactions (ADR)

The Penn Adverse Drug Reactions (ADR; Nikfarjam et al. 2015) dataset is an annotated collection of tweets giving informal adverse reactions to prescription drugs. It's thus a different kind of clinical text than in our two previous experiments – public self-reports by patients, rather than private technical descriptions by healthcare professionals.

The original dataset contained 1,340 labeled tweets for training and 444 for testing. However, due to restrictions on redistributing Twitter data, the project team was unable to release the tweets, but rather only a script for downloading them. Due to tweet deletions, we were able to download only 749 train examples and 272 test examples. This limits our ability to compare against prior work on this dataset, but the small size further tests our hypothesis that our combined model can get traction with relatively few examples.

For our hand-built feature functions, we follow the protocol specified in the ADRMine CRF package released by Nikfarjam et al. (2015). Key components include tokenization (Gimpel et al., 2011), spelling correction (Cutting, 1999; Atkinson, 2018), lemmatization, and featurization (Loper and Bird, 2002). Thus our combined model is a strict extension of this publicly available package (setting aside differences related to implementation and optimization). We follow Nikfarjam et al. (2015) in using Inside/Outside/Beginning (IOB; Ramshaw and Marcus 1995) tags.

Our test-set results, given in table 2, column 3, show the power of our combined model. For context, the best results reported by Nikfarjam et al. are 72.1, for a CRF that includes hand-built features as well as features based on the cluster indices of distributional word representations. That is, their model draws on similar insights to our own. Though we only have half of the training samples, our unified model is still able to get traction on this dataset.

3.4 Chemical–Disease Relations (CDR)

The Biocreative V Chemical Disease Relation dataset of Wei et al. (2015) captures relationships

---

	Diagnosis Detection	Prescription Reasons	Penn Adverse Drug Reactions (ADR)	Chemical–Disease Relations (CDR)	Drug–Disease Relations
rand-LSTM-CRF	77.3 ± 0.05	69.6 ± 0.25	53.8 ± 0.88	85.1 ± 0.10	48.2 ± 1.12
HB-CRF	82.0 ± 0.05	78.5 ± 0.01	58.8 ± 0.12	86.2 ± 0.02	42.3 ± 0.30
ELMo-LSTM-CRF	83.9 ± 0.35	81.0 ± 0.20	65.7 ± 0.35	88.2 ± 0.34	50.6 ± 0.64
ELMo-LSTM-CRF-HB	$\mathbf{85.3 \pm 0.24}$***	$\mathbf{82.0 \pm 0.03}$***	$\mathbf{68.5 \pm 1.67}$*	$\mathbf{89.9 \pm 0.12}$***	$\mathbf{51.9 \pm 0.52}$**

Table 2: Per-token macro-F1 scores. For ADR, the F1 scores are for chunks via approximate matching (Nikfarjam et al., 2015; Tsai et al., 2006). 'rand-LSTM' is an LSTM with randomly initialized word vectors. 'ELMo-LSTM' is an LSTM initialized with pretrained ELMo embeddings. 'HB' signals sparse, high-dimensional feature representations based on hand-built feature functions. The mean values and standard deviations are calculated using F1 scores of three runs of repeated experiments, as discussed in section 3. Statistical significance notation for the last two rows (two top-performing models) is *: $p < 0.05$; **: $p < 0.01$; ***: $p < 0.001$.

between chemicals and diseases in the titles and abstracts for scientific publications. It contains 1,000 training texts and 500 test texts. Its labels are CHEMICAL, DISEASE, and OTHER. This dataset is not only from a different domain than our others, but it also involves much longer texts.

Our hand-built feature function is exactly the one used for the Prescription Reasons experiments. We report results for the standard test set. The power of the combined model is again evident in the results in table 2, column 4.

3.5 Drug–Disease Relations

Our final experiments are on a new annotated dataset that we will be releasing along with this paper.[2] The underlying corpus is FDA Drug Labels, which contains all the official labels for all drugs licensed for sale in the U.S. These labels include a wide range of information, including active ingredients, warnings, and approved usages. Our annotation project focused on capturing the relationship between these drugs and mentioned diseases. The resulting labels are TREATS, PREVENTS, UNRELATED and CONTRAINDICATED-FOR. Figure A1 describes the corpus-building process in more detail.

Since FDA Drug Labels is a public dataset, we used this as an opportunity to see whether we could obtain good labels via crowdsourcing. This effort proceeded in two phases. In the first, annotators identified disease spans, working from an annotation manual that provided guidance on how to delimit such phrases and lexical resources to help them identify diseases. In the second phase, annotators assigned the span labels from our label set, again using an annotation manual we created to

guide their choices.

We launched our task on Figure Eight with 10,000 sentences. It was completed within a few days. The job was done by 1,771 people from 72 countries, the majority from Venezuela. No special qualifications were imposed. To infer a label for each example, we applied Expectation Maximization (EM), essentially as in Dawid and Skene (1979). The inter-annotator agreement between these labels and those we inferred via EM is 0.83 for both tasks. For assessment, a team of experts independently labeled 500 examples from the same pool of sentences, using the same criteria and annotation manuals as the crowdworkers. The inter-annotator agreement between the labels inferred from the crowd and those from the experts is 0.82, suggesting that the inferred labels are good.

We expect the crowdsourced labels to be used only for training. Our test set consists entirely of non-train examples with labels assigned by experts. This allows us to train on noisy labels, to check for robustness, while still assessing on truly gold labels. Our results for this experiment are given in table 2, column 5, and point to the superiority of our combined model.

4 Discussion

Our discussion seeks to show that the combined model, which shows superior performance in all tasks (table 2), is making meaningful use of both kinds of features (hand-built and ELMo) and both of the major model components (LSTM and CRF).

4.1 The Role of Text Length

We expect the LSTM to handle short texts very effectively, but that its performance will be degraded for long ones. In contrast, the CRF might fall short of the LSTM on short texts, but it should be more

---

[2]`https://github.com/roamanalytics/roamresearch/tree/master/BlogPosts/Features_for_healthcare`

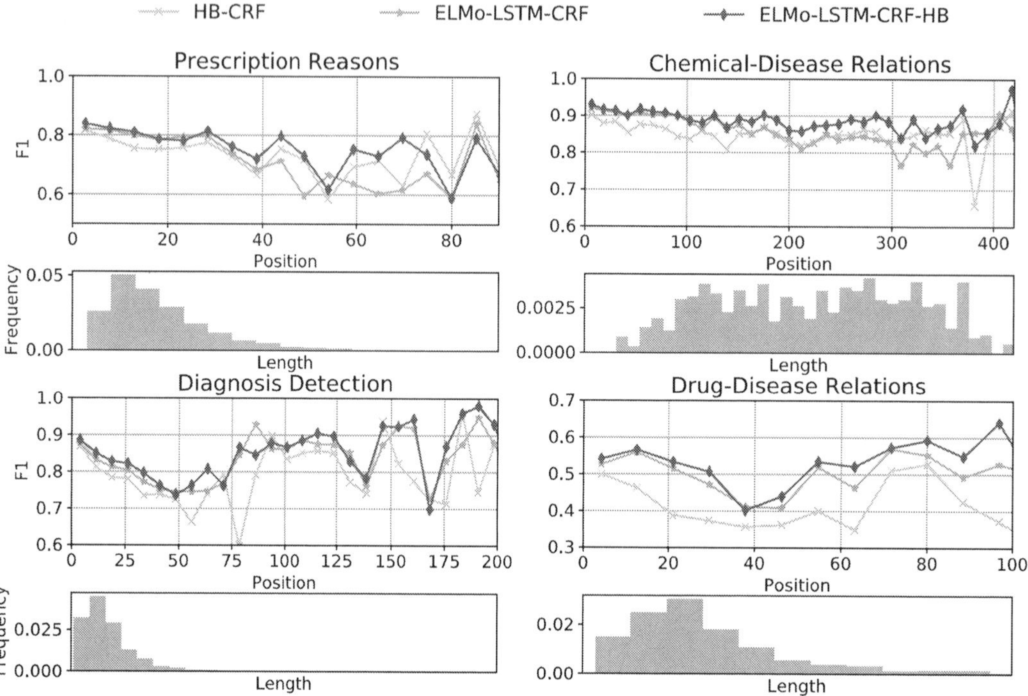

Figure 2: Text-length experiments. Along with the distribution of text lengths, per-token macro-F1 scores of words that fall into specific bins in the sentences are shown. For the top two datasets, the ELMo-LSTM-CRF is better at earlier positions, while the HB-CRF is better at later ones. For the bottom two datasets, the ELMo-LSTM-CRF is always better than the HB-CRF. In all these cases, the combined model takes advantage of both models and always outperforms the base models. ADR dataset results are given in figure A2 due to space limitations.

robust on long ones. We thus hypothesize that the combined model will learn to take advantage of these comparative strengths.

We find strong support for this hypothesis in our data. Figure 2 illustrates this. These plots track the macro-F1 scores (y-axes) of tokens in specific linear positions (x-axes). There are two major trends.

First, in the Prescription Reasons and CDR datasets (top two panels), we see that the HB-CRF starts to outperform the ELMo-LSTM-CRF after about word 40 in Prescription Reasons (which contains many long texts that list patient history; section 3.3) and after about word 160 in CDR (which has paragraph-length texts; section 3.4).

Second, in the Diagnosis Detection and Drug–Disease Relations datasets (bottom two panels in figure 2), the ELMo-LSTM-CRF model outperforms the HB-CRF at all positions. However, there is still evidence that our full model is leveraging the strengths of both of its major components, as it outperforms both in all positions.

In summary, the performance curve of the combined model is roughly an upper envelope of the two base-model curves. The combined model is able to achieve better performance for both short and long texts, and for words in any position, by utilizing features from both base models.

4.2 Analysis of the CRF Potential Scores

The potential scores (also referred to as "unary scores" or "emissions" in some work) of the CRF provide another method for model introspection. These scores are the direct inputs to the final CRF layer, where the token-level label predictions are determined. When the potential score for a specific label is high, the CRF assigns a high weight to that label under the contraints of adjacent labels. Thus, by checking the potential scores for the feature dimensions deriving from each of our base models, we can gain insights into the relative importance of these models and how the combined model leverages features from both.

The potential scores of each word in the test set are shown in figure 3, where the left panels show the LSTM features and the right panels show the CRF (hand-built) features. Due to the general effectiveness of the ELMo-LSTM, we always have higher average potential scores from those features. This is reflected in the mean scores at left and in the comparatively large amount of white (high scores) in the panels. However, the hand-built features always make substantial contributions, especially in Diagnosis Detection, Prescription Reasons, and CDR. We note also that, where the performance of the two base models is very similar (table 2), the potential scores in the combined model are also more similar.

4.3 Major Improvements in Minor Categories

One of our central motivations for this work is that clinical datasets tend to be small due to the challenges of getting quality labels on quality data. These size limitations impact model performance, and the hardest hit categories tend to be the smallest ones. Unfortunately, these are often the most important categories, identifying rare but significant events. We are thus especially interested in whether our combined model can address this problem.

Table 3 suggests that the combined model does make progress here, in that the largest gains, across all relevant datasets, tend to be for the smallest categories. This is very dramatically true for the Drug–Disease Relations dataset, where only the combined model is able to get any traction on the smallest categories; it achieves 103.5% and 71.3% improvements in F1 score over the HB-CRF model for the two smallest categories. It seems clear that, in transferring compact embedding representations learned from other large text datasets, the combined model can elevate performance on small categories to an acceptable level.

5 Prior Work

5.1 Clinical Text Labeling

Apache cTAKEs (Savova et al., 2010) extracts information from clinical text. Its labeling module implements a dictionary look-up of concepts in the UMLS database, and the concept is then mapped into different semantic types (labels). Similar extractions play a role in our hand-built features, but only as signals that our models learn to weight against each other to make decisions.

ADRMine (Nikfarjam et al., 2015) is closer to our own approach; it focuses on extracting adverse drug reaction mentions from noisy tweets. It combines hand-built features and word embedding cluster features for label prediction. However, our model is more powerful in the sense that we directly utilize the word embeddings and feed them into the LSTM.

Habibi et al. (2017) use a combined LSTM-CRF to achieve better NER results on 33 biomedical datasets than both available NER tools and entity-agnostic CRF methods, though they do not incorporate hand-built features.

There are also competitions related to labeling tasks in the context of clinical text. The i2b2 Challenge (Sun et al., 2013) includes event detection as one of the task tracks, which is basically a labeling task. The best results on this task came from a team using a simple CRF. The Biocreative V Chemical–Disease relation (CDR) competition (Wei et al., 2015) released a widely used dataset for researchers to evaluate their NER tools for biomedical text, and Verga et al. (2018) report state-of-the-art results for a self-attention encoder, using a dataset that extends CDR.

5.2 Efficient Annotation

Obtaining accurate annotations is expensive and time consuming in many domains, and a rich line of research seeks to ease this annotation burden. Ratner et al. (2016) and Hancock et al. (2018) propose to synthesize noisy labeling functions to infer gold training labels, and thus make better use of annotators' time, by allowing them to focus on writing high-level feature functions (and perhaps label individual examples only for evaluation). These efforts are potentially complementary to our own, and our experiments on our new Drug–Disease dataset (section 3.5) suggest that our combined model is especially robust to learning from noisy labels compared with base models.

5.3 Related Models

A large body of work explores combined LSTM and CRF models for text labeling. Huang et al. (2015) use an LSTM-CRF for sequence tagging, and Ma and Hovy (2016) propose a bi-directional LSTM-CNNs-CRF for the same task. In addition to word embeddings, Lample et al. (2016) utilize character embedding information as the input to a LSTM-CRF. Jagannatha and Yu (2016) integrate pairwise potentials into the LSTM-CRF model, which improves sequence-labeling performance in clinical text. Wang et al. (2018) and Crichton et al. (2017) use multi-task learning based on the ba-

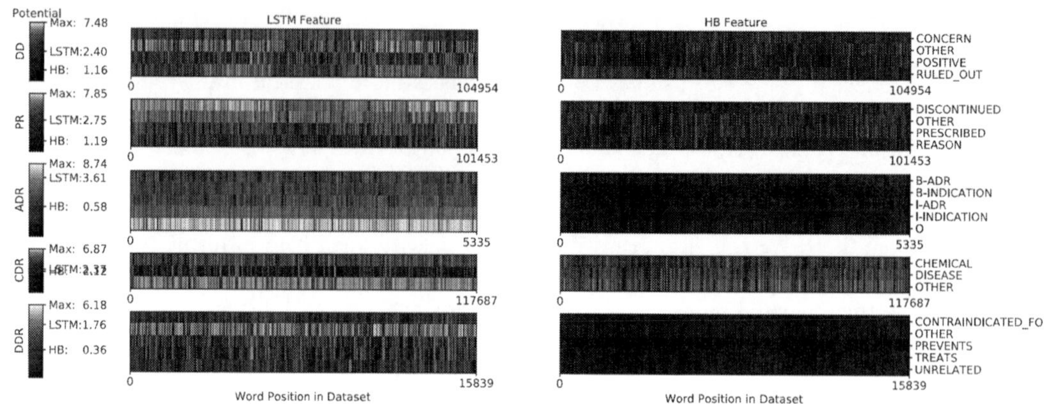

Figure 3: Potential score experiments. Potential scores from the ELMo-LSTM and HB modules of all five datasets are shown. Mean potential scores of both features are calibrated in the left colorbar. Higher potential scores (lighter cells) indicate greater importance for the feature. In all five datasets, the combined model pays more attention to the ELMo-LSTM features, but the hand-built features always contribute. Comparing with the results in table 2, we note that when the performance of two base models is comparable, their potential scores in the combined model are also closer.

		Diagnosis Detection					Prescription Reasons	
Label	Support	F1 score	Improvement		Label	Support	F1 score	Improvement
OTHER	74888	95.3	1.4%		OTHER	83618	95.8	0.9%
POSITIVE	24489	86.1	4.4%		REASON	9114	64.7	8.6%
RULED-OUT	2797	86.4	3.6%		PRESCRIBED	5967	84.7	4.4%
CONCERN	2780	72.1	5.6%		DISCONTINUED	2754	82.7	5.6%

		Chemical–Disease Relations (CDR)					Drug–Disease Relations	
Label	Support	F1 score	Improvement		Label	Support	F1 score	Improvement
OTHER	104530	98.3	0.5%		OTHER	10634	90.8	2.3%
DISEASE	6887	84.2	6.3%		TREATS	3671	76.0	5.7%
CHEMICAL	6270	87.0	6.7%		UNRELATED	1145	53.8	71.3%
					PREVENTS	320	41.1	103.5%
					CONTRAINDICATED-FOR	69	0	–

Table 3: Relative F1 score improvements of different labels. For each label, we give the number of supporting examples (Support), the F1 score of our combined model, and the relative improvements over the HB-CRF model. The F1 scores of minor labels suffer from insufficient training data, and thus have lower values. However, the combined model shows the largest relative improvements in these categories. ADR results are shown in table A4.

sic LSTM-CRF structure to improve NER performance in biomedical text. Our model provides an effective method for fully utilizing the sparse ontology-driven features left out of by the above work, which are complementary to dense embeddings and therefore boost performance of clinical concept extraction with limited training data (section 4).

There are also a number of models that mix dense and sparse feature representations. Gormley et al. (2015) and Cheng et al. (2016) combine both unlexicalized hand-crafted features and word embeddings to improve the performance of relation extraction in recommender systems. However, they focus on simple multi-layer perceptron models, rather than considering a more expressive LSTM structure. Similarly, Wang et al. (2019) utilize both sparse UMLS features and unpretrained word embeddings as the input to an LSTM for genetic association inferences from medical literature. While their UMLS features are a single look-up table of semantic types, our model relies on much richer resources of medical knowledge and includes more heterogeneous and expressive hand-built features that capture the semantic, morphological and contextual information of words (section 2).

6 Conclusion

Clinical text datasets are expensive to label and thus tend to be small, but the questions they can answer are often very high-impact. It is thus incumbent upon us to make maximally efficient use of these resources. One way to do this is to draw heavily on lexicons and other structured resources to write feature functions. Another way is to leverage unlabeled data to create dense feature vectors.

The guiding hypothesis of this paper is that the best models will make use of both kinds of information. To explore this hypothesis, we defined a new LSTM-CRF architecture that brings together these two kinds of feature, and we showed that this combined model yields superior performance on five very different healthcare-related tasks. We also used a variety of introspection techniques to gain an understanding of how the combined model balances its different sources of information. These analyses show that the combined model learns to pay attention to the most reliable sources of information for particular contexts, and that it is most effective, as compared to its simpler variants, on smaller categories, which are often the most crucial and the hardest to generalize about.

We also introduced the publicly available Drug–Disease Relations dataset, which contains a large training set of crowdsourced labels and a smaller test set of gold labels assigned by experts. This dataset can be used to learn facts about drug–disease relationships that have medical significance, and it shows that combined models like ours can learn effectively in noisy settings.

References

Kevin Atkinson. 2018. SCOWL (Spell Checker Oriented Word Lists). Accessed: September, 2018.

James Bergstra and Yoshua Bengio. 2012. Random search for hyper-parameter optimization. *Journal of Machine Learning Research*, 13:281–305.

Ciprian Chelba, Tomas Mikolov, Mike Schuster, Qi Ge, Thorsten Brants, Phillipp Koehn, and Tony Robinson. 2013. One billion word benchmark for measuring progress in statistical language modeling. ArXiv:1312.3005.

Heng-Tze Cheng, Levent Koc, Jeremiah Harmsen, Tal Shaked, Tushar Chandra, Hrishi Aradhye, Glen Anderson, Greg Corrado, Wei Chai, Mustafa Ispir, Rohan Anil, Zakaria Haque, Lichan Hong, Vihan Jain, Xiaobing Liu, and Hemal Shah. 2016. Wide & deep learning for recommender systems. In *Proceedings of the 1st Workshop on Deep Learning for Recommender Systems*, DLRS 2016, pages 7–10, New York, NY, USA. ACM.

Gamal Crichton, Sampo Pyysalo, Billy Chiu, and Anna Korhonen. 2017. A neural network multi-task learning approach to biomedical named entity recognition. *BMC Bioinformatics*, 18(1):368.

Doug Cutting. 1999. Apache Lucene. Accessed: September, 2018.

Alexander Philip Dawid and Allan M Skene. 1979. Maximum likelihood estimation of observer error-rates using the EM algorithm. *Applied statistics*, pages 20–28.

Kevin Gimpel, Nathan Schneider, Brendan O'Connor, Dipanjan Das, Daniel Mills, Jacob Eisenstein, Michael Heilman, Dani Yogatama, Jeffrey Flanigan, and Noah A. Smith. 2011. Part-of-speech tagging for Twitter: Annotation, features, and experiments. In *Proceedings of the 49th Annual Meeting of the Association for Computational Linguistics: Human Language Technologies: Short Papers - Volume 2*, HLT '11, pages 42–47, Stroudsburg, PA, USA. Association for Computational Linguistics.

Xavier Glorot and Yoshua Bengio. 2010. Understanding the difficulty of training deep feedforward neural networks. In *International Conference on Artificial Intelligence and Statistics*, pages 249–256.

Matthew R. Gormley, Mo Yu, and Mark Dredze. 2015. Improved relation extraction with feature-rich compositional embedding models. In *Proceedings of the 2015 Conference on Empirical Methods in Natural Language Processing*, pages 1774–1784. Association for Computational Linguistics.

Maryam Habibi, Leon Weber, Mariana Neves, David Luis Wiegandt, and Ulf Leser. 2017. Deep learning with word embeddings improves biomedical named entity recognition. *Bioinformatics*, 33(14):i37–i48.

Braden Hancock, Paroma Varma, Stephanie Wang, Martin Bringmann, Percy Liang, and Christopher Ré. 2018. Training classifiers with natural language explanations. In *Proceedings of the 56th Annual Meeting of the Association for Computational Linguistics (Volume 1: Long Papers)*, pages 1884–1895. Association for Computational Linguistics.

Geoffrey E. Hinton, Nitish Srivastava, Alex Krizhevsky, Ilya Sutskever, and Ruslan R. Salakhutdinov. 2012. Improving neural networks by preventing co-adaptation of feature detectors. ArXiv:1207.0580.

Sepp Hochreiter and Jürgen Schmidhuber. 1997. Long short-term memory. *Neural Computation*, 9(8):1735–1780.

Zhiheng Huang, Wei Xu, and Kai Yu. 2015. Bidirectional LSTM-CRF models for sequence tagging. ArXiv 1508.01991.

Abhyuday Jagannatha and Hong Yu. 2016. Structured prediction models for RNN based sequence labeling in clinical text. In *Proceedings of the 2016 Conference on Empirical Methods in Natural Language Processing*, pages 856–865. Association for Computational Linguistics.

Warren A Kibbe, Cesar Arze, Victor Felix, Elvira Mitraka, Evan Bolton, Gang Fu, Christopher J Mungall, Janos X Binder, James Malone, Drashtti Vasant, et al. 2014. Disease Ontology 2015 update: An expanded and updated database of human diseases for linking biomedical knowledge through disease data. *Nucleic acids research*, 43(D1):D1071–D1078.

Diederik P. Kingma and Jimmy Ba. 2014. Adam: A method for stochastic optimization. ArXiv 1412.6980.

John Lafferty, Andrew McCallum, and Fernando Pereira. 2001. Conditional random fields: Probabilistic models for segmenting and labeling sequence data. In *Proceedings of ICML-01*, pages 282–289.

Guillaume Lample, Miguel Ballesteros, Sandeep Subramanian, Kazuya Kawakami, and Chris Dyer. 2016. Neural architectures for named entity recognition. In *Proceedings of the 2016 Conference of the North American Chapter of the Association for Computational Linguistics: Human Language Technologies*, pages 260–270. Association for Computational Linguistics.

Edward Loper and Steven Bird. 2002. NLTK: The natural language toolkit. In *Proceedings of the ACL-02 Workshop on Effective Tools and Methodologies for Teaching Natural Language Processing and Computational Linguistics - Volume 1*, ETMTNLP '02, pages 63–70, Stroudsburg, PA, USA. Association for Computational Linguistics.

Xuezhe Ma and Eduard Hovy. 2016. End-to-end sequence labeling via bi-directional LSTM-CNNs-CRF. In *Proceedings of the 54th Annual Meeting of the Association for Computational Linguistics (Volume 1: Long Papers)*, pages 1064–1074, Berlin, Germany. Association for Computational Linguistics.

Bryan McCann, James Bradbury, Caiming Xiong, and Richard Socher. 2017. Learned in translation: Contextualized word vectors. In I. Guyon, U. V. Luxburg, S. Bengio, H. Wallach, R. Fergus, S. Vishwanathan, and R. Garnett, editors, *Advances in Neural Information Processing Systems 30*, pages 6294–6305. Curran Associates, Inc.

Azadeh Nikfarjam, Abeed Sarker, Karen O'Connor, Rachel Ginn, and Graciela Gonzalez. 2015. Pharmacovigilance from social media: Mining adverse drug reaction mentions using sequence labeling with word embedding cluster features. *Journal of the American Medical Informatics Association*, 22(3):671–681.

Matthew Peters, Mark Neumann, Mohit Iyyer, Matt Gardner, Christopher Clark, Kenton Lee, and Luke Zettlemoyer. 2018. Deep contextualized word representations. In *Proceedings of the 2018 Conference of the North American Chapter of the Association for Computational Linguistics: Human Language Technologies, Volume 1 (Long Papers)*, pages 2227–2237. Association for Computational Linguistics.

Alec Radford, Karthik Narasimhan, Tim Salimans, and Ilya Sutskever. 2018. Improving language understanding by generative pre-training. Ms, OpenAI.

Lance Ramshaw and Mitch Marcus. 1995. Text chunking using transformation-based learning. In *Third Workshop on Very Large Corpora*.

Alexander J Ratner, Christopher M De Sa, Sen Wu, Daniel Selsam, and Christopher Ré. 2016. Data programming: Creating large training sets, quickly. In D. D. Lee, M. Sugiyama, U. V. Luxburg, I. Guyon, and R. Garnett, editors, *Advances in Neural Information Processing Systems 29*, pages 3567–3575. Curran Associates, Inc.

Guergana K Savova, James J Masanz, Philip V Ogren, Jiaping Zheng, Sunghwan Sohn, Karin C Kipper-Schuler, and Christopher G Chute. 2010. Mayo clinical text analysis and knowledge extraction system (cTAKES): Architecture, component evaluation and applications. *Journal of the American Medical Informatics Association*, 17(5):507–513.

Lynn Marie Schriml, Cesar Arze, Suvarna Nadendla, Yu-Wei Wayne Chang, Mark Mazaitis, Victor Felix, Gang Feng, and Warren Alden Kibbe. 2011. Disease Ontology: A backbone for disease semantic integration. *Nucleic acids research*, 40(D1):D940–D946.

Kent A Spackman, Keith E Campbell, and Roger A Côté. 1997. SNOMED RT: A reference terminology for health care. In *Proceedings of the AMIA Annual Fall Symposium*, page 640. American Medical Informatics Association.

Weiyi Sun, Anna Rumshisky, and Ozlem Uzuner. 2013. Evaluating temporal relations in clinical text: 2012 i2b2 challenge. *Journal of the American Medical Informatics Association*, 20(5):806–813.

Charles Sutton and Andrew McCallum. 2011. An introduction to conditional random fields. *Foundations and Trends in Machine Learning*, 4(4):267–373.

Richard Tzong-Han Tsai, Shih-Hung Wu, Wen-Chi Chou, Yu-Chun Lin, Ding He, Jieh Hsiang, Ting-Yi Sung, and Wen-Lian Hsu. 2006. Various criteria in the evaluation of biomedical named entity recognition. *BMC Bioinformatics*, 7(1):92.

Ozlem Uzuner, Yuan Luo, and Peter Szolovits. 2007. Evaluating the state-of-the-art in automatic de-identification. *Journal of the American Medical Informatics Association : JAMIA*, 14(5):550–563.

Patrick Verga, Emma Strubell, and Andrew McCallum. 2018. Simultaneously self-attending to all mentions for full-abstract biological relation extraction. In *Proceedings of the 2018 Conference of the North American Chapter of the Association for Computational Linguistics: Human Language Technologies, Volume 1 (Long Papers)*, pages 872–884. Association for Computational Linguistics.

Denny Vrandečić and Markus Krötzsch. 2014. Wikidata: A free collaborative knowledgebase. *Communications of the ACM*, 57(10):78–85.

Haohan Wang, Xiang Liu, Yifeng Tao, Wenting Ye, Qiao Jin, William W Cohen, and Eric P Xing. 2019. Automatic human-like mining and constructing reliable genetic association database with deep reinforcement learning. *Pacific Symposium on Biocomputing*.

Xuan Wang, Yu Zhang, Xiang Ren, Yuhao Zhang, Marinka Zitnik, Jingbo Shang, Curtis Langlotz, and Jiawei Han. 2018. Cross-type biomedical named entity recognition with deep multi-task learning. *Bioinformatics*, page bty869.

Chih-Hsuan Wei, Yifan Peng, Robert Leaman, Allan Peter Davis, Carolyn J Mattingly, Jiao Li, Thomas C Wiegers, and Zhiyong Lu. 2015. Overview of the BioCreative V chemical disease relation (CDR) task. In *Proceedings of the 5th BioCreative Challenge Evaluation Workshop*, pages 154–166.

Sentence	Hand-built features of word *bacteria*	
antiseptic	**Adjacent words features**:	
handwash	word-4:antiseptic, word-3:handwash, word-2:to, word-1:decrease,	
to	word:bacteria, word+1:on, word+2:the, word+3:skin, word+4:..	
decrease	**Adjacent POS tags features**:	
bacteria	tag-4:JJ, tag-3:NN, tag-2:TO, tag-1:VB,	
on	tag:NNS, tag+1:IN, tag+2:DT, tag+3:NN, tag+4:..	
the	**Semantic environment features**:	
skin	bias:1, is_upper:0, is_title:0, is_punctuation:0,	
.	in_left_context_of_negative_cues:0,	in_right_context_of_negative_cues:0,
	in_left_context_of_prevents_cues:0,	in_right_context_of_prevents_cues:0,
	in_left_context_of_treats_cues:0,	in_right_context_of_treats_cues:0,
	in_left_context_of_treats_symptoms_cues:0,	in_right_context_of_treats_symptoms_cues:0,
	in_left_context_of_contraindicated_cues:0,	in_right_context_of_contraindicated_cues:0,
	in_left_context_of_affliction_adj_cues:0,	in_right_context_of_affliction_adj_cues:0,
	in_left_context_of_indication_cues:0,	in_right_context_of_indication_cues:0,
	in_left_context_of_details_cues:0,	in_right_context_of_details_cues:0.

Table A1: Hand-built features of the word *bacteria* in a Drug–Disease Relations dataset example. These features describe the word's adjacent words, adjacent POS tags, and semantic environment (section 2). The detailed meanings of hand-built features in the table are described as below: **Adjacent words features**: "word($\pm$1/2/3/4)" feature the word and adjacent words within a window size of 9. **Adjacent POS tags features**: "tag($\pm$1/2/3/4)" feature the tags of word and its adjacent words within a window size of 9. **Semantic environment features**: "bias" is always 1 for all words; "is_upper" specifies whether the word is upper case or lower case; "is_title" features whether the word is in the title or not; "is_punctuation" specifies whether the token is actually a word or a punctuation. "in_left/right_context_of_negative/prevents/treats(_symptoms)/contraindicted/afflicition_adj/indication/details_cues" feature whether the word is in the left or right context (of specific window size like 4) of cue-words from specific lexicons. Features related to 8 lexicons are shown in this example. Concrete examples: *not, none* and *no* are three cue-words of lexicon "negative_cues", *prevent* and *avoid* are two cue-words of lexicon "prevents_cues", *treat, solve* and *alleviate* are three cue-words of lexicon "treats_cues" etc. Different semantic environments are defined in the five datasets by carefully defining the lexicons/cue-words from various sources which possibly contain corresponding domain knowledge, as discussed in section 2 and section 3.

Statistics	Diagnosis Detection	Prescription Reasons	Penn Adverse Drug Reactions (ADR)	Chemical–Disease Relations (CDR)	Drug–Disease Relations
# texts	6042	5179	–	–	–
# training texts	–	–	749	1000	9494
# test texts	–	–	272	500	500
mean text length	17	19	19	227	30
max text length	374	258	40	623	542
# labels	4	4	5	3	5

Table A2: Statistics for our five datasets. The sample size varies from around 1,000 to 10,000. The mean text length (measured as the number of words) varies from 17 (short sentences) to 227 (full paragraphs). The number of labels varies from 3 to 5. ADR, CDR, and Drug–Disease Relations are already partitioned into training and test sets, while Diagnosis Detection and Prescription Reasons do not have predefined splits.

Models	Hyperparams	Diagnosis Detection	Prescription Reasons	Penn Adverse Drug Reactions (ADR)	Chemical–Disease Relations (CDR)	Drug–Disease Relations
rand-LSTM-CRF	η	1e-4	1e-4	1e-4	1e-4	1e-4
	$\text{epoch}_{\text{tune}}$	3	3	513	10	13
	$\text{epoch}_{\text{train}}$	34	40	3076	164	130
	$\mathcal{R}_{c1}$			{ 0, 3e-5, 1e-4, 3e-4, 1e-3 }		
	$\mathcal{R}_{c2}$			{ 0, 3e-4, 1e-3, 3e-3, 1e-2 }		
HB-CRF	η	1e-2	1e-2	3e-2	1e-2	1e-4
	$\text{epoch}_{\text{tune}}$	1	1	10	2	3
	$\text{epoch}_{\text{train}}$	3	4	82	10	35
	$\mathcal{R}_{c1}$			{ 0, 3e-6, 1e-5, 3e-5, 1e-4 }		
	$\mathcal{R}_{c2}$			{ 0, 3e-5, 1e-4, 3e-4, 1e-3 }		
ELMo-LSTM-CRF	η	1e-3	1e-3	1e-4	1e-3	5e-6
	$\text{epoch}_{\text{tune}}$	1	1	10	2	3
	$\text{epoch}_{\text{train}}$	3	4	82	10	35
	$\mathcal{R}_{c1}$			{ 0, 3e-5, 1e-4, 3e-4, 1e-3 }		
	$\mathcal{R}_{c2}$			{ 0, 3e-4, 1e-3, 3e-3, 1e-2 }		
ELMo-LSTM-CRF-HB	η	1e-3	1e-3	1e-4	1e-3	1e-5
	$\text{epoch}_{\text{tune}}$	1	1	10	2	3
	$\text{epoch}_{\text{train}}$	3	4	82	5	35
	$\mathcal{R}_{c1}$			{ 0, 3e-7, 1e-6, 3e-6, 1e-5 }		
	$\mathcal{R}_{c2}$			{ 0, 3e-6, 1e-5, 3e-5, 1e-4 }		

Table A3: Hyperparameters for our experiments. The step size η is first manually tuned within the training set when the ℓ_1 and ℓ_2 regularizers are set to be zeros. The coefficients c_1 and c_2 of the ℓ_1 and ℓ_2 regularizers are determined via random search (for 10 settings) from ranges $\mathcal{R}_{c1}$ and $\mathcal{R}_{c2}$ during tuning (Bergstra and Bengio, 2012). Epochs of tuning $\text{epoch}_{\text{tune}}$ are set to 1~3 to reduce tuning time for most datasets (which consumes most of the time for the experiments). It is set to 10 for ADR since that dataset is so small that it is hard to see clear trends after just one epoch. Epochs of training $\text{epoch}_{\text{train}}$ are set to be large enough until the training converges. The 'rand-LSTM-CRF' model requires many more epochs for tuning and training because of the updates to the randomly initialized embeddings.

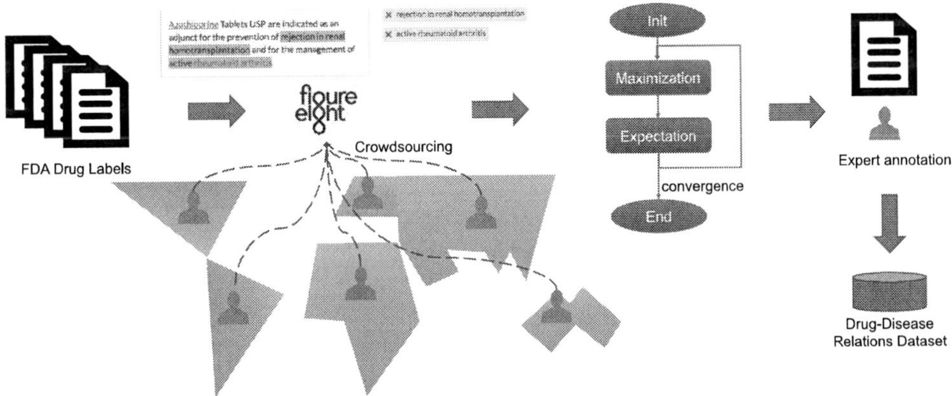

Figure A1: Procedure for building the Drug–Disease Relations dataset. 10,000 raw sentences from the FDA Drug Labels corpus were annotated by participants from 72 countries on the Figure Eight platform (crowdsourcing). Expectation Maximization was used to infer labels for all the annotated sentences used for training. A team of experts independently labeled different examples for testing. The resulting dataset consists of 9,500 crowdsourced examples and 500 expert-annotated examples.

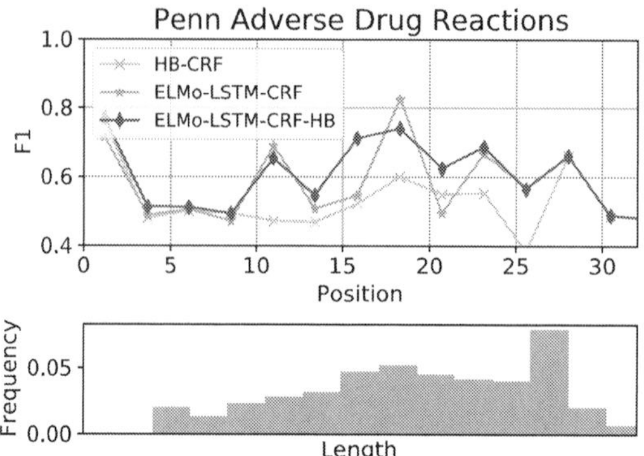

Figure A2: Text-length experiment for the Penn Adverse Drug Reactions (ADR) dataset. Since ADR uses the IOB tag format, in order to calculate per-token F1 scores, we collapse test-set labels starting with 'B-' and 'I-' into the same labels. The ELMo-LSTM-CRF always performs better than the HB-CRF, while the combined model takes advantage of both models and always outperforms both base models. Figure 2 provides comparable plots for the other four datasets.

| | Penn Adverse Drug Reactions (ADR) | | |
Label	Support	F1 score	Improvement
OTHER	5023	98.0	0.3%
ADR	283	57.1	17.7%
INDICATION	29	35.9	178.3%

Table A4: Relative F1 score improvements of different labels in the Penn Adverse Drug Reactions (ADR) dataset. To bring the IOB tag format of this dataset in line with our others, ADR merges B-ADR and I-ADR, and INDICATION merges B-INDICATION and I-INDICATION. Consistent with table 3, the combined model gains most in the smallest categories.

An Analysis of Attention over Clinical Notes for Predictive Tasks

Sarthak Jain
Northeastern University
jain.sar@husky.neu.edu

Ramin Mohammadi
Northeastern university
mohammadi.r@husky.neu.edu

Byron C. Wallace
Northeastern University
b.wallace@northeastern.edu

Abstract

The shift to electronic medical records (EMRs) has engendered research into machine learning and natural language technologies to analyze patient records, and to predict from these clinical outcomes of interest. Two observations motivate our aims here. First, unstructured notes contained within EMR often contain key information, and hence should be exploited by models. Second, while strong predictive performance is important, *interpretability* of models is perhaps equally so for applications in this domain. Together, these points suggest that neural models for EMR may benefit from incorporation of *attention* over notes, which one may hope will both yield performance gains and afford transparency in predictions. In this work we perform experiments to explore this question using two EMR corpora and four different predictive tasks, that: (i) inclusion of *attention mechanisms* is critical for neural encoder modules that operate over notes fields in order to yield competitive performance, but, (ii) unfortunately, while these boost predictive performance, it is decidedly less clear whether they provide meaningful support for predictions. Code to reproduce all experiments is available at https://github.com/successar/AttentionExplanation.

1 Introduction

The adoption of electronic medical records (EMRs) has spurred development of machine learning (ML) and natural language processing (NLP) methods that analyze the data these records contain; for a recent survey of such efforts, see (Shickel et al., 2018). Key information for downstream predictive tasks (e.g., forecasting whether a patient will need to be readmitted within 30 days) may be contained within unstructured notes fields (Boag et al., 2018; Jin et al., 2018).

In this work we focus on the modules within neural network architectures responsible for encoding text (notes) into a fixed-size representation for consumption by downstream layers. Patient histories are often long and may contain information mostly irrelevant to a given target. Encoding this may thus be difficult, and text encoder modules may benefit from *attention mechanisms* (Bahdanau et al., 2014), which may be imposed to emphasize relevant tokens.

In addition to mitigating noise introduced by irrelevant tokens, attention mechanisms are often seen as providing interpretability, or insight into model behavior. However, recent work (Jain and Wallace, 2019) has argued that treating attention as explanation may, at least in some cases, be misguided. Interpretability is especially important for clinical tasks, but incorrect or misleading rationales supporting predictions may be particularly harmful in this domain; this motivates our focused study in this space.

To summarize, our **contributions** are as follows. First, we empirically investigate whether incorporating standard attention mechanisms into RNN-based text encoders improves the performance of predictive models learned over EMR. We find that they do; inclusion of standard additive attention mechanism in LSTMs consistently yields absolute gains of ~ 10 points in AUC, compared to an LSTM without attention.[1] Second, we evaluate the induced attention distributions with respect to their ability to 'explain' model predictions. We find mixed results here, similar to (Jain and Wallace, 2019): attention distributions correlate only weakly (though almost always significantly) with

---

[1]Indeed, across both corpora and all tasks considered, inattentive LSTMs perform considerably worse than logistic regression and bag-of-words (BoW); introducing attention makes the neural variants competitive, but not decisively better. We hope to explore this point further in future work.

Proceedings of the 2nd Clinical Natural Language Processing Workshop, pages 15–21
Minneapolis, Minnesota, June 7, 2019. ©2019 Association for Computational Linguistics

gradient measures of feature importance, and we are often able to identify very different attention distributions that nonetheless yield equivalent predictions. Thus, one should not in general treat attention weights as meaningful explanation of predictions made using clinical notes.

2 Models

We experiment with multiple standard encoding architectures, including: (i) a standard BiLSTM model; (ii) a convolutional model, and (iii) an embedding projection based model. We couple each of these with an attention layer, following (Jain and Wallace, 2019). Concretely, each encoder yields hidden state vectors $\{h_1, ..., h_T\}$, and an attention distribution $\{\alpha_1, ..., \alpha_T\}$ is induced over these according to a scoring function ϕ: $\hat{\alpha} = \text{softmax}(\phi(\mathbf{h})) \in \mathbb{R}^T$. In this work we consider *Additive* similarity functions $\phi(\mathbf{h}) = \mathbf{v}^T \tanh(\mathbf{W_1 h} + \mathbf{b})$ (Bahdanau et al., 2014), where $\mathbf{v}, \mathbf{W_1}, \mathbf{b}$ are model parameters. Predictions are made on the basis of induced representations: $\hat{y} = \sigma(\boldsymbol{\theta} \cdot h_\alpha) \in \mathbb{R}^{|\mathcal{Y}|}$, where $h_\alpha = \sum_{t=1}^{T} \hat{\alpha}_t \cdot h_t$ and $\boldsymbol{\theta}$ are top-level discriminative (e.g., softmax) parameters.

3 Datasets and Tasks

We consider five tasks over two independent EMR datasets. The first EMR corpus is MIMIC-III (Johnson et al., 2016), a publicly available set of records from patients in the Intensive Care Unit (ICU). We follow prior work in modeling aims and setup on this dataset. Specifically we consider the following predictive tasks on MIMIC.

1. **Readmission.** The task here is to predict patient readmission within 30 days of discharge or transfer from the ICU. We follow the cohort selection of (Lin et al., 2018). We assume the model has access to all notes from patient admission up until the discharge or transfer from the ICU (the point of prediction).

2. **Retrospective 1-yr mortality**. We aim to predict patient mortality within one year. In this we follow the experimental setup of (Ghassemi et al., 2014). The model is provided all notes up until patient discharge (excluding the discharge summary).

3. **Phenotyping**. Here we aim to predict the top 25 acute care phenotypes for patients (associated at discharge with the admission). For

this we again rely on the framing established in prior work (Harutyunyan et al., 2017). The model has access to all notes from admission up until the end of the ICU stay. Note that this may be viewed as a multilabel classification task, similar to (Harutyunyan et al., 2017; Lipton et al., 2015).

The second EMR dataset we use comprises records for 7174 patients from Mass General Hospital who underwent hip or knee arthroplasty procedures. Use of this data was approved by an Institutional Review Board (IRB protocol number 2016P002062) at Partners Healthcare.

1. **Predicting Hip and Knee Surgery Complications**. We consider patients who underwent hip or knee arthroplasty procedure; we aim to classify these patients with respect to whether or not they will be readmitted within 30 days due to surgery-related complications. We run experiments over hip and knee surgery patients separately.

4 Experiments

Following the analysis of (Jain and Wallace, 2019) but focusing on clinical tasks, we perform a set of experiments on these corpora that aim to assess the degree to which attention mechanisms aid (or hamper) predictive performance, and the degree to which the induced attention weights might be viewed as providing explanations for predictions.

The latter can be assessed in many ways, depending on one's view of interpretability. To address the question of whether it is reasonable to treat attention as providing interpretability broadly, we perform experiments that interrogate multiple properties we might expect these weights to exhibit if so. Specifically, we: probe the degree to which attention weights correlate with alternative gradient-based feature importance measures, which have a more straight-forward interpretation (Ross et al., 2017; Li et al., 2016); evaluate whether we are able to identify 'counterfactual' attention distributions that change the attention weights (focus) but not the prediction; and, in an exercise novel to the present work, we consider replacing attention weights with log odds scores from a logistic regression (linear) model. We provide a web interface to interactively browse the plots for all datasets, model variants, and experiment types: `https://successar.github. io/AttentionExplanation/docs/`.

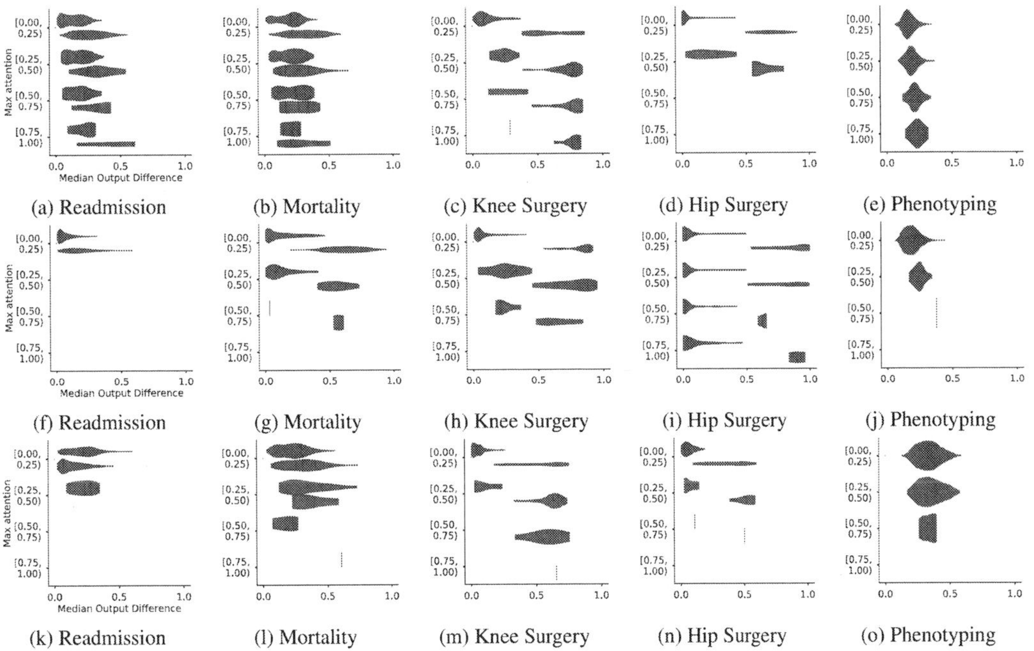

Figure 1: **Median change in output** $\Delta \hat{y}^{med}$ (x) densities in relation to the **max attention** $(\max \hat{\alpha})$ (y) obtained by randomly permuting instance attention weights. Colors denote classes: negative (■) and positive (■); phenotyping (e) is not binary. **Top row shows results for BiLSTM encoders; middle for CNNs; bottom for Embedding Projection.**

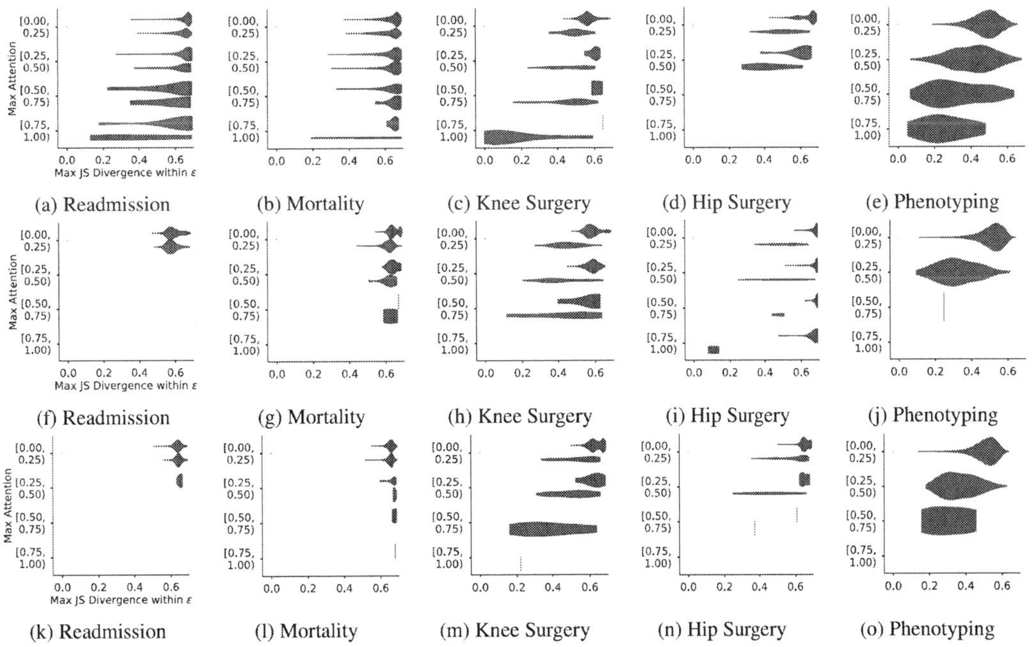

Figure 2: Densities of **maximum JS divergences** (ϵ-**max JSD**) (x-axis) as a function of the **max attention** (y-axis) in each instance for obtained between original and adversarial attention weights. Colors are as above. **Top row shows results for BiLSTM encoders; middle for CNNs; bottom for Embedding Projection.**

Dataset	Class	Mean ± Std.	Sig. Frac.
LSTM Encoder			
Readmission	0	0.37 ± 0.04	1.00
	1	0.38 ± 0.05	1.00
Mortality	0	0.33 ± 0.05	1.00
	1	0.35 ± 0.06	1.00
Knee Surgery	0	0.38 ± 0.07	1.00
	1	0.49 ± 0.08	1.00
Hip Surgery	0	0.24 ± 0.07	1.00
	1	0.33 ± 0.09	1.00
Phenotyping	Overall	0.24 ± 0.06	1.00
Projection Encoder			
Readmission	0	0.65 ± 0.03	1.00
	1	0.64 ± 0.03	1.00
Mortality	0	0.76 ± 0.02	1.00
	1	0.76 ± 0.02	1.00
Knee Surgery	0	0.65 ± 0.05	1.00
	1	0.60 ± 0.06	1.00
Hip Surgery	0	0.59 ± 0.09	1.00
	1	0.55 ± 0.09	1.00
Phenotyping	Overall	0.89 ± 0.02	1.00

Table 1: Mean and std. dev. of correlations between gradient importance measures and attention weights. *Sig. Frac.* columns report the fraction of instances for which this correlation is statistically significant.

4.1 Gradient Experiments

To evaluate correlations between attention weights and gradient based feature importance scores, we compute Kendall-τ measure (Table 1) between attention scores and gradients with respect to the tokens comprising documents. Across both corpora and all tasks we observe only a modest correlation between the two for BiLSTM model (the projection based model have higher correspondence, which is expected for such simple architectures). This may be problematic for attention as an explanatory mechanism, given the explicit relationship between gradients and model outputs. (Although we note that gradient based methods themselves pose difficulty with respect to interpretation (Feng et al., 2018)).

4.2 Counterfactual Experiments

We investigate if model predictions *would* have differed, had the model attended to different words (i.e., under *counterfactual* attention distributions).

We follow the two strategies from (Jain and Wallace, 2019) for constructing counterfactual attention distributions. In the first we randomly permute the empirical weights obtained from the attention module prior to inducing the weighted representation $\mathbf{h}_\alpha$. We repeat this process 100 times and record the median change in output.

The second strategy is *adversarial*; we explicitly aim to identify attention weights that are maximally different from the observed weights, with

Model	ROC AUC	PR AUC
Readmission		
LR + BoW	0.70	0.29
LSTM	0.63	0.22
LSTM + Additive Attention	0.71	0.30
LSTM + Additive Attention (Log Odds at Test)	0.69	0.26
LSTM + Log Odds Attention	0.71	0.29
Mortality		
LR + BoW	0.82	0.46
LSTM	0.74	0.29
LSTM + Additive Attention	0.83	0.47
LSTM + Additive Attention (Log Odds at Test)	0.80	0.41
LSTM + Log Odds Attention	0.82	0.42
Knee Surgery Complication		
LR + BoW	0.80	0.39
LSTM	0.66	0.18
LSTM + Additive Attention	0.79	0.35
LSTM + Additive Attention (Log Odds at Test)	0.81	0.34
LSTM + Log Odds Attention	0.81	0.38
Hip Surgery Complication		
LR + BoW	0.76	0.32
LSTM	0.63	0.16
LSTM + Additive Attention	0.75	0.24
LSTM + Additive Attention (Log Odds at Test)	0.74	0.26
LSTM + Log Odds Attention	0.78	0.29
Phenotyping		
LR + BoW	0.86	0.59
LSTM	0.78	0.41
LSTM + Additive Attention	0.86	0.58
LSTM + Additive Attention (Log Odds at Test)	0.81	0.48
LSTM + Log Odds Attention	0.85	0.56

Table 2: Predictive results across all datasets and tasks using different models and attention variants.

the constraint that this does not change the model output by more some small value ϵ. In both cases, all other model parameters are held constant.

In Figures 1 and 2, we observe that predictions are unchanged under alternative attention configurations in a significant majority of cases across all architectures. Thus, attention cannot be viewed casually in the sense of 'the model made these predictions *because* these words were attended to'. Alternative attention distributions that yield equivalent predictions would seem to be equally plausible under the view of attention as explanation.

4.3 Log Odds Experiments

As a novel exercise, we also consider swapping log-odds scores for features (from an LR model operating over BoW) in for attention weights in BiLSTM model. Specifically, we induce a 'log odds attention' over an input by substituting the absolute value of log odds (as estimated via LR) of

Original vs Adversarial Attention Difference : Sed dolorem sed adipisci ipsum dolor dolorem. Ut adipisci magnam tempora. Modi # eius : tempora change ipsum adipisci tempora tracheobronchomalacia quaerat dolor. Numquam est dolore labore est neque. respiratory failure Ipsum quiquia etincidunt labore modi. Dolorem aliquam dolore amet. Amet est consectetur modi neque. Porro respiratory failure etincidunt quaerat est neque dolor quaerat. Est quaerat est adipisci ipsum. Sit dolore quisquam ipsum non neque quiquia aliquam. Ut ipsum adipisci labore tempora quaerat tempora labore. Ipsum numquam voluptatem consectetur. Aliquam voluptatem , eius numquam. Velit generalized ut non numquam magnam sed modi. Consectetur porro . heart etincidunt eius consectetur , quaerat amet. Amet dolorem is difficult dolor consectetur etincidunt sed effusions quiquia aliquam. Porro etincidunt dolore labore no dolore dolorem aliquam. Tempora etincidunt quisquam aliquam numquam eius ut. tracheostomy Modi modi amet voluptatem

Original Output: 0.694 **Adversarial Output:** 0.699

Original vs Log Odds Attention Difference : Non magnam quiquia magnam magnam quaerat. Ut etincidunt magnam voluptatem velit eius. Dolorem dolorem velit dolor porro ut etincidunt. Consectetur dolor voluptatem cystic brain mass quaerat surgical resection est magnam etincidunt. Ipsum neque dolorem sed consectetur est. Magnam modi voluptatem dolorem tempora sed ut. Dolore dolor tempora eius aliquam quisquam. Dolor quisquam eius sed labore dolore sit velit. Magnam aliquam quisquam numquam. Aliquam sed sed modi neque. Dolor chronic quiquia voluptatem adipisci quaerat adipisci. . . . . . . Magnam velit quaerat adipisci. Ut cystic brain mass adipisci velit modi. Sed aliquam astrocytoma est porro. Labore resection eius voluptatem sit quisquam consectetur modi. Est ipsum tumor dolore

Original Output: 0.798 **Log Odds Output :** 0.800

Figure 3: Heatmaps showing difference in Original and counterfactual attention distributions over clinical notes from MIMIC, where we have replaced text with *lorem ipsum* for all but the most relevant tokens in order to preserve privacy (red implies counterfactual attention is higher and blue vice-versa). These show different cases where we can significantly change the attention distribution (either **adversarial (Top)** or using **Log Odds (Bottom)**) while barely affecting the prediction.

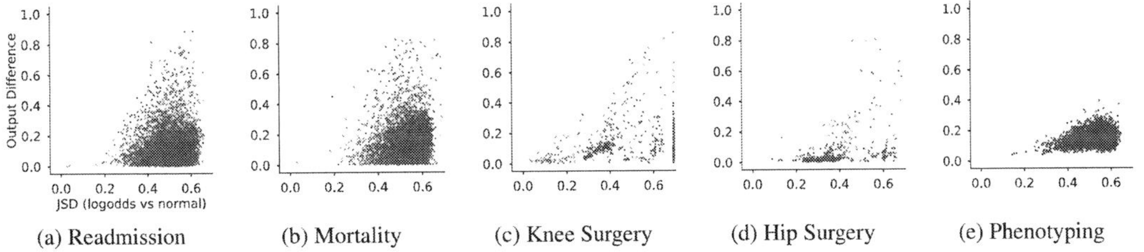

(a) Readmission (b) Mortality (c) Knee Surgery (d) Hip Surgery (e) Phenotyping

Figure 4: Change in output (y-axis) using original attention vs Log Odds attention during predictions against JSD between these two distributions (x-axis). These results are for LSTM encoders.

the word present at each position and passing this through a softmax: $\alpha^{LO} = \text{softmax}_t(\{\beta_{w_t}\}_{t=1}^{T})$ where w_t is the word at position t and β are log-odds estimates.

These scores enjoy a clear interpretation under a linear regime. We thus explore two ways of using them with attentive neural models: (1) Swapping in these in as attention weights place of $\mathbf{h}_\alpha$ at test (prediction) time; (2) Use the (fixed) 'log-odds attention' during training, in place of learning the attention distribution end-to-end.

Table 2 shows that using log odds attention at test time does not degrade the performance significantly in most datasets (and actually improves performance for the Knee Surgery Complications task). Similarly, using log odds attention during training also yields similar performance to standard attention variants. But as we see in Figure 4, log odds attention distributions can differ considerably from learned attention distributions, again highlighting the difficulty of interpreting attention weights.

5 Discussion and Conclusions

Across two EMR datasets and five predictive tasks, we have shown that (i) attention mechanisms substantially boost the performance of LSTM text encoders passed over clinical notes, but, (ii) treating attention weights as 'explanations' for predictions is unwarranted. The latter confirms that the recent general findings of (Jain and Wallace, 2019) hold in the clinical domain; this is important because interpretability in this space is critical for obvious reasons.

We hope that this paper inspires work on transparent attention mechanisms for models that make predictions on the basis of EMR.

Acknowledgments

This work was supported by the Army Research Office (ARO), award W911NF1810328.

References

Dzmitry Bahdanau, Kyunghyun Cho, and Yoshua Bengio. 2014. Neural machine translation by jointly learning to align and translate. *arXiv preprint arXiv:1409.0473*.

Willie Boag, Dustin Doss, Tristan Naumann, and Peter Szolovits. 2018. What's in a note? unpacking predictive value in clinical note representations. *AMIA Summits on Translational Science Proceedings*, 2017:26.

Shi Feng, Eric Wallace, Alvin Grissom II, Pedro Rodriguez, Mohit Iyyer, and Jordan Boyd-Graber. 2018. Pathologies of neural models make interpretation difficult. In *Empirical Methods in Natural Language Processing*.

Marzyeh Ghassemi, Tristan Naumann, Finale Doshi-Velez, Nicole Brimmer, Rohit Joshi, Anna Rumshisky, and Peter Szolovits. 2014. Unfolding physiological state: Mortality modelling in intensive care units. In *Proceedings of the 20th ACM SIGKDD international conference on Knowledge discovery and data mining*, pages 75–84. ACM.

Hrayr Harutyunyan, Hrant Khachatrian, David C Kale, and Aram Galstyan. 2017. Multitask learning and benchmarking with clinical time series data. *arXiv preprint arXiv:1703.07771*.

Sarthak Jain and Byron C Wallace. 2019. Attention is not explanation. *arXiv preprint arXiv:1902.10186*.

Mengqi Jin, Mohammad Taha Bahadori, Aaron Colak, Parminder Bhatia, Busra Celikkaya, Ram Bhakta, Selvan Senthivel, Mohammed Khalilia, Daniel Navarro, Borui Zhang, et al. 2018. Improving hospital mortality prediction with medical named entities and multimodal learning. *arXiv preprint arXiv:1811.12276*.

Alistair EW Johnson, Tom J Pollard, Lu Shen, H Lehman Li-wei, Mengling Feng, Mohammad Ghassemi, Benjamin Moody, Peter Szolovits, Leo Anthony Celi, and Roger G Mark. 2016. Mimic-iii, a freely accessible critical care database. *Scientific data*, 3:160035.

Jiwei Li, Will Monroe, and Dan Jurafsky. 2016. Understanding neural networks through representation erasure. *arXiv preprint arXiv:1612.08220*.

Yu-Wei Lin, Yuqian Zhou, Faraz Faghri, Michael J Shaw, and Roy H Campbell. 2018. Analysis and prediction of unplanned intensive care unit readmission using recurrent neural networks with long short-term memory. *bioRxiv*.

Zachary C Lipton, David C Kale, Charles Elkan, and Randall Wetzel. 2015. Learning to diagnose with lstm recurrent neural networks. *arXiv preprint arXiv:1511.03677*.

Sampo Pyysalo, Filip Ginter, Hans Moen, Tapio Salakoski, and Sophia Ananiadou. 2013. Distributional semantics resources for biomedical text processing. *Proceedings of LBM*, pages 39–44.

Andrew Slavin Ross, Michael C Hughes, and Finale Doshi-Velez. 2017. Right for the right reasons: Training differentiable models by constraining their explanations. *arXiv preprint arXiv:1703.03717*.

Benjamin Shickel, Patrick James Tighe, Azra Bihorac, and Parisa Rashidi. 2018. Deep ehr: A survey of recent advances in deep learning techniques for electronic health record (ehr) analysis. *IEEE journal of biomedical and health informatics*, 22(5):1589–1604.

An Analysis of Attention over Clinical Notes for Predictive Tasks: Appendix

A   Dataset Statistics

Task	$|V|$	Avg. length	Train size	Test size
Readmission	36464	3865	23790 / 5499	4265 / 735
Mortality	34030	3901	21347 / 4675	4323 / 677
Hip Surgery Complications	10842	2624	3281 / 369	719 / 75
Knee Surgery Complications	10842	2586	2664 / 324	582 / 48
Phenotyping	10842	3641	31075	5000

Table 3: Dataset characteristics. For train and test size, we list the cardinality for each class, where applicable: 0/1 for binary classification and overall for multilabel. Average length is in tokens.

The Phenotypes studied in Phenotyping task are -

Acute and unspecified renal failure, Acute cerebrovascular disease, Acute myocardial infarction, Cardiac dysrhythmias, Chronic kidney disease, Chronic obstructive pulmonary disease and bronchiectasis, Complications of surgical procedures or medical care, Conduction disorders, Congestive heart failure - nonhypertensive, Coronary atherosclerosis and other heart disease, Diabetes mellitus with complications, Diabetes mellitus without complication, Disorders of lipid metabolism, Essential hypertension, Fluid and electrolyte disorders, Gastrointestinal hemorrhage, Hypertension with complications and secondary hypertension, Other liver diseases, Other lower respiratory disease, Other upper respiratory disease, Pleurisy - pneumothorax - pulmonary collapse, Pneumonia (except that caused by tuberculosis or sexually transmitted disease), Respiratory failure - insufficiency - arrest (adult), Septicemia (except in labor), Shock .

B   Model Details

For all datasets, we use spaCy for tokenization. We map out of vocabulary words to a special <unk> token and map any word with numeric characters to 'qqq'. Each word in the vocabulary was initialized using pretrained embeddings (Pyysalo et al., 2013). We initialize words not present in the vocabulary using samples from a standard Gaussian ($\mu = 0$, $\sigma^2 = 1$).

B.1   BiLSTM

We use an embedding size of 300 and hidden size of 128 for all datasets. The model was regularized with L_2 regularization ($\lambda = 10^{-5}$) applied to all parameters. We use a sigmoid activation function for all binary classification tasks. We treat each phenotype classification as binary classification and take the mean loss over labels during training. We trained the model using maximum likelihood loss function with Adam Optimizer with default parameters in PyTorch.

B.2   CNN

We use an embedding size of 300 and 4 kernels of sizes [1, 3, 5, 7], each with 64 filters, giving a final hidden size of 256. We use ReLU activation function on the output of the filters. All other configurations remain same as BiLSTM.

B.3   Average

We use the embedding size of 300 and a projection size of 256 with ReLU activation on the output of the projection matrix. All other configurations remain same as BiLSTM.

Extracting Adverse Drug Event Information with Minimal Engineering

Timothy Miller[1], Alon Geva[1], and Dmitriy Dligach[2]

[1]Computational Health Informatics Program, Boston Children's Hospital
[1]Harvard Medical School
[1]{firstname.lastname}@childrens.harvard.edu
[2]Department of Computer Science, Loyola University Chicago
[2]ddligach@luc.edu

Abstract

In this paper we describe an evaluation of the potential of classical information extraction methods to extract drug-related attributes, including adverse drug events, and compare to more recently developed neural methods. We use the 2018 N2C2 shared task data as our gold standard data set for training. We train support vector machine classifiers to detect drug and drug attribute spans, and pair these detected entities as training instances for an SVM relation classifier, with both systems using standard features. We compare to baseline neural methods that use standard contextualized embedding representations for entity and relation extraction. The SVM-based system and a neural system obtain comparable results, with the SVM system doing better on concepts and the neural system performing better on relation extraction tasks. The neural system obtains surprisingly strong results compared to the system based on years of research in developing features for information extraction.

1 Introduction

Adverse drug events (ADEs) describe undesirable signs and symptoms that occur consequent to administration of a medication. ADEs may be identified in randomized controlled trials (RCTs), observational studies, spontaneous reports such as those gathered in the Food and Drug Administrations (FDAs) Adverse Event Reporting System (FAERS), or manual chart review of data in electronic health records (EHRs). RCTs have notable limitations for pharmacoepidemiology, including strict inclusion and exclusion criteria that limit their generalizability, small cohort sizes that make them under-powered for detecting rarer ADEs, and time-limited study periods that prevent detection of ADEs that occur with longer drug administration (Sanson-Fisher et al., 2007; Sultana

et al., 2013; McMahon and Dal Pan, 2018). Although drug manufacturers are required to submit postmarket adverse event reports to the FDA, this information is not uniformly available to clinicians (Maxey et al., 2013). Therefore, the 21st Century Cures Act directs the FDA to use real-world data (RWD) in the drug approval process.

Use of RWD is particularly important for medications that are commonly used off-label, for example, those targeted for treatment of rare diseases such as pulmonary hypertension in children (Maxey et al., 2013). Electronic health records (EHRs) provide an opportunity to capture such data reflecting real-world use of approved medications. Most studies of pharmacovigilance using RWD are based on health care insurance claims—for instance, the FDAs Sentinel program—because claims data contains longitudinal information about medication dispensing and clinical diagnoses (Platt et al., 2018). However, claims data may lack sensitivity for identification of ADEs, since not all signs and symptoms are submitted to insurers for billing purposes (Nadkarni, 2010). Reliance on claims data may also lead to incongruous results, such as a Mini-Sentinel study that found—contrary to data from several large RCTs—that dabigatran was associated with a lower risk of gastrointestinal bleeding than warfarin (Sipahi et al., 2014).

Limiting studies using RWD to structured data alone neglects the rich data that may be found in the unstructured, free text portion of the EHR. However, this data is not readily available for computation. Extracting this information requires natural language processing (NLP) methods. The NLP sub-task of information extraction is concerned with finding concepts in text and the relations between them (Jurafsky and Martin, 2014). Examples of information extraction are named entity recognition (e.g., finding the names of peo-

Proceedings of the 2nd Clinical Natural Language Processing Workshop, pages 22–27
Minneapolis, Minnesota, June 7, 2019. ©2019 Association for Computational Linguistics

ple, organizations, etc.) and relation extraction (e.g., determining whether the employment relation holds between a detected person like *Tim Cook* and a detected organization like *Apple*). A recent National NLP Clinical Challenge (n2c2)-hosted shared task annotated ADEs in clinical text in a style that is amenable to an information extraction approach. Specifically, annotations for things like drug names or drug attributes, including dosages, routes, and adverse events are entity-like spans, while the pairing of attributes and drugs are naturally represented as relations to be extracted. The benefit of framing the ADE task as an information extraction task is that decades of research in information extraction can be brought to bear on the task, before even considering the specifics of the domain or the task. In this work, we sought to evaluate a number of standard information extraction methods, including both standard clinical NLP tools and general domain methods, with the goals of setting strong baselines, learning how much performance is dependent on domain knowledge, and comparing classical machine learning to new deep learning approaches.

2 Methods

2.1 Data

This work describes methods for participating in the National NLP Clinical Challenge (n2c2) Track 2 shared task: Adverse Drug Events and Medication Extraction in EHRs. The data consists of 500 discharge summaries from the MIMIC (Medical Information Mart for Intensive Care) III database (Johnson et al., 2016). The n2c2 data was labeled with eight concept types: Drugs, Strengths, Dosages, Durations, Forms, Routes, Reasons, and ADEs. In addition, seven relations are labeled, between Drug mentions and the other seven concept types.

We participated in all three tracks of the shared task: entity recognition, relation classification given entities, and end-to-end relation extraction.

2.2 Methods

Our methods explore how well standard information extraction methods perform. One of our primary motivations is the prevalence of neural network methods in recent work, often motivated by their elimination of resource-intensive manual feature engineering, and thus judged superior to classical machine learning methods even if accuracy

is similar. Unfortunately, in work comparing neural networks to classical methods, baseline classical machine learning systems can appear to be under-developed, while one is left wondering how much effort was actually required to engineer the network architecture and tune hyperparameters for the neural system. We used this dataset and task as an opportunity to invert that dynamic. We design a comparison that uses well-engineered features in a simple linear classifier without actually doing the engineering ourselves – we use features engineered over years of research in information extraction, and packaged in open source software such as Apache cTAKES (Savova et al., 2010) and ClearTK (Bethard et al., 2014). We then complete the comparison by comparing against off-the-shelf neural network tools and architectures for information extraction.

2.2.1 Entity extraction

To classify entities, we used a BIO tagger over tokens with a support vector machine classifier, with one classifier for each entity type. These classify every token in a document as the [B]eginning, [I]nside, or [O]utside of the entity type that classifier handles. We used Apache cTAKES (Savova et al., 2010) default pipeline to pre-process the data and the ClearTK (Bethard et al., 2014) machine learning API to extract features and train the models with Liblinear (Fan et al., 2008). The features used by the classifiers are standard features from information extraction, including:

- The previous token's BIO classification decision

- Word identity and part of speech for the current token

- Word identities and parts of speech in the surrounding context

- Sub-word character type features

- Word semantic features

For token and token context features, we represent features in two forms, first as bags of words within a window and also with relative positional information. Character type features extract the character sequence in both the target token and the context tokens to model the fact that many attributes are typically numbers, or include numbers. This feature maps tokens to strings representing character types inside the token—for example, lower case characters map to l, upper case to u, punctuation to p, and digits to d, so the phrase *Mar 10, 2019* would map to *Ull ddp dddd*. Finally, we used semantic type information of the current token, as extracted with the cTAKES dictionary lookup module, to create a feature representing whether a token is a sign/symptom, disease/disorder, procedure, drug mention (as detected by cTAKES), or anatomical site, as well as the UMLS (Bodenreider, 2004) Type Unique Identifier (TUI).

During development, we manually partitioned the data so that we could empirically optimize the value of C in the linear SVM classifier on held out data. We tuned a single value of C that optimized the micro-F score on the held-out part of the training data. It may be possible to squeeze out slightly better performance by tuning C separately for each classifier, but the classifiers were pretty stable in the range we experimented with. We compare this system to an off-the-shelf neural network-based system called Flair (Akbik et al., 2018). This system is pre-trained using one billion words of text (Chelba et al., 2013) to learn a multi-layer Long Short-Term Memory (LSTM) (Hochreiter and Schmidhuber, 1997) network language model. Given the pre-trained network, this system passes in the tokens for an input sequence, and receives back the values at the deepest hidden layer at each index of the multi-layer LSTM, and this sequence of vectors is called contextual embeddings. Like regular word embeddings (Turian et al., 2010; Mikolov et al., 2013; Pennington et al., 2014), there is one vector per input token, but since they are extracted from the output layer of the pre-trained LSTM they are expected to contain more information about the surrounding sentence context.

To train an entity extractor in Flair, we again model the task as a BIO tagging task, but instead of using linguistic features we simply pass the contextual embeddings for each token to a standard LSTM tagger. This LSTM has a hidden state with 256 dimensions, and is optimized with Adam (Kingma and Ba, 2014). We train for 50 epochs, and the model that performs best on the held out validation set during training is used to prevent overfitting.

2.2.2 Relation Extraction

We built relation extraction classifiers relating each extracted attribute to drug mentions. Relation candidate pairs were extracted by comparing all drug mentions with the relevant attribute mention within the same paragraph, where paragraphs were defined to be delimited by two newline characters. We use the same feature set as previous work extracting relations to find anatomical site modifiers (Dligach et al., 2014). In the end-to-end version of the task, we considered drug mentions discovered both by the BIO tagger model and by cTAKES's dictionary lookup module, which increased our recall. Any drug mentions discovered by cTAKES but not used in a relation were not output as *Drug* entities.

Finally, during preliminary work, we found that ADE and Reason entities actually behave more like relations, since they typically needed a nearby drug argument and some trigger words to be annotated. Therefore, instead of trying to detect ADE and Reason entities directly, we first train Drug-ADE and Drug-Reason relation classifiers, where the candidates for ADE and Reason arguments are all signs/symptoms and disease/disorders detected by cTAKES. If the relation classifier classifies a candidate pair as a Drug-ADE relation, we not only create the Drug-ADE relation but we create an ADE entity out of the non-Drug argument (and the Reason entity detector works the same way).

For relation extraction with the Flair neural model, we use a representation based on previous work on extracting temporal narrative container relations from sentences (Dligach et al., 2017). For each relation candidate consisting of a (Drug, Attribute) tuple, we insert xml-like start and stop tokens into the sentence around each of the candidate arguments indicating their position. For example, the sentence: *He does feel episodes of hypoglycemia if he does not eat following insulin* becomes: *He does feel episodes of <ADE> hypoglycemia </ADE> if he does not eat following <Drug> insulin </Drug>*. This augmented sentence representation is then passed into the pre-trained Flair bi-directional LSTM sequence model, and the final states in each direction are concatenated into a feature vector. This feature vector is then passed through a linear layer to a softmax function over the output space to classify the relation.

For Track 3 (end-to-end relation extraction), the

Track 1	Precision		Recall		F1	
	SVM	Neural	SVM	Neural	SVM	Neural
Drug	0.96	0.96	0.92	0.90	0.94	0.93
Strength	0.98	0.97	0.95	0.97	0.97	0.97
Duration	0.82	0.91	0.63	0.65	0.71	0.76
Route	0.96	0.95	0.91	0.83	0.94	0.89
Form	0.97	0.93	0.92	0.95	0.95	0.94
ADE	0.66	0.58	0.20	0.18	0.31	0.27
Dosage	0.94	0.92	0.88	0.92	0.91	0.92
Reason	0.78	0.71	0.38	0.56	0.51	0.63
Frequency	0.98	0.98	0.93	0.95	0.95	0.96
Average	0.95	0.94	0.86	0.87	0.91	0.90

Table 1: Results of entity recognition experiments with SVM vs. Neural systems.

Track 2	Precision		Recall		F1	
	SVM	Neural	SVM	Neural	SVM	Neural
Drug-Strength	0.93	0.99	0.96	0.98	0.94	0.98
Drug-Duration	0.81	0.93	0.83	0.86	0.82	0.89
Drug-Route	0.93	0.97	0.95	0.94	0.94	0.96
Drug-Form	0.96	0.99	0.97	0.95	0.97	0.97
Drug-ADE	0.75	0.77	0.78	0.80	0.76	0.79
Drug-Dosage	0.95	0.98	0.96	0.93	0.95	0.95
Drug-Reason	0.74	0.91	0.76	0.65	0.75	0.76
Drug-Frequency	0.90	0.98	0.92	0.94	0.91	0.96
Average	0.90	0.97	0.92	0.90	0.91	0.93

Table 2: Results of relation classification experiments (gold standard entity arguments) with SVM vs. Neural systems.

Track 3	Precision		Recall		F1	
	SVM	Neural	SVM	Neural	SVM	Neural
Drug-Strength	0.92	0.96	0.91	0.94	0.91	0.95
Drug-Duration	0.73	0.83	0.51	0.57	0.60	0.67
Drug-Route	0.92	0.94	0.86	0.77	0.89	0.85
Drug-Form	0.95	0.94	0.89	0.89	0.92	0.91
Drug-ADE	0.60	0.50	0.18	0.15	0.28	0.23
Drug-Dosage	0.92	0.92	0.84	0.84	0.88	0.88
Drug-Reason	0.66	0.65	0.31	0.46	0.42	0.54
Drug-Freq	0.90	0.96	0.86	0.87	0.88	0.92
Average	0.90	0.90	0.76	0.78	0.82	0.84

Table 3: Results of relation extraction experiments (system-generated entity arguments) with SVM vs. Neural systems.

entity pairs found by the system in Track 1 were used to create candidate relations during training and testing. For Track 2, we used the gold standard entity pairs to create the candidate relations.

Results are scored with the scoring tool distributed by the organizers of the challenge. This tool reports scores for precision ($\frac{\#TruePositives}{\#Predictions}$), recall ($\frac{\#TruePositives}{\#GoldPositives}$), and F1 score ($\frac{2*precision*recall}{precision+recall}$). For concepts, true positives can be strict (the system concept span must match a gold concept spans begin and end exactly) or lenient (a system concept span must overlap a gold concept span). For relations, a true positive is one where the gold set has a relation where both arguments match, and the relation category is the same. For both concepts and relations, we report micro-averaged results of the lenient evaluation, since that was the metric used to score the shared task.

3 Evaluation

The tables show results on the concept extraction (Table 1), relation classification (Table 2), and end-to-end relation extraction (Table 3). In the concept extraction task, the systems perform very similarly on average, with the SVM feature-engineered approach obtaining a micro-averaged F-score of 0.91 and the neural system scoring 0.90 (final row). By comparison, the best performing system at the n2c2 shared task scored 0.94 on the concept extraction task. The middle rows of Table 1 show the performance for different concept types. The two systems perform similarly across concept types, except that the SVM-based system performs much better on Route, while the neural system is much better at extracting Reason and Duration concepts.

For relation classification with gold standard concepts given as input (Table 2, top), the neural system is at least as good as the SVM-based system for every relation type, and the micro-averaged neural system is 0.93 compared to the 0.91 for the SVM-based system. Most improvement is seen in the Drug-Duration and Drug-Frequency categories. By comparison, the best performing system in the n2c2 challenge scored 0.96 on Track 2.

In the end-to-end relation extraction task (Table 3, bottom), the neural system is again two points better than the SVM in F1 score. The SVM performs better on Drug-Route and Drug-ADE, while the neural system performs better in Drug-Duration and Drug-Reason. The best performing system in the n2c2 challenge scored 0.89 on Track 3.

4 Conclusion

Despite minimal engineering effort, neural systems pre-trained on non-medical text obtain similar performance to feature engineered systems with features specific to clinical text. This is perhaps somewhat surprising, and provides some evidence that standard neural architectures for sequence tagging and relation extraction tasks are already quite mature. One caveat to these results is that, while our feature-based approach used standard feature sets with history of success in the literature, one could argue that to mirror the tuning that is done with neural networks we could have done more extensive tuning of feature hyperparameters, by, for example, testing configurations where certain groups of features are turned on or off.

While the performance of the neural system in this work is impressive, one might expect them to perform even better if they could be pre-trained on clinical text. Future work will investigate language model pre-training in Flair and other neural architectures on large amounts of clinical data from electronic health record systems. The code developed to participate in the n2c2 challenge and run these experiments is available open source.[1]

Acknowledgements

Research reported in this publication was supported by the National Library Of Medicine of the National Institutes of Health under Award Number R01LM012918. The content is solely the responsibility of the authors and does not necessarily represent the official views of the National Institutes of Health.

References

Alan Akbik, Duncan Blythe, and Roland Vollgraf. 2018. Contextual string embeddings for sequence labeling. In *Proceedings of the 27th International Conference on Computational Linguistics*, pages 1638–1649.

S Bethard, PV Ogren, and L Becker. 2014. ClearTK 2.0: Design Patterns for Machine Learning in UIMA. *LREC*.

Olivier Bodenreider. 2004. The unified medical language system (UMLS): integrating biomedical terminology. *Nucleic acids research*, 32(suppl_1):D267–D270.

Ciprian Chelba, Tomas Mikolov, Mike Schuster, Qi Ge, Thorsten Brants, Phillipp Koehn, and Tony Robinson. 2013. One Billion Word Benchmark for Measuring Progress in Statistical Language Modeling. *arXiv:1312.3005 [cs]*. ArXiv: 1312.3005.

Dmitriy Dligach, Steven Bethard, Lee Becker, Timothy Miller, and Guergana K Savova. 2014. Discovering body site and severity modifiers in clinical texts. *Journal of the American Medical Informatics Association : JAMIA*, 21(3):448–54.

Dmitriy Dligach, Tim Miller, Chen Lin, Steven Bethard, and Guergana Savova. 2017. Neural Temporal Relation Extraction. In *Proceedings of the 15th Annual Meeting of the European Association for Computational Linguistics*, pages 746–751, Valencia, Spain.

Rong-En Fan, Kai-Wei Chang, Cho-Jui Hsieh, Xiang-Rui Wang, and Chih-Jen Lin. 2008. LIBLINEAR: A Library for Large Linear Classification. *Journal of Machine Learning Research*, 9:1871–1874.

S Hochreiter and J Schmidhuber. 1997. Long short-term memory. *Neural computation*.

Alistair E.W. Johnson, Tom J. Pollard, Lu Shen, Liwei H. Lehman, Mengling Feng, Mohammad Ghassemi, Benjamin Moody, Peter Szolovits, Leo Anthony Celi, and Roger G. Mark. 2016. MIMIC-III, a freely accessible critical care database. *Scientific Data*, 3:160035.

Dan Jurafsky and James H Martin. 2014. *Speech and language processing*, volume 3. Pearson London.

Diederik P Kingma and Jimmy Lei Ba. 2014. Adam: Amethod for stochastic optimization. In *Proc. 3rd Int. Conf. Learn. Representations*.

Dawn M Maxey, D Dunbar Ivy, Michelle T Ogawa, and Jeffrey A Feinstein. 2013. Food and Drug Administration (FDA) postmarket reported side effects and adverse events associated with pulmonary hypertension therapy in pediatric patients. *Pediatric cardiology*, 34(7):1628–1636.

Ann W McMahon and Gerald Dal Pan. 2018. Assessing Drug Safety in ChildrenThe Role of Real-World Data. *The New England journal of medicine*, 378(23):2155.

Tomas Mikolov, Kai Chen, Greg Corrado, and Jeffrey Dean. 2013. Distributed Representations of Words and Phrases and their Compositionality arXiv : 1310 . 4546v1 [cs . CL] 16 Oct 2013. *arXiv preprint arXiv:1310.4546*, pages 1–9.

Prakash M Nadkarni. 2010. Drug safety surveillance using de-identified EMR and claims data: issues and challenges. *Journal of the American Medical Informatics Association*, 17(6):671–674.

Jeffrey Pennington, Richard Socher, and Christopher D Manning. 2014. GloVe: Global Vectors for Word Representation. In *Proceedings of EMNLP*.

Richard Platt, Jeffrey S. Brown, Melissa Robb, Mark McClellan, Robert Ball, Michael D. Nguyen, and Rachel E. Sherman. 2018. The FDA Sentinel Initiative - An Evolving National Resource. *The New England journal of medicine*, 379(22):2091–2093.

---

[1] https://github.com/tmills/ctakes-ade

Robert William Sanson-Fisher, Billie Bonevski, Lawrence W Green, and Cate DEste. 2007. Limitations of the randomized controlled trial in evaluating population-based health interventions. *American journal of preventive medicine*, 33(2):155–161.

GK Savova, JJ Masanz, and PV Ogren. 2010. Mayo clinical Text Analysis and Knowledge Extraction System (cTAKES): architecture, component evaluation and applications. *Journal of the American Medical Informatics Association.*

Ilke Sipahi, Seden Celik, and Nurdan Tozun. 2014. A comparison of results of the US food and drug administrations mini-sentinel program with randomized clinical trials: the case of gastrointestinal tract bleeding with dabigatran. *JAMA internal medicine*, 174(1):150–151.

Janet Sultana, Paola Cutroneo, and Gianluca Trifir. 2013. Clinical and economic burden of adverse drug reactions. *Journal of pharmacology & pharmacotherapeutics*, 4(Suppl1):S73.

Joseph Turian, Lev Ratinov, and Yoshua Bengio. 2010. Word representations: A simple and general method for semi-supervised learning. In *Proc. of ACL 2010.*

Hierarchical Nested Named Entity Recognition

Zita Marinho[†][*]   **Afonso Mendes**[†]   **Sebastião Miranda**[†]   **David Nogueira**[†]

zam@priberam.com,   amm@priberam.com,   ssm@priberam.com,   dan@priberam.com

[†]Priberam Labs, Alameda D. Afonso Henriques, 41, 2°, 1000-123 Lisboa, Portugal
[*] Instituto de Sistemas e Robótica, Instituto Superior Técnico, 1049-001 Lisboa, Portugal

Abstract

In the medical domain and other scientific areas, it is often important to recognize different levels of hierarchy in entity mentions, such as those related to specific symptoms or diseases associated with different anatomical regions. Unlike previous approaches, we build a transition-based parser that explicitly models an arbitrary number of hierarchical and nested mentions, and propose a loss that encourages correct predictions of higher-level mentions. We further propose a set of modifier classes which introduces certain concepts that change the meaning of an entity, such as absence, or uncertainty about a given disease. Our model achieves state-of-the-art results in medical entity recognition datasets, using both nested and hierarchical mentions.

1 Introduction

One of the most common studied tasks in NLP lies in extracting semantic information from unstructured text in the form of entities and detecting entity mentions across a single document, in particular where the mention is located (its span) and its corresponding classification or entity semantic type, such as person (PER), location (LOC), organization (ORG), etc. The task of entity recognition has long been studied and applied to different higher level tasks such as question answering (Abney et al., 2000), coreference resolution (Fragkou, 2017), relation extraction (Mintz et al., 2009; Miwa and Bansal, 2016; Liu et al., 2017), entity linking (Gupta et al., 2017; Guo and Barbosa, 2014) and event extraction (Feng et al., 2016). Most of the existing work in Named Entity Recognition and Classification focuses on flat mentions, usually corresponding to the longest outer mention (Ling and Weld, 2012; Marcinczuk, 2015; Leaman and Lu, 2016), or using nested mentions that can capture overlapping mentions within different nested levels (Finkel and Manning, 2009;

Lu and Roth, 2015; Wang et al., 2018; Ju et al., 2018). One of the main disadvantages of using simple independent classes to model different hierarchies is that there is no information that conveys an explicit hierarchical nature, in a way that lower level classes help to disambiguate the nature of higher level classes.

The most common approach to circumvent this issue involves projecting each lower level class to an individual label throwing away all of the inherent structure of the ontology. This approach is limited, since it does not propagate information to higher level classes and it does not use common information of all children in the ontology. The ability to identify hierarchical entities is very useful in many fields, in particular in the medical domain, where we associate medication, symptoms and other pathological conditions with more specific subtypes giving a more refined classification.

Additionally, we introduce the concept of modifier classes that can alter the meaning of a given class. Often, in medical records, the doctor states either the absence or presence of a particular condition, for that purpose we created a modifier level that acts on a particular class and is associated with the degree of relevance of that class, for example in the medical domain it may identify the absence or probability of certain symptoms/diseases, or refer to their duration (chronic, acute), etc. This concept is of particular use if we consider a hierarchical model to identify where this modifier actuates.

We test our model against other state-of-the-art methods modelling nested mentions whose classification is defined by their projected lower levels. We make use of hierarchical datasets in the medical field, where these notions are of extreme importance. We evaluate our model using the GENIA (Ohta et al., 2002) dataset, a bigger and more complex proprietary medical corpus (MED18) with higher hierarchical dependencies and modifier classes. To summarize, this paper

28

Proceedings of the 2nd Clinical Natural Language Processing Workshop, pages 28–34
Minneapolis, Minnesota, June 7, 2019. ©2019 Association for Computational Linguistics

makes the following contributions:

- we introduce a novel Hierarchical and Nested Named Entity Recognition (HNNER) model based on a neural transition based approach (Dyer et al., 2015), that is able to handle different levels of nested mentions and hierarchy,

- we further propose a model that can learn from modifier classes, allowing to model more complex and fine grained relations, such as degree of importance/variants of each class.

- we obtain state-of-the-art performance when compared with existing nested models with lower level projected labels (corresponding to the same hierarchical levels).

2 Related Work

Named entity recognition and classification has long been a popular task in NLP (Zhou and Su, 2002; McDonald et al., 2005; Ratinov and Roth, 2009; Wang et al., 2013). The first contribution on detecting nested mentions was proposed by Shen et al. (2003); Zhang et al. (2004); GuoDong (2004) and relied mostly on rule-based models. Later Finkel and Manning (2009) introduced a constituency parser as the first model-based approach for nested recognition, followed by work of Alex et al. (2007) using models based on linear-Conditional Random Fields (CRFs). Lu and Roth (2015); Muis and Lu (2017) handcrafted features to extract nested mentions without modelling their hidden dependencies using mention hypergraphs, that can capture nested dependencies with unbounded lengths.

With the success of neural based approaches for NER (Collobert et al., 2011; Chiu and Nichols, 2016; Ma and Hovy, 2016), several work has been done in classifying nested mentions: Ju et al. (2018) dynamically modeled each nested layer as a Long-Short-Term-Memory (LSTM)-CRF layer (Lample et al., 2016), requiring the knowledge of the number of nested overlapps to be known a priori. Katiyar and Cardie (2018) proposed a recurrent neural network to extract features to learn an hypergraph structure of nested mentions, using a BILOU encoding scheme. This required the creation of additional hyperarcs whenever a nested mention is encountered. More recently Wang et al. (2018) used a model based on a shift reduce parser that builds a forest structure for nested mentions. This neural approach can only be applied to classify nested mentions of different spans, meaning a single span cannot correspond to different mentions.

All of the proposed approaches so far, allow nested mentions classification but have never attempted to model explicit hierarchical and nested structures. Furthermore, our proposed model architecture is more expressive since it allows the same sequence of words to correspond to distinct mentions possibly with different hierarchical or nested levels.

3 Hierarchical Nested Named Entity Recognition (HNNER)

For a given input sequence of words $\{w_1, w_2, \ldots, w_n\}$ our model generates a sequence of actions that identifies nested and hierarchical mentions simultaneously.

Our transition-based model allows for several mentions to start and end at a given location in the sequence. We make use of an additional stack to store temporarily the terms corresponding to each mention, which we denote as *word stack*. The system state s is represented by a stack of words S containing all the temporary words pertaining to a mention (the word stack), a buffer of words to be parsed B, and a stack of actions corresponding to all mentions to be parsed M (the *mention stack*) and an output buffer that encode the entity mentions and other words O. Initially, we define the starting state as $s_0 = [M = \emptyset, S = \emptyset, B = \{w_1, \ldots, w_n\}], O = \emptyset$.

At each state, we apply an action a_n and change the state of the system s_n: by adding elements or resetting the word stack and moving the resulting mention to the output buffer, popping the top most word of the buffer and adding or popping actions from the mention stack. We consider four types of possible system actions $a \in \mathcal{A}$:

- OUT pops the top element of the buffer, and moves it to the output unaltered,

- SHIFT shifts the top element of the buffer to the word stack,

- TRANSITION(a) indicates the start of a mention, adds action label a to the mention stack,

- REDUCE(a) indicates the end of a mention and pops all elements of the mention stack until the last recorded transition and inserts the resulting mention (encoded as the output of an LSTM) in the output buffer. Since we only allow reductions of actions that remain in the top of the mention stack, we transition first to longer mentions, whenever more than one mention starts at the same point in the word sequence.

For each state of the system s_n we consider the subset of all possible valid actions $\mathcal{A}(a_{n-1}, s_n)$,

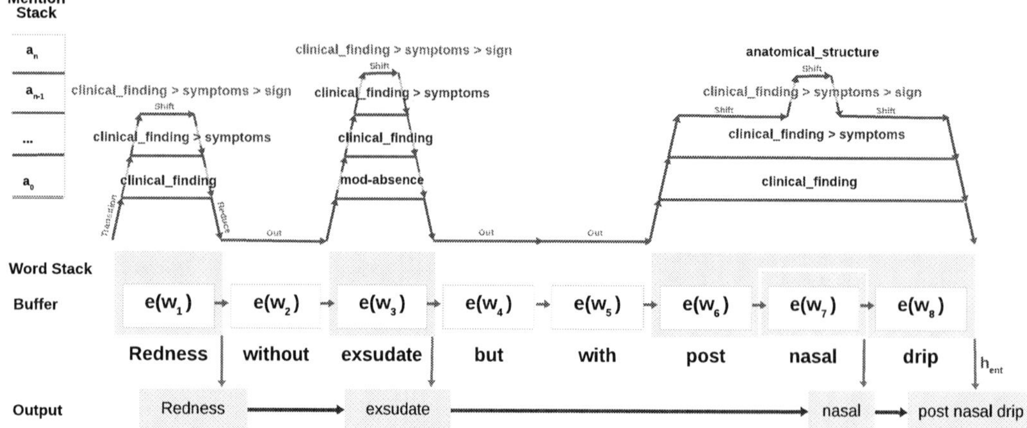

Figure 1: Transition-shift-reduce mechanism for hierarchical nested mention recognition. *Transition* is indicated by arrows pointing upwards, *Reduce* by downward arrows, *Out* horizontal arrows when mention stack is empty, and *Shift* action when non-empty. Different levels of the mention stack indicate the number of nested layers, while mention color indicates the hierarchical level (darker blue for level 0 and lighter as we go up in the hierarchy).

that depends on the previous action generated and the current parser state, in particular the mention stack. We consider a simple set of rules: for hierarchical mentions we only allow transitions to lower levels in the hierarchy if the upper levels exist in the mention buffer, meaning transitions of the form TRANSITION($a > b$) where the symbol $>$ indicates that b is a lower level hierarchy of class a and is only admitted if TRANSITION(a) exists in the mention stack. Our model allows an arbitrary number of hierarchies since, without knowing this number beforehand; we only allow reductions of the top most element in the mention stack, this step requires an ordering of nested mentions from longer to shorter spanning windows; we also only allow SHIFT actions if the mention stack is non-empty.

A mention containing a single word requires three actions to be considered: TRANSITION(a), SHIFT and REDUCE(a). Using this approach, we can model consecutive transitions of different mentions, multiple hierarchical as well as nested mentions, as long as they remain without overlaps.[1] For modifier classes, we model each individual modifier as a top level class. Figure 2 provides an example of a sequence of hierarchical and nested mentions. The terminal state is achieved when the word buffer is empty and all the elements of the mention stack have been reduced.

4   HNNER Model

Our transition-based model draws inspiration from the transition based parser proposed by Dyer et al. (2015). For a given sequence of input words $W = \{w_1, \ldots, w_N\}$ we represent each word as a low dimensional vector $e(w_n) \in \mathbb{R}^{d_w}$ for each word in the vocabulary $w_n \in [V]$. To better capture morphological and orthographic features of words, we consider each word vector the product of concatenating a fixed word lookup embedding $l(w_n)$ with its learned character sequence representation $c(w_n)$, such that $e(w_n) = [l(w_n); c(w_n)]$. We compute the character embeddings using a bidirectional LSTM following work of Ma and Hovy (2016); Lample et al. (2016). We initialize character embeddings randomly, while each word embedding is retrieved from a pretrained look-up representation. For words out-of-vocabulary we consider the word's character based representation and we train a representation of the unknown word embedding.

We associate an LSTM with the word stack $\text{LSTM}_S(\{e(w_j)\}_{w_j \in S})$ whose inputs correspond to the words shifted from the buffer, another with the mention stack $\text{LSTM}_M(\{a_n\}_{a_n \in M})$ with inputs from mentions that the system initialized, and a last LSTM that models the output of the system $\text{LSTM}_O(\{e(o_n)\}_{o_n \in O})$, whose inputs correspond to the latest state of the word LSTM or the word embeddings, depending on whether the word is in the word stack or not, respectively. We start by filling the input buffer $B_0 = [w_n, w_n - 1, \ldots, w_0]$ with the sequence of word embeddings

---

[1] We consider only non overlapping mentions disregarding any occurrences of the form TRANSITION(a)- SHIFT- TRANSITION(b)- SHIFT- REDUCE(a)- SHIFT- REDUCE(b).

Models	GENIA flat NER		
	P	R	F1
Finkel et al. (2004)	71.62	68.56	70.06
GuoDong (2004)	75.99	69.42	72.55
HNNER	**76.11**	**69.43**	**72.62**

Table 1: Results on JNLPBA with flat mentions.

to be parsed in reverse order, and leave the first word at the top of the buffer. For a given state of the system $s_i = [M, S, B, O]$ we compute the system state representation p_i for each action i as a nonlinear transformation of the last LSTM state of the word stack $h_w \in \mathbb{R}^{d_w}$, the last LSTM state of the mention stack $h_m \in \mathbb{R}^{d_m}$ and the top most element of the buffer $b_n \in \mathbb{R}^{d_w}$ and the last element of the output LSTM $o_n \in \mathbb{R}^{d_o}$:

$$p_i = \tanh(W[h_w; h_m; b_n; o_n] + b),$$

with the bias $b \in \mathbb{R}^k$ and linear weights $W \in \mathbb{R}^{(2d_w + d_m + d_o) \times k}$.

The system state p_i contains all the information required to make predictions about the current action of the parser $a_i \in \mathcal{A}$, according to a set of possible valid actions that we compute with simple rules $\mathcal{V}(a_{n-1}, s_n)$. Namely, we consider only as viable actions: SHIFT actions if it follows after a TRANSITION; REDUCE actions can only be applied in the reverse order of the previously applied TRANSITIONS; OUT actions are only allowed if there is no action to be reduced, and hierarchies must respect their parent transitions, meaning TRANSITION(a¿b) is not allowed if TRANSITION(a) has not been created first. Modifier classes are considered as a separate class of labels that may be applied in any hierarchical level.

The system greedily decides the current action based on:

$$p(a_n = a \mid p_n) = \frac{\exp \alpha_a^\top p_n}{\sum_{a' \in \mathcal{V}} \exp \alpha_{a'}^\top p_n}$$

We train our model to maximize the log-likelihood of each action in a batch of M sequences:

$$\mathcal{L} = -\sum_{i=1}^{M} \sum_{n=1}^{N} \beta^{H - L(a_n)} \log p(a_n \mid p_n),$$

weighted by a different value for each hierarchical level $\beta < 1$, where the level of each action $L(a_n) = 0$ for the top levels and decreases as we go down in the hierarchy, and H denotes the total number of levels.

Datasets	GENIA			MED18		
	train	dev	test	train	dev	test
vocabulary	74,560			51,879		
pretrained vocab.	23,813			49,782		
sentences	13,416	3,147	1,656	73,099	4,216	4,018
mentions	35,506	8738	4,492	495,148	29,522	28,458
hier. L0	17,753	4,369	2,246	230,912	13,702	13,271
hier. L1	17,753	4,369	2,246	139,665	8,353	7,933
hier. L2	–	–	–	123,291	7,372	7,132
hier. L3	–	–	–	1,200	95	122
flat actions	5			26		
hier. actions	23			531		
hier. L0	5			66		
hier. L1	18			126		
hier. L2	–			325		
hier. L3	–			14		

Table 2: Dataset description: total number of mentions, sentences, words and actions. Number of mentions and types of actions per hierarchical layer

5 Experimental Results

Datasets: We compare our HNNER model using different nested and hierarchical scenarios. First, we compare against standard baselines for flat NER using the splits and the JNLPBA dataset (Gridach, 2017), considering only flat and the topmost entities in the GENIA dataset (Ohta et al., 2002), following the same splits and entity types used by Finkel and Manning (2009). We used the GENIA dataset (Ohta et al., 2002), consisting of 2000 MEDLINE abstracts with 36 fine-grained entity categories. We also employed the same conversion to the main 5 entity types (and left the DNA and RNA subtypes the hierarchical experiments). We used pretrained word embeddings for GENIA using PUBMED dataset.[2] We further tested on a more complex medical dataset MED18, [3] comprising 3000 documents of annotated clinical reports in Portuguese. We consider 4 levels of hierarchy and 531 fine-grained entity categories. We trained word embeddings for this dataset using word2vec (Mikolov et al., 2013) on over around 10M documents of clinical records.

Table 2 in 5 shows a description of the datasets. The MED18 dataset is larger and more complex than GENIA, containing a total of 509869 mentions, 531 different hierarchical classes with 4 levels of hierarchy, while GENIA altough initialy contains 36 fine-grained classes, we only report on 23 different classes with 2 levels of hierarchy.

Models and Baselines: We evaluate our HNNER model against state-of-the-art models for

<hr>

[2]Embeddings available in `http://bio.nlplab.org/#source-data`

[3]a proprietary dataset for Portuguese Medical Diagnosis

Nested Models	Nested GENIA		
	P	R	F1
Finkel and Manning (2009)	75.4	65.9	70.3
Lu and Roth (2015)	72.5	65.2	68.7
Muis and Lu (2017)	75.4	66.8	70.8
Wang et al. (2018)	**76.0**	69.4	71.6
HNNER	74.0	**72.0**	**73.0**

Table 3: Results on GENIA with nested mentions.

nested mentions: a CRF-based constituency parser (Finkel and Manning, 2009); a nested NER model using mention hypergraphs (Lu and Roth, 2015); a multigraph representation with mention separators for overlapping mentions (Muis and Lu, 2017); a neural layered model for each nested layer (Ju et al., 2018); and a neural shift-reduce neural parser for nested mentions (Wang et al., 2018). We also, evaluated HNNER against the non-hierarchical nested version with the same number of hierarchical levels projected as a different independent class (HNNER+SUB). We train our model using Adam gradient updates (Kingma and Ba, 2014) using a learning rate of 0.001 and a batch size of 32 sentences. We employed dropout of 0.1 on all input layers (Srivastava et al., 2014). We used $\beta = 0.8$ for GENIA and $\beta = 1.0$ for MED18. For higher level datasets this value should be closer to one in order to not overshadow the effect of lower hierarchies, which are often the most frequent ones.

Results Our HNNER model obtains state-of-the-art results when compared with other flat (Table 1) and nested NER models (Table 3).

Learning hierarchical mentions explicitly using our model (HNNER) achieves better performance than using a set of projected subcategories independently, (HNNER+SUB) in Table 4. The proposed approach is still able to perform well when we deal with higher levels of hierarchy and more nested classes, which we can observe in the results using the MED18 dataset. As we progress towards higher level hierarchies the gap performance increases between projected subclasses and explicit hierarchical modeling. The performance of level $L3$ drops when compared with lower level levels, because of the scarce number of existing mentions for this level (see §5).

6 Conclusions and Future Work

We propose a hierarchical model based on a transition-based parser that is able to recognize hierarchical and nested mentions with undefined levels of complexity. We tested the performance

Hierarchical Models	L2-GENIA			L3-MED18		
	P	R	F1	P	R	F1
HNNER+SUB	69.3	64.5	66.8	73.2	71.7	72.5
HNNER+SUB-L0	73.5	68.4	70.9	74.4	71.3	72.8
HNNER+SUB-L1	65.1	60.6	62.8	72.7	72.7	72.7
HNNER+SUB-L2	-	-	-	72.1	72.1	72.1
HNNER+SUB-L3	-	-	-	37.5	36.9	37.2
HNNER	69.5	68.5	**70.0**	73.7	72.7	**73.2**
HNNER-L0	73.6	72.6	**73.1**	74.2	73.1	**73.6**
HNNER-L1	65.3	64.4	**64.8**	73.8	72.8	**73.3**
HNNER-L2	-	-	-	73.3	72.3	**72.8**
HNNER-L3	-	-	-	38.9	40.2	**39.5**

Table 4: Results on GENIA and MED18 with nested mentions with all the subcategories, and performance per hierarchical layer.

of our model using two medical datasets GENIA and MED18, and reported state-of-the-art results on flat, nested and hierarchical datasets. We leave as future work extending this approach to more general overlapping mentions with non projective overlaps and exploiting schedule sampling techniques to make the algorithm less prone to errors during test-time.

References

Steven Abney, Michael Collins, and Amit Singhal. 2000. Answer extraction. In *Proceedings of the Sixth Conference on Applied Natural Language Processing*. Association for Computational Linguistics, Stroudsburg, PA, USA, ANLC '00, pages 296–301. https://doi.org/10.3115/974147.974188.

Beatrice Alex, Barry Haddow, and Claire Grover. 2007. Recognising nested named entities in biomedical text. In *Proceedings of the Workshop on BioNLP 2007: Biological, Translational, and Clinical Language Processing*. Association for Computational Linguistics, Stroudsburg, PA, USA, BioNLP '07, pages 65–72.

Jason Chiu and Eric Nichols. 2016. Named entity recognition with bidirectional lstm-cnns. *Transactions of the Association for Computational Linguistics* 4:357–370. http://aclweb.org/anthology/Q16-1026.

Ronan Collobert, Jason Weston, Léon Bottou, Michael Karlen, Koray Kavukcuoglu, and Pavel Kuksa. 2011. Natural language processing (almost) from scratch. *J. Mach. Learn. Res.* 12:2493–2537. http://dl.acm.org/citation.cfm?id=1953048.2078186.

Chris Dyer, Miguel Ballesteros, Wang Ling, Austin Matthews, and Noah A. Smith. 2015. Transition-based dependency parsing with stack long short-term memory. *Proceedings of the 53rd Annual Meeting of the Association for Computational Linguistics and the 7th International Joint Conference on Natural Language Processing (Volume 1: Long Papers)*.

Xiaocheng Feng, Bing Qin, and Ting Liu. 2016. A language-independent neural network for event detection. *Science China Information Sciences* 61(9):092106. https://doi.org/10.1007/s11432-017-9359-x.

Jenny Rose Finkel, Shipra Dingare, Huy Nguyen, Malvina Nissim, Christopher D. Manning, and Gail Sinclair. 2004. Exploiting context for biomedical entity recognition: From syntax to the web. In *Proceedings of the International Joint Workshop on Natural Language Processing in Biomedicine and its Applications, NLPBA/BioNLP 2004, Geneva, Switzerland, August 28-29, 2004*.

Jenny Rose Finkel and Christopher D. Manning. 2009. Nested named entity recognition. In *Proceedings of the 2009 Conference on Empirical Methods in Natural Language Processing: Volume 1 - Volume 1*. Association for Computational Linguistics, Stroudsburg, PA, USA, EMNLP '09, pages 141–150.

Pavlina Fragkou. 2017. Applying named entity recognition and co-reference resolution for segmenting english texts. *Progress in Artificial Intelligence* 6. https://doi.org/10.1007/s13748-017-0127-3.

Mourad Gridach. 2017. Character-level neural network for biomedical named entity recognition. *Journal of Biomedical Informatics* 70:85 – 91.

Zhaochen Guo and Denilson Barbosa. 2014. Robust entity linking via random walks. In *Proceedings of the 23rd ACM International Conference on Conference on Information and Knowledge Management*. ACM, New York, NY, USA, CIKM '14, pages 499–508. https://doi.org/10.1145/2661829.2661887.

Zhou GuoDong. 2004. Recognizing names in biomedical texts using hidden markov model and svm plus sigmoid. In *Proceedings of the International Joint Workshop on Natural Language Processing in Biomedicine and Its Applications*. Association for Computational Linguistics, Stroudsburg, PA, USA, JNLPBA '04, pages 1–7. http://dl.acm.org/citation.cfm?id=1567594.1567596.

Nitish Gupta, Sameer Singh, and Dan Roth. 2017. Entity linking via joint encoding of types, descriptions, and context. In *Proceedings of the 2017 Conference on Empirical Methods in Natural Language Processing*. Association for Computational Linguistics, pages 2681–2690. https://doi.org/10.18653/v1/D17-1284.

Meizhi Ju, Makoto Miwa, and Sophia Ananiadou. 2018. A neural layered model for nested named entity recognition. In *Proceedings of the 2018 Conference of the North American Chapter of the Association for Computational Linguistics: Human Language Technologies, Volume 1 (Long Papers)*. Association for Computational Linguistics, pages 1446–1459. https://doi.org/10.18653/v1/N18-1131.

Arzoo Katiyar and Claire Cardie. 2018. Nested named entity recognition revisited. In *Proceedings of the 2018 Conference of the North American Chapter of the Association for Computational Linguistics: Human Language Technologies, Volume 1 (Long Papers)*. Association for Computational Linguistics, pages 861–871. https://doi.org/10.18653/v1/N18-1079.

Diederik P. Kingma and Jimmy Ba. 2014. Adam: A method for stochastic optimization. *CoRR* abs/1412.6980. http://arxiv.org/abs/1412.6980.

Guillaume Lample, Miguel Ballesteros, Sandeep Subramanian, Kazuya Kawakami, and Chris Dyer. 2016. Neural architectures for named entity recognition. *CoRR* abs/1603.01360.

Robert Leaman and Zhiyong Lu. 2016. Taggerone: joint named entity recognition and normalization with semi-markov models. *Bioinformatics* 32(18):2839–2846.

Xiao Ling and Daniel S. Weld. 2012. Fine-grained entity recognition. In *In Proc. of the 26th AAAI Conference on Artificial Intelligence*.

Liyuan Liu, Xiang Ren, Qi Zhu, Shi Zhi, Huan Gui, Heng Ji, and Jiawei Han. 2017. Heterogeneous supervision for relation extraction: A representation learning approach. *Proceedings of the 2017 Conference on Empirical Methods in Natural Language Processing* https://doi.org/10.18653/v1/d17-1005.

Wei Lu and Dan Roth. 2015. Joint mention extraction and classification with mention hypergraphs. In *Proceedings of the 2015 Conference on Empirical Methods in Natural Language Processing*. Association for Computational Linguistics, pages 857–867. https://doi.org/10.18653/v1/D15-1102.

Xuezhe Ma and Eduard Hovy. 2016. End-to-end sequence labeling via bi-directional lstm-cnns-crf. In *Proceedings of the 54th Annual Meeting of the Association for Computational Linguistics (Volume 1: Long Papers)*. Association for Computational Linguistics, pages 1064–1074. https://doi.org/10.18653/v1/P16-1101.

Michal Marcinczuk. 2015. Automatic construction of complex features in conditional random fields for named entities recognition. In *Recent Advances in Natural Language Processing, RANLP 2015, 7-9 September, 2015, Hissar, Bulgaria*. pages 413–419.

Ryan McDonald, Fernando Pereira, Seth Kulick, Scott Winters, Yang Jin, and Pete White. 2005. Simple algorithms for complex relation extraction with applications to biomedical ie. In *Proceedings of the 43rd Annual Meeting on Association for Computational Linguistics*. Association for Computational Linguistics, Stroudsburg, PA, USA, ACL '05, pages 491–498. https://doi.org/10.3115/1219840.1219901.

Tomas Mikolov, Ilya Sutskever, Kai Chen, Greg S Corrado, and Jeff Dean. 2013. Distributed representations of words and phrases and their compositionality. In C. J. C. Burges, L. Bottou, M. Welling, Z. Ghahramani, and K. Q. Weinberger, editors, *Advances in Neural Information Processing Systems 26*, Curran Associates, Inc., pages 3111–3119. http://papers.nips.cc/paper/5021-distributed-representations-of-words-and-phrases-and-their-compositionality.pdf.

Mike Mintz, Steven Bills, Rion Snow, and Dan Jurafsky. 2009. Distant supervision for relation extraction without labeled data. In *Proceedings of the Joint Conference of the 47th Annual Meeting of the ACL and the 4th International Joint Conference on Natural Language Processing of the AFNLP: Volume 2 - Volume 2*. Association for Computational Linguistics, Stroudsburg, PA, USA, ACL '09, pages 1003–1011. http://dl.acm.org/citation.cfm?id=1690219.1690287.

Makoto Miwa and Mohit Bansal. 2016. End-to-end relation extraction using lstms on sequences and tree structures. In *Proceedings of the 54th Annual Meeting of the Association for Computational Linguistics (Volume 1: Long Papers)*. Association for Computational Linguistics, pages 1105–1116. https://doi.org/10.18653/v1/P16-1105.

Aldrian Obaja Muis and Wei Lu. 2017. Labeling gaps between words: Recognizing overlapping mentions with mention separators. In *Proceedings of the 2017 Conference on Empirical Methods in Natural Language Processing*. Association for Computational Linguistics, pages 2608–2618. https://doi.org/10.18653/v1/D17-1276.

T. Ohta, Y. Tateisi, and J.D. Kim. 2002. The genia corpus: An annotated research abstract corpus in molecular biology domain. In *the Human Language Technology Conference*.

Lev Ratinov and Dan Roth. 2009. Design challenges and misconceptions in named entity recognition. In *Proceedings of the Thirteenth Conference on Computational Natural Language Learning*. Association for Computational Linguistics, Stroudsburg, PA, USA, CoNLL '09, pages 147–155. http://dl.acm.org/citation.cfm?id=1596374.1596399.

Dan Shen, Jie Zhang, Guodong Zhou, Jian Su, and Chew-Lim Tan. 2003. Effective adaptation of a hidden markov model-based named entity recognizer for biomedical domain. In *Proceedings of the ACL 2003 Workshop on Natural Language Processing in Biomedicine - Volume 13*. Association for Computational Linguistics, Stroudsburg, PA, USA, BioMed '03, pages 49–56. https://doi.org/10.3115/1118958.1118965.

Nitish Srivastava, Geoffrey Hinton, Alex Krizhevsky, Ilya Sutskever, and Ruslan Salakhutdinov. 2014. Dropout: A simple way to prevent neural networks from overfitting. *J. Mach. Learn. Res.* 15(1):1929–1958. http://dl.acm.org/citation.cfm?id=2627435.2670313.

Bailin Wang, Wei Lu, Yu Wang, and Hongxia Jin. 2018. A neural transition-based model for nested mention recognition. In *Proceedings of the 2018 Conference on Empirical Methods in Natural Language Processing*. Association for Computational Linguistics, pages 1011–1017.

Mengqiu Wang, Wanxiang Che, and Christopher D. Manning. 2013. Effective bilingual constraints for semi-supervised learning of named entity recognizers. In *Proceedings of the Twenty-Seventh AAAI Conference on Artificial Intelligence*. AAAI Press, AAAI'13, pages 919–925.

Jie Zhang, Dan Shen, Guodong Zhou, Jian Su, and Chew-Lim Tan. 2004. Enhancing hmm-based biomedical named entity recognition by studying special phenomena. *J. of Biomedical Informatics* 37(6):411–422. https://doi.org/10.1016/j.jbi.2004.08.005.

GuoDong Zhou and Jian Su. 2002. Named entity recognition using an hmm-based chunk tagger. In *Proceedings of the 40th Annual Meeting on Association for Computational Linguistics*. Association for Computational Linguistics, Stroudsburg, PA, USA, ACL '02, pages 473–480. https://doi.org/10.3115/1073083.1073163.

Towards Automatic Generation of Shareable Synthetic Clinical Notes Using Neural Language Models

Oren Melamud
IBM T. J. Watson Research Center
Yorktown Heights, NY, USA.
oren.melamud@ibm.com

Chaitanya Shivade
IBM Almaden Research Center
San Jose, CA, USA.
cshivade@us.ibm.com

Abstract

Large-scale clinical data is invaluable to driving many computational scientific advances today. However, understandable concerns regarding patient privacy hinder the open dissemination of such data and give rise to suboptimal siloed research. De-identification methods attempt to address these concerns but were shown to be susceptible to adversarial attacks. In this work, we focus on the vast amounts of unstructured natural language data stored in clinical notes and propose to automatically generate synthetic clinical notes that are more amenable to sharing using generative models trained on real de-identified records. To evaluate the merit of such notes, we measure both their privacy preservation properties as well as utility in training clinical NLP models. Experiments using neural language models yield notes whose utility is close to that of the real ones in some clinical NLP tasks, yet leave ample room for future improvements.

1 Introduction

Clinical data and clinical notes specifically, are an important factor for the advancement of computational methods in the medical domain. Suffice to say that the recently introduced *MIMIC-III* clinical database alone (Johnson et al., 2016) already has hundreds of cites on Google Scholar. However, understandable privacy concerns yield strict restrictions on clinical data dissemination, thus inhibiting scientific progress. De-identification techniques provide some relief (Dernoncourt et al., 2017), but are still far from providing the privacy guarantees required for unrestricted sharing (Ohm, 2009; Shokri et al., 2017).

In this work, we investigate the possibility of disseminating clinical notes data by computationally generating synthetic notes that are safer to share than real ones. To this end, we introduce a clinical notes generation task, where synthetic notes are to be generated based on a set of real de-identified clinical discharge summary notes, henceforth referred to as *MedText*, which we extracted from MIMIC-III. The evaluation includes a new measure of the privacy preservation properties of the synthetic notes, as well as their utility on three clinical NLP tasks. We use neural language models to perform this task and discuss the potential and challenges of this approach. Resources associated with this paper are available for download.[1]

2 Background

2.1 Clinical Notes

Electronic health records contain a wealth of information about patients in the form of both structured data and unstructured text. While structured data is critical for purposes like billing and administration, unstructured clinical notes contain important information entered by doctors, nurses, and other staff associated with patient care, which is not captured elsewhere. To this end, researchers have found that although structured data is easily accessible, clinical notes remain indispensable for understanding a patient record (Birman-Deych et al., 2005; Singh et al., 2004). Rosenbloom et al. (2011) argued that clinical notes are considered to be more useful for identifying patients with specific disorders. A study by Köpcke et al. (2013) found that 65% of the data required to determine eligibility of a patient into clinical trials was not found in structured data and required examination of clinical notes. Similar findings were also reported by Raghavan et al. (2014).

Due to their importance, it is no wonder that clinical notes are used extensively in medical NLP

---

[1] https://github.com/orenmel/synth-clinical-notes.

35

Proceedings of the 2nd Clinical Natural Language Processing Workshop, pages 35–45
Minneapolis, Minnesota, June 7, 2019. ©2019 Association for Computational Linguistics

research. Unfortunately, however, due to privacy concerns, explained further below, it is very common that the data is exclusively available only to researchers collaborating with or working for a particular healthcare provider (Choi et al., 2016; Afzal et al., 2018; Liu et al., 2018).

2.2 De-identification

Clinical notes contain sensitive personal information required for medical investigations, which is protected by law. For example, in the United States, the Health Insurance Portability and Accountability Act (HIPAA)[2] defines 18 types of protected health information (PHI) that needs to be removed to de-identify clinical notes (e.g. name, age, dates and contact details). Both manual and automated methods for de-identification have been investigated with varying degrees of success. Neamatullah et al. (2008) reported a recall ranging from 0.63 to 0.94 between 14 clinicians for manually identifying PHI in 130 clinical notes. Since human annotations for clinical data are costly (Douglass et al., 2004), researchers have investigated automated and semi-automated methods for de-identification (Gobbel et al., 2014; Hanauer et al., 2013). Automated methods range from rule-based systems (Morrison et al., 2009) to statistical methods such as support vector machines and conditional random fields (Stubbs et al., 2015), with more recent use of recurrent neural networks (Liu et al., 2017; Dernoncourt et al., 2017).

Unfortunately, despite strong results reported for clinical data de-identification methods, it is usually hard to determine to what extent they are resistant to re-identification attacks on healthcare data (Ohm, 2009; El Emam et al., 2011; Gkoulalas-Divanis et al., 2014). Therefore, in practice, de-identified patient data is almost never shared freely, and complementary privacy protection techniques, such as the one described in the following section, are being actively investigated.

2.3 Differential Privacy

Collections of private individual data records are commonly used to compute aggregated statistical information or train statistical models that are made publicly available. Possible use cases include collections of search queries used to provide intelligent auto-completion suggestions to users of search engines and medical records used to train computer-based clinical expert systems. While this is not always transparent, providing access to such aggregated information may be sufficient for attackers to infer some individual private data. One example to such well crafted attacks are the *membership inference* attacks proposed by Shokri et al. (2017). In these attacks, the adversary has only black-box access to a machine learning model that was trained on a collection of records, and tries to learn how to infer whether any given data record was part of that model's train set or not. Susceptibility to such attacks is an indication that private information may be compromised.

Differential privacy (DP) is, broadly speaking, a guarantee that the personal information of each individual record within a collection is reasonably protected even when the aggregated statistical information is exposed. A model that is trained on some record collection as its input and makes its outputs publicly available, will provide stronger DP guarantees the less those outputs depend on the presence of any individual record in the collection.

More formally, a randomized function K provides $\epsilon-$differential privacy if for all collections C_1 and C_2 differing by at most one element, and all $S \subseteq Range(K)$:

$$\log p(K(C_1) \in S) - \log p(K(C_2) \in S) \leq \epsilon$$

A mechanism K satisfying this definition addresses concerns of personal information leakage from any individual record since the inclusion of that record will not result in any publicly exposed outputs becoming significantly more or less likely (Dwork, 2008).

Differential privacy is an active research field, with various techniques proposed to provide DP guarantees to various machine learning models (Abadi et al., 2016; Papernot et al., 2018). However, while DP shares some motivation with traditional machine learning techniques, such as the need to avoid overfitting, it is unfortunately not always easy to achieve good differential privacy guarantees, and they typically come at the cost of some accuracy degradation and computational complexity.

2.4 Language Modeling

Language models (LMs) learn to estimate the probability of a next word given a context of preceding words, i.e. $\hat{P}(w_i|w_{1..i-1})$, where w_i is the

---

[2] Office for Civil Rights H. Standards for privacy of individually identifiable health information. Final rule. Federal Register. 2002;67:53181.

word in position i in the text. They were found useful in many NLP tasks, including text classification (Howard and Ruder, 2018), machine translation (Luong et al., 2015) and speech recognition (Chen et al., 2015). They are also commonly used for generating text (Sutskever et al., 2011; Radford et al., 2018) as we do in this paper. To generate text, a trained model is typically used to estimate the conditional probability distribution of the next word $\hat{P}(w_i|w_{1..i-1})$. Next, it samples a word for position i from this distribution and then goes on to sample the next one based on $\hat{P}(w_{i+1}|w_{1..i})$ and so on. The predominant model design used to implement LMs today used to be Recurrent Neural Networks (RNNs) due to their ability to capture long distance contexts (Jozefowicz et al., 2016), but recently, the attention-based *Transformer* architecture surpassed state of the art results (Radford et al., 2018; Dai et al., 2019).

3 The Clinical Notes Generation Task

To establish the merit of synthetic clinical notes generated by statistical models, we propose a task setup that consists of: (1) real de-identified clinical notes datasets used to train models, which in turn generate synthetic notes; (2) privacy measures used to estimate the privacy preservation properties of the synthetic notes; and (3) utility benchmarks used to estimate the usefulness of the notes. To be considered successful, a model needs to score well both on privacy and utility measures.

3.1 Original Clinical Notes Data

As our source for composing the real clinical notes datasets, we used MIMIC-III (v1.4) (Johnson et al., 2016), a large de-identified database that comprises nearly 60,000 hospital admissions for 38,645 adult patients. Despite having been stripped of patient identifiers, MIMIC's records are available to researchers only under strict terms of use that include careful access restrictions and completion of sensitive data training[3] due to privacy concerns.

Training language models is expensive in terms of time and compute power. It is a common practice (Merity et al., 2017) to evaluate language models that were trained on both a small dataset that is relatively quick to train on and a medium-sized dataset which can demonstrate some bene-

fits of scale while still being manageable. Therefore, within MIMIC-III, following Dernoncourt et al. (2017), we focused on the discharge summary notes due to their content diversity and richness in natural language text. Further, we followed the recently introduced WikiText-2 and WikiText-103 datasets (Merity et al., 2017) to determine plausible size, splits and most of the preprocessing of our datasets. These datasets include text from Wikipedia articles and are commonly used to benchmark general-domain language models. We name our respective benchmarks, MedText-2 and MedText-103.

To create the MedText datasets, we first extracted the full text of the discharge summary notes from the NOTEEVENTS table available from MIMIC-III. Since the text includes arbitrary line splits, presumably for formatting reasons, we merged lines and then performed sentence splitting and word tokenization using the NLP toolkit spaCy.[4] We then randomly sampled notes to create the MedText-2 and MedText-103 datasets. Each of these datasets was split into train/validation/test subsets, with MedText-2 and MedText-103 comprising approximately 2 and 103 million word train sets, respectively, and sharing the same $\sim$200K-word validation and test sets. Finally, we replaced all words with an occurrence count below 3 with an *unk* token.[5]

Table 1 describes more precise statistics of the resulting MedText datasets, compared to the respective WikiText datasets. As seen, compared to the WikiText datasets, which are nearly identical in terms of word counts, we note that MedText exhibits notably smaller vocabulary sizes (24K vs. 33K and 135K vs. 267K) and Out-Of-Vocabulary (OOV) rates (1.5% vs. 2.6% and 0.3% vs. 0.4%). We hypothesize that this is one of the artifacts of MedText being more domain-specific than WikiText, as it is restricted only to discharge summary notes. To this end, we note that to the best of our knowledge, unlike the general domain where popular language modeling benchmarks, such as WikiText, PTB and WMT (Chelba et al., 2014), are commonly used, there are no equivalent benchmarks specific to the medical domain. Therefore, as an independent contribution, we propose MedText as such a benchmark.

[3]https://mimic.physionet.org/gettingstarted/access/

[4]https://spacy.io/
[5]This was done separately for MedText-2 and MedText-103 resulting in a discrepancy between their validation/test sets in terms of the *unk* tokens.

	Train	Valid	Test
	MedText-2		
Notes	1280	128	128
Words	2,259,966	228,795	219,650
Vocab	24,052		
OOV	1.5%		
	MedText-103		
Notes	59,396	128	128
Words	103,590,422	228,795	219,650
Vocab	135,220		
OOV	0.3%		

	Train	Valid	Test
	WikiText-2		
Articles	600	60	60
Words	2,088,628	217,646	245,569
Vocab	33,278		
OOV	2.6%		
	WikiText-103		
Articles	28,475	60	60
Words	103,227,021	217,646	245,569
Vocab	267,735		
OOV	0.4%		

Table 1: MedText vs. WikiText dataset statistics

3.2 The Privacy Measure

As mentioned in the Background section, while traditional de-identification methods, such as deleting patient identifiers, are an essential prerequisite to protecting the privacy of patient data, it is well understood that they are not sufficient to provide strong privacy guarantees. To address this, we propose to share the output of statistical models that were trained to generate synthetic data based on real de-identified data. While this intuitively seems to increase privacy preservation compared to sharing the real data, it is still not necessarily sufficient, due to potential private information leakage from such models.

To quantify the risk involved in sharing synthetic clinical notes, we propose to use an empirical measure of private information leakage. This measure is meant to serve two purposes: (1) help drive the development of synthetic clinical notes generation methods that preserve privacy; and (2) inform decision makers regarding the concrete risk in releasing any given synthetic notes dataset.

Our proposed measure is adopted from the field of Differential Privacy (DP). Recently, Long et al. (2017) proposed an empirical differential privacy measure, called Differential Training Privacy (DTP). Unlike DP guarantees, which are analyzed theoretically and apply only to specific models designed for DP, DTP is a local property of any model and a concrete training set. It can be derived by means of empirical computation to any trained model regardless of whether it has theoretical DP guarantees, and provides an estimate of the privacy risks associated with sharing the outputs of that concrete trained model. In this work, we base our privacy measures on the *Pointwise Differential Training Privacy* (PDTP) metric (Long et al.,

2017), a more computationally efficient variant of DTP:

$$PDTP_{M,T}(t) = \qquad (1)$$

$$\max_{y \in Y}(|\log p_{M(T)}(y|t) - \log p_{M(T \setminus \{t\})}(y|t)|)$$

for a classification model M, a set of possible class predictions Y, a training set T, and a specific target record $t \in T$ for which the risk is measured. The rationale for this measure is that to protect the privacy of t, the difference in the predictions of a model trained with t versus those of a model trained without it, should be as small as possible, and in particular when it comes to predictions made when the model is applied to t itself.

For the purpose of measuring privacy, we make the assumption that the model M that was trained to generate the synthetic notes can be queried for the conditional probability $\log p_{M(T)}(w_i^c|w_{1..i-1}^c)$, where w_i^c is the i-th word in clinical note c, which is our equivalent of a record. [6] We note that unlike in the setting of Long et al. (2017), where a single class y is predicted for each record, for synthetic notes, we can view every generated word w_i^c in c as a separate class prediction. Accordingly, we propose Sequential-PDTP:

$$S - PDTP_{M,T}(c)$$
$$= \max_{i \in 1..|c|} \left(|\log p_{M(T)}(w_i^c|w_{1..i-1}^c) \qquad (2) \right.$$
$$\left. - \log p_{M(T \setminus \{c\})}(w_i^c|w_{1..i-1}^c)| \right)$$

S-PDTP estimates the privacy risk for clinical note c as the largest absolute difference between the conditional probability predictions made by

---

[6] If M does not disclose this information, then the synthetic notes it generates could be used to train a language model M' that does, as an approximation for M.

$M(T)$ and $M(T \setminus \{c\})$ for any of the words in c given their preceding context. Finally, our proposed privacy score for notes generated by a model M trained on a benchmark dataset T, is the expected privacy risk, where a higher score indicates a higher expected risk:

$$S - PDTP_{M,T} = \mathbb{E}_{c \in T}[S - PDTP_{M,T}(c)] \quad (3)$$

Intuitively, a high S-PDTP score means that the output of the trained model is sensitive to the presence of at least some individual records in its training set and therefore revealing that output may compromise the private information in those records. In practice, since it is challenging computationally to train and test $|T|$ different models, we use an estimated measure based on a sample of 30 notes from T.

3.3 Utility Benchmarks

We compare the utility of synthetic vs. real clinical notes by using them as training data in the following clinical NLP tasks.

3.3.1 Estimating lexical-semantic association

As a measure of the quality of the lexical semantic information contained in clinical notes, we use them to train word2vec embeddings (Mikolov et al., 2013) with 300 dimensions and a 5-word window [7]. Then, we evaluate these embeddings on the medical word similarity and relatedness benchmarks, UMNSRS-Sim and UMNSRS-Rel (Pakhomov et al., 2010; Chiu et al., 2016). These benchmarks comprise 566 and 587 word pairs, which were manually rated with a similarity and relatedness score, respectively.

To evaluate each set of embeddings, we compute its estimated similarity scores, as the cosine similarity between the embeddings of the words in each pair. Since our MedText datasets are domain-specific and not huge in size, our learned embeddings do not include a representation for many of the words in the UMNSRS benchmarks. Therefore, to ensure that we do have an embedding for every word included in the evaluation, we limit our datasets only to pairs, whose words occur at least 20 times and 30 times in MedText-2 and MedText-103, respectively. Accordingly, the number of pairs we use from UMNSRS-Sim/UMNSRS-Rel is 110/105 in the case of MedText-2 and 317/305 in the case of MedText-103. Finally, each set of

embeddings is evaluated according to the Spearman's correlation between the pair rankings induced by the embeddings' scores and the one induced by the manual scores.

3.3.2 Natural language inference (NLI)

We also probe the utility of clinical notes for performing natural language inference (NLI) – a sentence level task. The task is to determine whether a given hypothesis sentence can be inferred from a given premise sentence. NLI, also known as recognizing textual entailment (RTE) (Dagan et al., 2013), is a fundamental popular task in natural language understanding.

For our NLI task, we use MedNLI, the first clinical domain NLI dataset, recently released by Romanov and Shivade (2018). The dataset includes sentence pairs with annotated relations that are used to train evaluated models. Romanov and Shivade (2018) report the performance of various neural network based models that typically benefit from the use of unsupervised pre-trained word embeddings. In our benchmark, we report the accuracy of their simple *BOW model* (also called *sum of words*) with input embeddings that are pre-trained on MedText clinical notes and kept fixed during the training with the MedNLI sentence pairs. The pre-trained embeddings used were the same as the ones used for the lexical-semantic association task. In all of our experiments, we used the implementation of Romanov and Shivade (2018) with its default hyperparameters .[8]

3.3.3 Recovering letter case information

Our third task goes beyond word embeddings, using clinical notes to train a recurrent neural network model end-to-end. More specifically, we use MedText to train letter casing (capitalization) models. These models are trained based on parallel data comprising the original text and an all-lowered-case version of the same. Then, they are evaluated on their ability to recover casing for a test lower-cased text. The appealing aspect of this task is that the parallel data can be easily obtained in various languages and domains.

We note that sequential information is important in predicting the correct casing of words. The simplest example in English is that the first word of every sentence usually begins with a capital letter, but title casing, and ambiguous words in context (such as the word 'bid' that may need to

---

[7]We used default word2vec hyperparameters, except for 10 negative samples and 10 iterations.

[8]`https://github.com/jgc128/mednli`

be mapped to 'BID', i.e. 'twice-a-day', in the clinical prescription context), are other examples. Arguably, for this reason, the state-of-the-art for this task is achieved by sequential character-RNN models (Susanto et al., 2016). We use their implementation[9] with default hyperparameters for our evaluation.[10] We use the dev and test splits of MedText to perform the letter case recovery task and report F1.

4 Experiments

In this section, we describe results obtained when using various models to perform the clinical notes generation task. We first generate synthetic clinical notes and evaluate their privacy properties. Then, assuming these notes were shared with another party we evaluate their utility to that party in training various clinical NLP models compared to that of the real notes.

4.1 Compared Methods

To generate the synthetic notes, we used primarily a standard LSTM language model implementation by PyTorch.[11] We trained 2-layer LSTM models with 650 hidden-units on the train sets of MedText-2 and MedText-103, and tuned their hyperparameters based on validation perplexity.[12]

To get more perspective on the efficacy of the LSTM models, we also trained a simple unigram baseline with Lidstone smoothing:

$$p_{unigram}(w_i = u|w_{1..i-1}) = \frac{count(u) + 1}{N + |V|} \quad (4)$$

where w_i is the word at position i, N is the total number of words in the train set and $|V|$ is the size of the vocabulary. As can clearly be seen, this is a very naive model that generates words based on a smoothed unigram distribution, disregarding

---

[9] https://github.com/raymondhs/char-rnn-truecase

[10] We use their 'small' model configuration for MedText-2 and 'large' model configuration for MedText-103.

[11] https://github.com/pytorch/examples/tree/master/word_language_model

[12] For MedText-2, we trained for 20 epochs, beginning with a learning rate of 20 and reducing it by a factor of 4 after every epoch for which the validation loss did not go down compared to the previous epoch. For the much larger MedText-103, we trained for 2 epochs, beginning with a learning rate of 20 and reducing it by a factor of 1.2 every $\frac{1}{40}$ epoch if the validation loss did not go down by at least 0.1, but never going below a minimum learning rate of 0.1. In all runs, we used SGD with gradients clipped to 0.25, back-propagation-through-time 35 steps, a batch size of 20 and tied input and output embeddings.

the context of the word in the note. Therefore, we expect that the utility of notes generated with this model would be low. However, on the other hand, since it captures much less information about the train data, we also expect it to have better privacy properties.

We then used the trained models to generate synthetic MedText-2-M and MedText-103-M datasets with identical word counts to the respective real note train datasets, and where M denotes a generative model being used. To that end, we iteratively sampled a next token from the model's predicted conditional probability distribution and then fed that token as input back to the model. We used an empty line as an indication of an end-of-note, hence a collection of clinical notes is represented by the model as a seamless sequence of text.

We study the effect that using dropout regularization (Srivastava et al., 2014; Zaremba et al., 2014) has on privacy and the tradeoffs between privacy and utility. Dropout, like other regularization methods, is a machine learning technique commonly applied to neural networks to minimize their prediction error on unseen data by reducing overfitting to the train data. It has also been shown that avoiding overfitting using regularization is helpful for protecting the privacy of the train data (Jain et al., 2015; Shokri et al., 2017; Yeom et al., 2017). Accordingly, we hypothesize that the higher dropout values used in our models are, the better the privacy scores would be. Utility, however, typically has a dropout optimum value over which it begins to degrade.

4.2 Qualitative Observations

We sought feedback from a clinician on the quality of the generated synthetic discharge summary notes. A generated note comprises various relevant sections indicated by plain text headers. These sections are mostly in the right order with a typical order being: admission details, medical history, treatment, medications and finally, discharge details. The text of a section is mostly topically coherent with its header. For instance, the text generated for a medical history section often includes sentences mentioning medical problems. On the other hand, although local linguistic expressions and phrases typically make sense, continuity across consecutive sentences makes little clinical sense and many sentences are unclear due to incorrect grammar. A simple but obvious error is change of gender for the same patient (e.g. the pronoun 'he' switches to 'she'). A different example for short range language modeling problem is generation of incorrect terms like "Hepatitis C deficiency". The quality of a generated section is typically much better when it is backed by a structure as in a numbered list of medications. Yet, a notable problem here is that lists frequently have repeated entries (e.g. same symptom listed more than once). In conclusion, to a human eye, the synthetic notes are clearly distinct from real ones, yet from a topical and shallow linguistic perspective they do carry genuine properties of the original content. A sample snippet of a synthetic clinical note is shown in Figure 1.

Admission Date :
⟨ deidentified ⟩
Discharge Date :
⟨ deidentified ⟩
Date of Birth :
⟨ deidentified ⟩ Sex :
F
Service :
SURGERY
Allergies :
Patient recorded as having No Known Allergies to Drugs
Attending :
⟨ deidentified ⟩
Chief Complaint :
Dyspnea
Major Surgical or Invasive Procedure :
Mitral Valve Repair
History of Present Illness :
Ms. ⟨ deidentified ⟩ is a 53 year old female who presents after a large bleed rhythmically lag to 2 dose but the patient was brought to the Emergency Department where he underwent craniotomy with stenting of right foot under the LUL COPD and transferred to the OSH on ⟨ deidentified ⟩ .
The patient will need a pigtail catheter to keep the sitter daily .

Figure 1: Sample snippet of a synthetic clinical note

4.3 Results

Table 2 shows the results we get when training the LSTM language models with varied dropout values. Starting with perplexity, we see that generally we achieve notably lower (better) perplexities on MedText, compared to results with LSTM on WikiText, which are around 100 for WikiText-2 and 50 for WikiText-103. [13] We hypothe-

size that this may be due to the highly domain-specific medical jargon and repeating note template characteristics that are presumably more predictable. We also see that best perplexity results are achieved with dropout values around 0.3-0.5 for MedText-2, and 0.0 (i.e. no dropout) for MedText-103, compared to the 0.5 dropout rate commonly used in general-domain language modeling (Zaremba et al., 2014; Merity et al., 2017). These differences reinforce our proposal of MedText as an interesting language modeling benchmark for medical texts. As a reference for future work, we report the perplexity results obtained on the test set data: 12.88 on MedText-2 (dropout = 0.5), and 8.15 on MedText-103 (dropout = 0.0).

Next, looking at privacy, we see that as predicted, more aggressive (higher) dropout values yield better (lower) privacy risk scores. We also see that privacy scores on the large MedText-103 are generally much better than the ones on the smaller MedText-2. This observation is intuitive in the sense that we would expect to generally get better privacy protection when any single personal clinical note is mixed with more, rather than fewer, notes in the train-set of a note-generating model.

For the utility evaluation, we chose three representative dropout values, for which we generated the MedText-M notes and compared them against the real MedText on the utility benchmarks. Looking at the results, we first see, as expected, that the performance with MedText-M is consistently lower than that with MedText, i.e. real notes are more useful than synthetic ones. However, the synthetic notes do seem to bear useful information. In particular, in the case of the letter case recovery task, they perform almost as well as the real ones. We also see as suspected, that privacy usually comes at some expense of utility.

Finally, looking at the unigram baseline, we see as expected that perplexity and utility is by far worse than that achieved by the LSTM models, while privacy is much better. This is yet further evidence of the utility vs. privacy trade-off. We hope that future work could reveal better models that can get closer to the privacy protection values exhibited by the unigram model, while achieving utility, which is closer to that of the real notes.

---

[13] https://www.salesforce.com/products/einstein/ai-research/the-wikitext-dependency-language-modeling-dataset/

note generation model	dropout	perplexity	privacy	similarity	relatedness	nli	case
MedText-2							
Baseline: Real notes				.459	.381	.713	.910
MedText-2-M							
LSTM	0.0	15.8	11.7	.227	.125	.678	.895
LSTM	0.3	12.5	11.8				
LSTM	0.5	12.5	9.6	.259	.160	.692	.895
LSTM	0.7	15.4	7.5				
LSTM	0.8	20.3	6.6	.146	.016	.699	.883
unigram	N/A	702.4	0.9	.027	-.072	.661	.488

note generation model	dropout	perplexity	privacy	similarity	relatedness	nli	case
MedText-103							
Baseline: Real notes				.608	.489	.724	.921
MedText-103-M							
LSTM	0.0	7.8	4.9	.415	.351	.697	.918
LSTM	0.2	8.4	4.0	.401	.337	.702	.915
LSTM	0.5	10.2	3.7	.315	.271	.713	.910
unigram	N/A	803.5	0.3	.094	.170	.644	.469

Table 2: Experimental results with the real MedText and synthetic MedText-M. 'dropout' is the dropout value used to train different LSTM models on MedText and then generate the respective synthetic MedText-M datasets (0.0 means no dropout applied); 'perplexity' is the perplexity obtained on the real MedText validation set for each note generation model M; 'privacy' is our privacy measure ($S - PDTP_{M,T}$ for every M, where T is MedText); 'similarity'/'relatedness' are UMNSRS word similarity/relatedness correlation results obtained using word embeddings trained on MedText and MedText-M; 'nli' is the accuracy obtained on the MedNLI test set using different MedText pre-trained word embeddings; and 'case' is the case restoration F1 measure.

4.4 Analysis

To better understand the factors determining our proposed privacy scores, we took a closer look at two note generating models, *MedText-2-0* and *MedText-103-0*, which are the models trained on MedText-2 and MedText-103, respectively, with dropout=0.0. First, we note that in 30 out of 30 and 25 out of 30 of the notes sampled to compute $S - PDTP_{M,T}(c)$ (Eq. 2) in MedText-2-0 and MedText-103-0, respectively, we observe that

$$\log p_{M(T)}(w_j^c | w_{1..j-1}^c) > \log p_{M(T \setminus \{c\})}(w_j^c | w_{1..j-1}^c)$$

where

$$j = argmax_{i \in 1..|c|} \left(|\log p_{M(T)}(w_i^c | w_{1..i-1}^c) - \log p_{M(T \setminus \{c\})}(w_i^c | w_{1..i-1}^c)| \right)$$

In other words, in the vast majority of the cases, the maximum differences in probability predictions are due to the model trained on train-set T, which includes note c, estimating a higher conditional probability to a word in c than the one estimated by the model trained on $T \setminus \{c\}$. This can be expected, since $M(T)$ has seen all the text in c during training, while $M(T \setminus \{c\})$ may or may not have seen similar texts.

Furthermore, when looking at the actual text positions j that determine the privacy scores, we indeed see that the prediction differences that contribute to the privacy risk measure, are typically due to rare words and/or sequences of words in note c that have no similar counterparts in $T \setminus \{c\}$. More specifically, several of the cases where $\log p_{M(T \setminus \{c\})}(w_j^c | w_{1..j-1}^c) \ll \log p_{M(T)}(w_j^c | w_{1..j-1}^c)$ occur when: (1) A particular rare word w_j^c, such as *cutdown*, appears only in a single clinical note c and never in $T \setminus \{c\}$. This happens, for example, in p("cutdown" | "Left popliteal");[14] (2) The rare word is at position $j - 1$ as is *Ketamine* in p("gtt" | "On POD # 2 Ketamine,"); and (3) The word w_j^c is not rare, but usually does not appear right after the sequence $w_{1..j-1}$ as in p("mouth" | "foaming at"), where in $T \setminus \{c\}$ there is always a determiner or pronoun before the word *mouth*, or p("pain" | "mild left

---

[14]POD stands for 'postoperative day'

should"), where *should* is a typo of *shoulder*.

These findings lead us to hypothesize that cases of PHI, such as full names of patients, inadvertently left in de-identified notes, might desirably increase the privacy risk measure output because of their rarity. This would be interesting to validate in future work.

For risk mitigation, we hypothesize that using pre-trained word embeddings including rare words and even more so, pre-training the language model on a larger public out-of-domain resource (Howard and Ruder, 2018), may help in reducing some of the above discrepancies between $p_{M(T\backslash\{c\})}$ and $p_{M(T)}$ and hence improve the overall privacy score of the models.

5 Related Work

Recently, Choi et al. (2017) proposed *medGAN*, a model for generating synthetic patient records that are safer to share than the real ones due to stronger privacy properties. However, unlike our work, their study is focused on discrete variable records and does not address the wealth of information embedded in natural language notes.

Boag et al. (2016) created a corpus of synthetically-identified clinical notes with the purpose of using this resource to train de-identification models. Unlike our synthetic notes, their notes only populate the PHI instances with synthetic data (e.g. replacing "[**Patient Name**] visited [**Hospital**]" with the randomly sampled names "Mary Smith visited MGH."

6 Conclusions and Future Work

We proposed synthetic clinical notes generation as means to promote open and collaborative medical NLP research. To have merit, the synthetic notes need to be useful and at the same time better preserve the privacy of patients. To track progress on this front, we suggested a privacy measure and a few utility benchmarks. Our experiments using neural language models demonstrate the potential and challenges of this approach, reveal the expected trade-offs between privacy and utility, and provide baselines for future work.

Further work is required to extend the range of clinical NLP tasks that can benefit from the synthetic notes as well as increase the levels of privacy provided. McMahan et al. (2018) introduced an LSTM neural language model with differential privacy guarantees that has just been publicly released.[15] Radford et al. (2018) and Dai et al. (2019) recently showed impressive improvement in language modeling performance using the novel attention-based *Transformer* architecture and larger model scales. These methods are example candidates for evaluation on our proposed clinical notes generation task. With sufficient progress, we hope that this line of research would lead to useful large synthetic clinical notes datasets that would be available more freely to a wider research community.

Acknowledgments

We would like to thank Ken Barker and Vandana Mukherjee for supporting this project. We would also like to thank Thomas Steinke for helpful discussions.

References

Martin Abadi, Andy Chu, Ian Goodfellow, H Brendan McMahan, Ilya Mironov, Kunal Talwar, and Li Zhang. 2016. Deep learning with differential privacy. In *Proceedings of the 2016 ACM SIGSAC Conference on Computer and Communications Security*.

Naveed Afzal, Vishnu Priya Mallipeddi, Sunghwan Sohn, Hongfang Liu, Rajeev Chaudhry, Christopher G Scott, Iftikhar J Kullo, and Adelaide M Arruda-Olson. 2018. Natural language processing of clinical notes for identification of critical limb ischemia. *International Journal of Medical Informatics*, 111:83–89.

Elena Birman-Deych, Amy D Waterman, Yan Yan, David S Nilasena, Martha J Radford, and Brian F Gage. 2005. Accuracy of icd-9-cm codes for identifying cardiovascular and stroke risk factors. *Medical Care*, pages 480–485.

Willie Boag, Tristan Naumann, and Peter Szolovits. 2016. Towards the creation of a large corpus of synthetically-identified clinical notes. In *In Proceedings of Machine Learning for Health Workshop at NIPS*.

C. Chelba, T. Mikolov, M.Schuster, Q. Ge, T. Brants, P. Koehn, and T. Robinson. 2014. One billion word benchmark for measuring progress in statistical language modeling. In *Proceedings of INTERSPEECH*.

Xie Chen, Tian Tan, Xunying Liu, Pierre Lanchantin, Moquan Wan, Mark JF Gales, and Philip C Woodland. 2015. Recurrent neural network language

---

[15]`https://github.com/tensorflow/privacy/`

model adaptation for multi-genre broadcast speech recognition. In *Sixteenth Annual Conference of the International Speech Communication Association*.

Billy Chiu, Gamal Crichton, Anna Korhonen, and Sampo Pyysalo. 2016. How to train good word embeddings for biomedical nlp. In *Proceedings of the 15th Workshop on Biomedical Natural Language Processing*.

Edward Choi, Mohammad Taha Bahadori, Andy Schuetz, Walter F Stewart, and Jimeng Sun. 2016. Doctor ai: Predicting clinical events via recurrent neural networks. In *Machine Learning for Healthcare Conference*, pages 301–318.

Edward Choi, Siddharth Biswal, Bradley Malin, Jon Duke, Walter F Stewart, and Jimeng Sun. 2017. Generating multi-label discrete patient records using generative adversarial networks. In *Proceedings of Machine Learning for Healthcare Conference*.

Ido Dagan, Dan Roth, Mark Sammons, and Fabio Massimo Zanzotto. 2013. Recognizing textual entailment: Models and applications. *Synthesis Lectures on Human Language Technologies*, 6(4):1–220.

Zihang Dai, Zhilin Yang, Yiming Yang, William W Cohen, Jaime Carbonell, Quoc V Le, and Ruslan Salakhutdinov. 2019. Transformer-xl: Attentive language models beyond a fixed-length context. *arXiv preprint arXiv:1901.02860*.

Franck Dernoncourt, Ji Young Lee, Ozlem Uzuner, and Peter Szolovits. 2017. De-identification of patient notes with recurrent neural networks. *Journal of the American Medical Informatics Association*, 24(3):596–606.

Margaret Douglass, Gari D Clifford, Andrew Reisner, George B Moody, and Roger G Mark. 2004. Computer-assisted de-identification of free text in the mimic ii database. In *Computers in Cardiology, 2004*, pages 341–344. IEEE.

Cynthia Dwork. 2008. Differential privacy: A survey of results. In *Proceedings of International Conference on Theory and Applications of Models of Computation*.

Khaled El Emam, Elizabeth Jonker, Luk Arbuckle, and Bradley Malin. 2011. A systematic review of re-identification attacks on health data. *PloS One*, 6(12):e28071.

Aris Gkoulalas-Divanis, Grigorios Loukides, and Jimeng Sun. 2014. Publishing data from electronic health records while preserving privacy: A survey of algorithms. *Journal of biomedical informatics*, 50:4–19.

Glenn T Gobbel, Jennifer Garvin, Ruth Reeves, Robert M Cronin, Julia Heavirland, Jenifer Williams, Allison Weaver, Shrimalini Jayaramaraja, Dario Giuse, Theodore Speroff, et al. 2014. Assisted annotation of medical free text using raptat.

Journal of the American Medical Informatics Association, 21(5):833–841.

David Hanauer, John Aberdeen, Samuel Bayer, Benjamin Wellner, Cheryl Clark, Kai Zheng, and Lynette Hirschman. 2013. Bootstrapping a de-identification system for narrative patient records: cost-performance tradeoffs. *International Journal of Medical Informatics*, 82(9):821–831.

Jeremy Howard and Sebastian Ruder. 2018. Fine-tuned language models for text classification. In *Proceedings of ACL*.

Prateek Jain, Vivek Kulkarni, Abhradeep Thakurta, and Oliver Williams. 2015. To drop or not to drop: Robustness, consistency and differential privacy properties of dropout. *arXiv preprint arXiv:1503.02031*.

Alistair EW Johnson, Tom J Pollard, Lu Shen, H Lehman Li-wei, Mengling Feng, Mohammad Ghassemi, Benjamin Moody, Peter Szolovits, Leo Anthony Celi, and Roger G Mark. 2016. MIMIC-III, a freely accessible critical care database. *Scientific data*, 3:160035.

R. Jozefowicz, O. Vinyals, M. Schuster, N. Shazeer, and Y. Wu. 2016. Exploring the limits of language modeling. *arXiv preprint arXiv:1602.02410*.

Felix Köpcke, Benjamin Trinczek, Raphael W Majeed, Björn Schreiweis, Joachim Wenk, Thomas Leusch, Thomas Ganslandt, Christian Ohmann, Björn Bergh, Rainer Röhrig, et al. 2013. Evaluation of data completeness in the electronic health record for the purpose of patient recruitment into clinical trials: a retrospective analysis of element presence. *BMC medical informatics and decision making*, 13(1):37.

Jingshu Liu, Zachariah Zhang, and Narges Razavian. 2018. Deep ehr: Chronic disease prediction using medical notes. *arXiv preprint arXiv:1808.04928*.

Zengjian Liu, Buzhou Tang, Xiaolong Wang, and Qingcai Chen. 2017. De-identification of clinical notes via recurrent neural network and conditional random field. *Journal of Biomedical Informatics*, 75:S34–S42.

Yunhui Long, Vincent Bindschaedler, and Carl A Gunter. 2017. Towards measuring membership privacy. *arXiv preprint arXiv:1712.09136*.

Thang Luong, Michael Kayser, and Christopher D Manning. 2015. Deep neural language models for machine translation. In *Proceedings of the Nineteenth Conference on Computational Natural Language Learning*.

H Brendan McMahan, Daniel Ramage, Kunal Talwar, and Li Zhang. 2018. Learning differentially private language models without losing accuracy. In *Proceedings of ICLR*.

S. Merity, C. Xiong, J. Bradbury, and R. Socher. 2017. Pointer sentinel mixture models. In *Proceedings of ICLR*.

T. Mikolov, I. Sutskever, K. Chen, G. Corrado, and J. Dean. 2013. Distributed representations of words and phrases and their compositionality. In *Advances in Neural Information Processing Systems*.

Frances P Morrison, Li Li, Albert M Lai, and George Hripcsak. 2009. Repurposing the clinical record: can an existing natural language processing system de-identify clinical notes? *Journal of the American Medical Informatics Association*, 16(1):37–39.

Ishna Neamatullah, Margaret M Douglass, H Lehman Li-wei, Andrew Reisner, Mauricio Villarroel, William J Long, Peter Szolovits, George B Moody, Roger G Mark, and Gari D Clifford. 2008. Automated de-identification of free-text medical records. *BMC Medical Informatics and Decision Making*, 8(1):32.

Paul Ohm. 2009. Broken promises of privacy: Responding to the surprising failure of anonymization. *Ucla L. Rev.*, 57:1701.

Serguei Pakhomov, Bridget McInnes, Terrence Adam, Ying Liu, Ted Pedersen, and Genevieve B Melton. 2010. Semantic similarity and relatedness between clinical terms: an experimental study. In *Proceedings of AMIA*.

Nicolas Papernot, Shuang Song, Ilya Mironov, Ananth Raghunathan, Kunal Talwar, and Úlfar Erlingsson. 2018. Scalable private learning with pate. In *Proceedings of ICLR*.

Alec Radford, Jeffrey Wu, Rewon Child, David Luan, Dario Amodei, and Ilya Sutskever. 2018. Language models are unsupervised multitask learners. Technical report, Technical report, OpenAi.

Preethi Raghavan, James L Chen, Eric Fosler-Lussier, and Albert M Lai. 2014. How essential are unstructured clinical narratives and information fusion to clinical trial recruitment? In *Proceedings of AMIA Summits on Translational Science*, volume 2014. American Medical Informatics Association.

Alexey Romanov and Chaitanya Shivade. 2018. Lessons from natural language inference in the clinical domain. In *Proceedings of EMNLP*.

S Trent Rosenbloom, Joshua C Denny, Hua Xu, Nancy Lorenzi, William W Stead, and Kevin B Johnson. 2011. Data from clinical notes: a perspective on the tension between structure and flexible documentation. *Journal of the American Medical Informatics Association*, 18(2):181–186.

Reza Shokri, Marco Stronati, Congzheng Song, and Vitaly Shmatikov. 2017. Membership inference attacks against machine learning models. In *Proceedings of IEEE Symposium on Security and Privacy*.

Jasvinder A Singh, Aaron R Holmgren, and Siamak Noorbaloochi. 2004. Accuracy of veterans administration databases for a diagnosis of rheumatoid arthritis. *Arthritis Care & Research*, 51(6):952–957.

Nitish Srivastava, Geoffrey Hinton, Alex Krizhevsky, Ilya Sutskever, and Ruslan Salakhutdinov. 2014. Dropout: A simple way to prevent neural networks from overfitting. *The Journal of Machine Learning Research*, 15(1):1929–1958.

Amber Stubbs, Christopher Kotfila, and Özlem Uzuner. 2015. Automated systems for the de-identification of longitudinal clinical narratives: Overview of 2014 i2b2/uthealth shared task track 1. *Journal of Biomedical Informatics*, 58:S11–S19.

Raymond Hendy Susanto, Hai Leong Chieu, and Wei Lu. 2016. Learning to capitalize with character-level recurrent neural networks: An empirical study. In *Proceedings of EMNLP*.

Ilya Sutskever, James Martens, and Geoffrey E Hinton. 2011. Generating text with recurrent neural networks. In *Proceedings of ICML*.

Samuel Yeom, Matt Fredrikson, and Somesh Jha. 2017. Privacy risk in machine learning: Analyzing the connection to overfitting. In *Procedings of the IEEE Computer Security Foundations Symposium*.

Wojciech Zaremba, Ilya Sutskever, and Oriol Vinyals. 2014. Recurrent neural network regularization. *arXiv preprint arXiv:1409.2329*.

A Novel System for Extractive Clinical Note Summarization using EHR Data

Jennifer Liang and Ching-Huei Tsou
IBM Research, Yorktown Heights, NY 10598
{jjliang, ctsou}@us.ibm.com

Abstract

While much data within a patient's electronic health record (EHR) is coded, crucial information concerning the patient's care and management remain buried in unstructured clinical notes, making it difficult and time-consuming for physicians to review during their usual clinical workflow. In this paper, we present our clinical note processing pipeline, which extends beyond basic medical natural language processing (NLP) with concept recognition and relation detection to also include components specific to EHR data, such as structured data associated with the encounter, sentence-level clinical aspects, and structures of the clinical notes. We report on the use of this pipeline in a disease-specific extractive text summarization task on clinical notes, focusing primarily on progress notes by physicians and nurse practitioners. We show how the addition of EHR-specific components to the pipeline resulted in an improvement in our overall system performance and discuss the potential impact of EHR-specific components on other higher-level clinical NLP tasks.

1 Introduction

EHRs are a longitudinal record of the patient's health information consisting of structured (e.g. vitals, medications, labs, procedures) and unstructured (e.g. progress notes, discharge summaries, diagnostic test reports) information. Clinical notes within EHRs are traditionally a rich source of data where detailed information about the patient's medical history and clinical care process is documented. However, physicians at the point of care are mostly unable to review much of this unstructured information due to the abundance of notes within a patient EHR and the time constraint inherent in the clinical setting. Also, the move from paper records to EHRs have unintentionally resulted in issues of note bloat, where use of templates and copy-paste have introduced unnecessary or redundant data into clinical notes, worsening the problem of information overload and making it more difficult for physicians to identify key clinical data with potentially negative consequences (Shoolin et al., 2013; Vogel, 2013).

In the clinical care process, what is considered key clinical data within a clinical document depends greatly on the user and their task; what is important for a physician to know while diagnosing a patient is different from what is important for a social worker to know when arranging post-discharge home care. Building off the idea of a problem-oriented medical record introduced by Dr. Lawrence Weed (1968), we decided to approach this problem of information overload within EHRs from a disease-specific perspective. We propose an automated summarization system that produces an extractive summary for each note containing only the most important information relevant for managing a patient's hypertension or diabetes mellitus at the point of care.

There are multiple challenges in generating a disease-specific extractive summary on clinical text. First of all, the abundance of domain-specific terminology and presence of non-standard abbreviations and misspellings make machine comprehension of clinical text a much more complex task (Demner-Fushman et al., 2009). Secondly, the use of temporal narratives with reference to multiple diseases and the inherent interrelatedness of different diseases and other clinical concepts makes it difficult to determine what is "disease-specific" in the context of our summary. Moreover, the heavy use of templates, copy-paste, and imported data within clinical notes (Shoolin et al., 2013; Vogel, 2013) suggests that medical NLP at the concept level is insufficient for differentiation between "important" and "unimportant" information. Last of all, due to the regulations surround-

Proceedings of the 2nd Clinical Natural Language Processing Workshop, pages 46–54
Minneapolis, Minnesota, June 7, 2019. ©2019 Association for Computational Linguistics

ing use and sharing of protected health information, and the need for expert annotation, clinical NLP systems typically only have access to a limited amount of labeled data. To address these concerns, we leverage individual components, trained on separate labeled datasets, that target lower level clinical NLP tasks such as identifying note structure and specific clinical events of interest, and chain these individual components together into a pipeline that automatically generates disease-specific summaries from clinical notes.

2   Related Work

EHR summarization efforts have mostly focused on extraction of clinical variables or visualization of structured and unstructured elements in the EHR as a longitudinal data display (Pivovarov and Elhadad, 2015), with the objective being to present an overview of the entire longitudinal patient record. Savova et al. (2010) built cTAKES, an open-source NLP system for information extraction from unstructured clinical text. Rogers et al. (2006) developed the CLEF chronicle, which uses a semantic network of concepts and interrelations to represent events in a patient's medical history, that could serve as a building block for future summarization efforts. CLAMP (Soysal et al., 2017) allows users to more efficiently build customized NLP pipelines and reported good performance on named entity recognition and concept encoding in their evaluation.

Some researchers approached EHR note summarization from a problem identification perspective. Cao et al. (2004) summarized discharge summaries as problem lists. Van Vleck and Elhadad (2010) identified a list of problems relevant to a physician seeing a new patient for a given set of clinical notes. Our work differs from previous published research in that our summarization system is (1) targeted toward a single clinical encounter represented by a note, (2) specific to the management of a given disease: hypertension and diabetes mellitus, (3) generates a human readable textual summary as opposed to a list of clinical variables, and (4) extends beyond basic medical NLP with concept recognition and relation detection to also include components specific to EHR data.

3   Method

The ultimate goal of the system is to generate a cohesive summary of a patient, similar to a summary written by an attending physician after reviewing the patient's chart. Such a system requires text summary from individual notes, reconciliation between structured data and unstructured narratives, temporal alignment of the clinical events, and natural language generation to produce the final abstractive summary. This paper focuses entirely on extracting informative sentences rather than cohesive sentences from a single clinical note. The output of the work presented here can be used as the input for downstream components to generate cohesive summaries across the longitudinal patient record.

3.1   Dataset

Our dataset consists of patient EHRs within a large ambulatory multi-specialty medical group in the US that contain a known diagnosis of hypertension and/or diabetes mellitus based on their structured encounter diagnosis list. We selected notes within these patient EHRs authored by physicians or nurse practitioners and manually reviewed approximately half of the selected notes to ensure that at least one of our diseases of interest, hypertension or diabetes mellitus, was addressed at the visit documented in that note. We made the decision to focus on physician and nurse practitioner notes because those providers are the primary decision-maker in the patients' clinical care management. Manual review was performed on approximately half of the notes to ensure a sufficient number of positive examples from the ground truth generation effort. The resulting corpus consisted of 3,453 outpatient clinical notes over 762 patients, with an average length of 138 sentences per note.

The corpus was annotated by 12 internal medicine or family medicine physicians over the course of 6 months. Physicians were asked to review each note and annotate information relevant to the physicians' decision-making for management of the patient's hypertension or diabetes mellitus, with the understanding that the annotated information would be presented together as a disease-focused summary of the note. Examples of relevant information included in the summary are statements about the current problem status, any signs or symptoms experienced by the patient, desirable and undesirable effects of current treat-

John Doe, a 58 yrs. male patient is here for follow up on:
* DIABETES MELLITUS: Since last visit patient has been well. **Patient has polyuria and polydypsia. Weight has been increased. Blood sugars have been worse. He is over eating. Pt is not motivated to take care of himself.**   GLU   222   12/1/17
GLUCOSEFAST   160   5/17/12
HGBA1C   8.3   12/1/17
* HYPERTENSION: <u>Since last visit BP has been elevated as per his home readings.</u> Patient complains of no side effects from medications. Patient denies any chest pain or shortness of breath. <u>Weight has increased.</u>
* OBESITY/OVERWEIGHT: Patient has not been following a weight reducing diet. Since last visit the weight is increased. Patient has not been able to do regular exercises.

Current outpatient prescriptions:
LISINOPRIL 40 MG TB 1 tablet daily
IBUPROFEN 600 MG TAB taking 3 tabs a day
METFORMIN 500 MG TAB 1 tablet twice daily
ATENOLOL 100 MG TAB Take 1 tab(s) orally once a day
ALLOPURINOL 300 MG TAB Take 1 tab(s) orally 1 times a day
AMLODIPINE 5 MG TAB 1 tablet daily

Blood pressure 160/102, pulse 74, weight 300 lb (136.079 kg). Estimated BMI is 45.61 kg/(m^2)
HEENT: TM's clear bilaterally, PERRLA, EOMI, no palpable nodes, thyroid normal to palpation
Chest: clear to auscultation
Cardiac: heart rate regular with no murmurs, gallops, or rubs
Abd: soft, non-tender, no masses
Extr: pulses normal throughout, no cyanosis, clubbing, or edema
Neuro: non focal, alert, oriented X 3 and gait nl

ASSESSMENT/PLAN:
- DIABETES MELLITUS: **sub-optimally controlled.** Plan Adjust medications: **Increase metformin to 1000mg from 500 mg bid, Recommend home blood sugar monitoring,** Encourage appointment with diabetes educator, Encourage better diet management, Encourage weight loss, Encourage annual eye exam due: next year.
- HYPERTENSION: <u>sub-optimally controlled.</u> Advised Change medications <u>Add hctz 25mg qday, Recommend home blood pressure monitoring and Labs today: Chem7 and now that gout is well controlled.</u>
- OBESITY/OVERWEIGHT: sub-optimally controlled. Discussed benefits of achieving ideal weight. Advised to push for more exercises. Dietary measures are emphasized. Resources for low fat diet are provided.
This visit lasted 25 minutes, including 15 minutes counseling the patient regarding the above problems.

Figure 1: Sample clinical note with extractive summaries for hypertension and diabetes mellitus. Underlined sentences together form the extractive summary for hypertension; sentences in bold together form the extractive summary for diabetes mellitus.

ment, and any changes to current treatment plan. Each note was independently reviewed and annotated by two physicians, and then adjudicated by a third MD. The inter-annotator agreement is reported in the "Results" section. Figure 1 shows an example of a clinical note and its extractive summaries for hypertension and diabetes mellitus.

3.2 Extractive Summarization

Current approaches of document summarization in the clinical domain have largely been extractive rather than abstractive, so the original text as written by the physicians are preserved.

Given a clinical note consisting of a sequence of sentences, $N = \{s_1, s_2, ...s_n\}$ a sentence level, single document, extractive summarization task can be defined as to create a summary NS by selecting m sentences ($m \leq n$) from N. One of the simplest approaches is to model the task as a supervised binary classification problem, where we find a model with model parameters θ that maximize the likelihood

$$p(Y|N, \theta) = \prod_{(i=1)}^{n} p(y_i|s_i, \theta) \qquad (1)$$

where $Y = \{y_1, y_2, ...y_n\}$ and $y_i \in \{0, 1\}$.

It is obvious that in (1) each sentence is classified solely on the information contained in the sentence itself. This rudimentary approach works reasonably well for many sentence classification tasks, provided the majority of the sentences are self-contained. For clinical notes, sentences are often short and the meaning depend heavily on the context. One way to address this is to model the problem as a sequence labeling task, where additional information at the document level is also considered,

$$p(Y|N, \theta) = \prod_{(i=1)}^{n} p(y_i|s_i, N, \theta) \qquad (2)$$

A simple example of sequence model is a linear-chain CRF (Lafferty et al., 2001), which takes the previously labeled sentence(s) into consideration when predicting the label of the current sentence. Recent advances in deep neural network based approaches have shown great promises in analyzing several types of EHR data (Shickel et al., 2018), but their application in extractive note summarization is largely unexplored (Alsentzer and Kim, 2018).

In this paper, we start by creating the baseline using the 3 approaches discussed above, i.e., a linear SVM for sentence classification, a linear chain CRF in which each note is modeled as a sequence, and a simple CNN-rand (Kim, 2014) for our summarization task. All 3 models used only the note

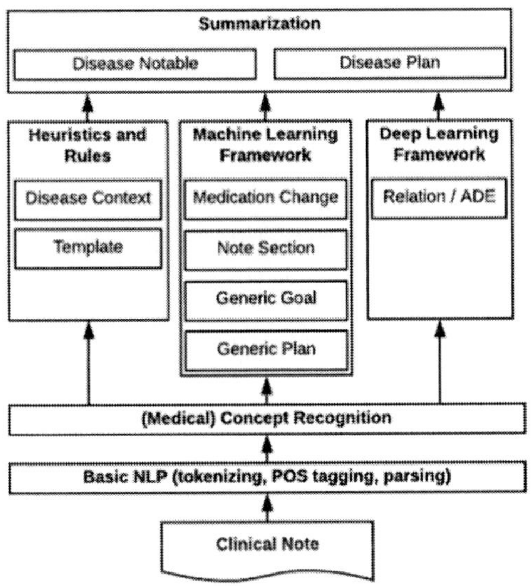

Figure 2: Single clinical document extractive summarization pipeline.

text as features: bag of n-grams for the SVM and the CRF, and randomly initialized word embeddings (updated during training) for CNN-rand. We report the F-scores for each of these models in the "Results" section.

3.3 Clinical Note Processing Pipeline

Each clinical note is ingested by a basic NLP processing layer that performs the standard NLP tasks including tokenization, lemmatization, sentence segmentation, POS tagging, and parsing, followed by a medical concept recognition component, where key medical concepts such as labs, procedures, medications, signs and symptoms, and diseases are identified. Our system used an English Slot Grammar (ESG) parser (McCord, 1990) followed by a proprietary medical concept annotator that maps terms into unified medical language system (UMLS) concepts (Bodenreider, 2004). This entity linking pipeline is similar to MetaMap (Aronson and Lang, 2010) but was optimized to process clinical notes, where sentences are not always well structured and abbreviation expansion and disambiguation plays an important role. These foundational NLP analytics, although crucial to the success of downstream components and remain an active research area, have become commodity in the recent years, for instance, CLAMP (Soysal et al., 2017), Amazon Comprehend Medical, (Amazon, 2019), and IBM Natural Language Understanding (IBM, 2019) and is not of interest in this paper.

We separate the components in the next layer into 3 categories based on how the analytics are developed, namely, heuristics and rules, assertions framework, and deep-learning framework (Figure 2). When labeled data is easier to obtain, data-driven approaches, such as deep neural network architectures, often outperform other methods due to their ability to effectively learn representations as well as model parameters. For instance, for adverse drug events (ADEs), we use an existing labeled dataset from the MADE1.0[1] NLP challenge to train a BiLSTM-CRF model with attention (Dandala et al., 2018). On the other hand, ground truth for extractive summarization requires human experts to read the entire note and is harder to acquire. With limited ground truth, we have learned that a hybrid system combining heuristics, less expressive models (e.g. linear SVM), and outputs from deep-learning based components as features generates better results than trying to train an end-to-end pure neural network based system. In the "Results" section, we will give one example from each category that has significant contribution to the overall system.

3.4 Evaluation

Evaluating a text summary is challenging. Generally, the ways of evaluating the performance of automatically generated summarizations can be categorized into intrinsic and extrinsic evaluation methods (Steinberger and Jezek, 2009). Intrinsic evaluation directly compares the generated summary to the ground truth summary. For example, co-selection measures calculate the precision, recall, and F-score at the sentence level; and content-based measures such as ROUGE (Lin, 2004) compares at word level using n-gram and/or longest common subsequence. Intrinsic evaluation can also be done qualitatively, by domain experts using a Likert-type scale. Extrinsic evaluation measures the quality of the automatic summaries indirectly, for a given task. For example, how much time a physician can save in their daily practice with or without the help of such summarization. In this work we present our results using intrinsic evaluation with co-selection measures. Studies using qualitative intrinsic measurements and quantitative extrinsic evaluation are being planned

[1]bio-nlp.org/index.php/announcements/39-nlp-challenges/

	Hypertension	Diabetes
Precision	0.723	0.726
Recall	0.646	0.671
F-score	0.682	0.697

Table 1: Inter-annotator agreement.

	Hypertension	Diabetes
SVM, linear	0.524	0.516
CRF, linear-chain	0.579	0.598
CNN	0.584	0.593

Table 2: F-scores for hypertension and diabetes mellitus summarization using different models.

	Hypertension	Diabetes
Unigram	0.555	0.581
+N-gram	0.579	0.598
+Concept	0.590	0.608
+Section	0.630	0.637
+Context	0.642	0.655
+Plan	0.646	0.662
All	0.657	0.679

Table 3: Ablation study - F-scores of disease-specific insights.

for the future; those results will be reported at a later time and are beyond the scope of this paper. In this work, we evaluated the system using the co-selection measures, i.e., calculating sentence level F-score between system-identified span and a physician-annotated span, using 10-fold cross validation.

4 Results

4.1 Inter-Annotator Agreement

Agreement was calculated at the sentence level, meaning that if two annotators each marked a different span of text within the same sentence, it was considered a match. On average, annotators marked 4 to 5 sentences per note to be included in the disease-specific summary. Because the number of sentences not included in a summary is significantly larger than the number of sentences marked by physician annotators, we use recall, precision, and F-score as surrogates for the typical Cohen's Kappa in reporting inter-annotator agreement. Using one annotator's annotations as reference, we calculate the recall, precision, and F-score of the second annotator as a measure of the inter-annotator agreement, as shown in Table 1. In the "Discussion' section, we will discuss reasons for the observed differences between annotators.

4.2 Summarization Models

Table 2 shows the results of 3 different approaches for our summarization task: classification with SVM, sequence labelling with CRF, and a simple CNN with randomly initialize word embeddings. Note that in our training corpus, notes on average have 138 sentences and only 3% of the sentences are annotated as summary. Although the F-

scores are at the fifties, the accuracies (including true-negatives) are well above high nineties.

We can see that considering the document level information (CRF & CNN) is important for the task, and CNN is performing reasonably well even with limited labeled data. In this paper, our goal is to identify useful information from the entire EHR, in the context of producing extractive clinical narrative summarization. Those document level and patient level features can be used in both neural network based and non-neural network based architectures. Our current system uses CRF at the top level to label the sentences, and several deep learning based models at the component level.

4.3 Impact of EHR Components

Table 3 shows the results of an ablation study on selected components. Here we only report the numbers using the CRF model. We started by using only bag-of-words (unigram) as features and introduce a new type of feature in the next row. The last row shows the final result of using all features, including all components shown in Figure 2, such as ADEs, goals, and medication changes.

4.4 Heuristics and Rules - Disease Context

As our summarization is disease-specific, it is intuitive that knowing the disease context of each sentence can be a useful feature. For example, in the sample clinical note in Figure 1, the phrase "sub-optimally controlled" appears 3 times, each under a different disease context: "*DIABETES MELLITUS*", "*HYPERTENSION*", and "*OBESITY/OVERWEIGHT*". Depending on the disease context, each specific instance of "sub-optimally controlled" may or may not be an insight we want to extract for a given target disease.

In practice, this disease context can be an explicit section header (as in Figure 1), or conveyed more implicitly, such as a disease mentioned in the previous sentence or an encounter diagnosis code in the structured data associated with that note. A common example of implicit disease context is in specialist notes; for example, an Endocrinology note consulting on a patient's newly diagnosed diabetes mellitus. Here, the specialty in the note metadata (*"Endocrinology"*) and the reason for consult (*"newly-diagnosed DM2"*) both serve as the context for the entire note.

Because the disease context can be far away from the current sentence, especially for cases of implicit context, heuristics are used until we have enough labeled data to train a model with long term memory, such as recurrent neural network with attention mechanism. These heuristics were developed with input from subject matter experts familiar with how to read and interpret clinical text. We can see from Table 3 that modeling disease context explicitly improved the overall performance.

4.5 Machine Learning Framework - Note Section

Although not required, healthcare providers often follow some common structures, for example, SOAP (Lew and Ghassemzadeh, 2018), when documenting a patient encounter in a clinical note. Knowing where a sentence resides with respect to these structures or sections, will undoubtfully help the system extract important insights from the note.

As there are no set rules for indicating sections, and headers and formats are not strictly enforced, pattern matching rules using regular expression yield mediocre results. To improve the accuracy, we model note section classification as a supervised sequence labeling task using linear-chain CRF - each sentence belongs to 1 of 14 predefined note sections, namely, chief complaint, history of present illness, past medical history, past surgical history, medications, allergies, social history, family history, review of systems, vital signs, physical exam, diagnostic test results, assessment and plan, and other, and both the results from regular expression (matching predefined format and headers) as well as the words in the sentence are used as features in the CRF model. Table 3 shows that note section is another useful global feature in extractive summarization.

5 Discussion

5.1 Reasons for Annotator Differences

Although we placed our extractive summarization task in the setting of a specific user (physician), disease (hypertension and diabetes mellitus), and task (disease management), there is still a subjective component in the ground truth generation process. Some practitioners prefer a very concise summary limited to only the disease of focus, while others prefer a more informative summary that includes not only information directly related to the disease of focus, but also to related co-morbidities. Also, redundancy in clinical notes means that the same information is often presented in different ways in different parts of the same note; for example, the patient's presentation is described in detail in the history of present illness (HPI) section at the top of the note, while the same information is summarized in a more concise way in the assessment and plan section (AP) at the end of the note. Some practitioners prefer the additional detail contained in the HPI section as part of their summary, while others prefer only seeing the more concise version in the AP section.

During the ground truth generation process, we aligned physicians' perspectives and preferences the best we could through multiple discussions of what types of information should (e.g. problem status, home monitoring results, changes in disease management) and should not (e.g. direct imports from structured data, routine labs and follow-up instructions) be included as part of the summary. The discussions helped ensure better consistency of the ground truth among different physician annotators, but still resulted in an observed IAA of 0.682 to 0.697. This reflects the inherent subjective nature of the task, and demonstrates the need for a third MD to adjudicate any disagreements between annotators to produce consistent ground truth to be used by our system.

5.2 Addressing Issues of Data Scarcity

One of the challenges common in developing analytics on clinical text is the limited labeled data available for training and testing due to health information privacy concerns and the expensive cost of expert annotations. Our automatic summarization system works around this limitation by using individual components that can be trained using separate ground truth. Some components, such as note section classification, do not require annotators with the same level of domain expertise and can more easily be done in-house by appropriately trained non-physician annotators. Other components, such as adverse drug events, make use of existing labeled datasets available through various clinical NLP challenges such as MADE1.0[2] and TAC[3]. Using separately trained components allows our system to make the most of the limited amount of available expert-annotated data.

5.3 Limitations in Evaluation

In this study, we use an intrinsic evaluation of our generated summary using precision, recall, and F-score to compare against ground truth created by physicians. However, these metrics do not fully capture the nuances of what should or should not be included in a clinical summary. The wide spectrum of what could be considered "important" to a physician means that not all false negatives are equivalent; some information is critical to patient management and should never be missed, while the importance and relevance of some other pieces of information are debatable amongst different physicians. Similarly, not all false positives are equivalent; some false positives are completely wrong and unrelated to the disease at hand, while others comprise of sentences that were not included in the ground truth but still provide relevant and useful information.

Adverse drug events are an example of important information that physicians are particularly sensitive to. ADEs have great impact on patient safety and is considered an important insight to extract per our annotation guidelines. These are rare yet important events for physicians to be aware of when managing a patient's care. We have been actively participating in recent ADE detection related challenges and developed our component using BiLSTM-CRF (Dandala et al., 2018). A major task for this component is to distinguish adverse drug events (e.g. *"His cough improved off lisinopril"*) from indication for a drug (e.g. *"His hypertension improved on lisinopril"*), i.e., to identify the type of relation between a drug and a sign or symptom. This is often impossible without medical knowledge, and is an example of why a generic summarization algorithm from other domains will not work on clinical narratives out of the box, as the importance of a sentence depends on medical

knowledge from outside of the document.

Because of the importance of ADEs to clinical care, a missed ADE by the system (false negative) or an incorrectly identified ADE (false positive) both negatively impact the overall quality of the summary significantly more compared to other types of information. As ADEs are rare, adding this component does not have significant impact to the overall summarization accuracy measure. However, we choose to discuss this component in this paper to demonstrate the need for a qualitative intrinsic evaluation that weighs each sentence based on its importance in order to capture the value that rare yet important events, such as ADEs, bring to the overall system.

Redundant information in clinical notes pose another challenge to the evaluation of our system. This redundancy led to observed cases where the ground truth has one sentence annotated while the system has annotated a different sentence containing essentially the same content. This is judged as a false negative (because the system missed the physician-annotated sentence) and a false positive (because the system-annotated sentence was not in the physician-annotated ground truth), reflecting negatively in the overall system evaluation without giving the system credit for the fact that the relevant information is still present in the generated summary. This demonstrates the need for a separate extrinsic evaluation of our generated summaries based on its usefulness in the clinical setting, which we have planned for the future.

We are planning future evaluations of our system using qualitative intrinsic measures to capture the importance of different information within the clinical summary, and quantitative extrinsic measures to evaluate the usefulness of the system-generated summaries for practicing physicians at the point of care.

6 Conclusions

We propose an automated system for disease-specific extractive summarization on a single clinical note. We describe our clinical note processing pipeline that includes a basic NLP processing layer as well as additional EHR-specific components such as note section classification, disease context identification, and adverse drug events detection. We show incremental improvement in overall system performance with addition of each component, from F-scores of 0.555 and 0.581 for

---

[2]bio-nlp.org/index.php/announcements/39-nlp-challenges/

[3]bionlp.nlm.nih.gov/tac2017adversereactions/

hypertension and diabetes mellitus, respectively, when using only unigrams, to 0.657 and 0.679 when all components are included in the pipeline. Our work demonstrates how analytics beyond concept recognition is necessary for a complex and higher-level clinical NLP task such as summarization. Also, until abundant labeled data in clinical narratives becomes available, generic summarization algorithms developed using non-EHR data will benefit from using EHR-specific components discussed here as global features.

References

Emily Alsentzer and Anne Kim. 2018. Extractive Summarization of EHR Discharge Notes. *arXiv:1810.12085*.

Amazon. 2019. Amazon Comprehend Medical.

Alan R Aronson and François-Michel Lang. 2010. An overview of MetaMap: historical perspective and recent advances. *Journal of the American Medical Informatics Association*, 17(3):229–236.

Olivier Bodenreider. 2004. The Unified Medical Language System (UMLS): integrating biomedical terminology. *Nucleic Acids Research*, 32:D267–D270.

Hui Cao, Michael F. Chiang, James J. Cimino, Carol Friedman, and George Hripcsak. 2004. Automatic Summarization of Patient Discharge Summaries to Create Problem Lists using Medical Language Processing. *Stud Health Technol Inform*, 107(2):1540.

Bharath Dandala, Venkata Joopudi, and Murthy Devarakonda. 2018. IBM Research System at MADE 2018: Detecting Adverse Drug Events from Electronic Health Records. In *Proceedings of the 1st International Workshop on Medication and Adverse Drug Event Detection*, volume 90 of *Proceedings of Machine Learning Research*, pages 39–47. PMLR.

Dina Demner-Fushman, Wendy W. Chapman, and Clement J. McDonald. 2009. What can natural language processing do for clinical decision support? *Journal of Biomedical Informatics*, 42(5):760–772. Biomedical Natural Language Processing.

IBM. 2019. IBM Natural Language Understanding.

Yoon Kim. 2014. Convolutional Neural Networks for Sentence Classification. In *Proceedings of the 2014 Conference on Empirical Methods in Natural Language Processing (EMNLP)*, pages 1746–1751, Doha, Qatar. Association for Computational Linguistics.

John D. Lafferty, Andrew McCallum, and Fernando C. N. Pereira. 2001. Conditional Random Fields: Probabilistic Models for Segmenting and Labeling Sequence Data. In *Proceedings of the Eighteenth International Conference on Machine Learning*, ICML '01, pages 282–289, San Francisco, CA, USA. Morgan Kaufmann Publishers Inc.

Valerie Lew and Sassan Ghassemzadeh. 2018. *SOAP Notes. [Updated 2019 Jan 19]. In: StatPearls [Internet]*. Treasure Island (FL): StatPearls Publishing.

Chin-Yew Lin. 2004. ROUGE: A Package for Automatic Evaluation of Summaries. In *Text Summarization Branches Out: Proceedings of the ACL-04 Workshop*, pages 74–81, Barcelona, Spain. Association for Computational Linguistics.

Michael C. McCord. 1990. Slot grammar. *Natural language and logic*, pages 118–145.

Rimma Pivovarov and Noémie Elhadad. 2015. Automated methods for the summarization of electronic health records. *Journal of the American Medical Informatics Association*, 22(5):938–947.

Jeremy Rogers, Colin Puleston, and Alan Rector. 2006. The CLEF Chronicle: Patient Histories Derived from Electronic Health Records. In *22nd International Conference on Data Engineering Workshops (ICDEW'06)*, pages x109–x109.

Guergana K Savova, James J Masanz, Philip V Ogren, Jiaping Zheng, Sunghwan Sohn, Karin C Kipper-Schuler, and Christopher G Chute. 2010. Mayo clinical Text Analysis and Knowledge Extraction System (cTAKES): architecture, component evaluation and applications. *Journal of the American Medical Informatics Association*, 17(5):507–513.

Benjamin Shickel, Patrick Tighe, Azra Bihorac, and Parisa Rashidi. 2018. Deep EHR: A Survey of Recent Advances in Deep Learning Techniques for Electronic Health Record (EHR) Analysis. *IEEE Journal of Biomedical and Health Informatics*, 22(5):1589–1604.

J. Shoolin, L. Ozeran, C. Hamann, and W. Bria. 2013. Association of Medical Directors of Information Systems Consensus on Inpatient Electronic Health Record Documentation. *Appl Clin Inform*, 4(2):293–303.

Ergin Soysal, Jingqi Wang, Min Jiang, Yonghui Wu, Hua Xu, Serguei Pakhomov, and Hongfang Liu. 2017. CLAMP a toolkit for efficiently building customized clinical natural language processing pipelines. *Journal of the American Medical Informatics Association*, 25(3):331–336.

Josef Steinberger and Karel Jezek. 2009. Evaluation Measures for Text Summarization. *Computing and Informatics*, 28:1001–1026.

Tielman T. Van Vleck and Noémie Elhadad. 2010. Corpus-Based Problem Selection for EHR Note Summarization. *AMIA Annu Symp Proc*, pages 817–821.

Lauren Vogel. 2013. Cut-and-paste clinical notes con-
fuse care, say US internists. *CMAJ*, 185(18):E826–
E826.

Lawrence L. Weed. 1968. Medical records that guide
and teach. *New England Journal of Medicine*,
278:652657.

Study of lexical aspect in the French medical language.
Development of a lexical resource

Agathe PIERSON[1] and **Cédrick FAIRON[1]**

(1) CENTAL, Collège Léon Dupriez, Place Montesquieu 3, 1348 Louvain-la-Neuve
agathe.pierson@uclouvain.be, cedrick.fairon@uclouvain.be

Abstract

This paper details the development of a new linguistic resource designed to integrate aspectual values in temporal information extraction systems. After a brief review of the linguistic notion of aspect and how it got a place in the NLP field, we present our clinical data and describe the five-step approach adopted in this study. Then, we describe our French linguistic resource and explain how we elaborated it and which properties were selected for the creation of the tables. Finally, we evaluate the coverage of our resource and we present several prospects and improvements to foresee.

1 Introduction

Being able to model the chronology of events is paramount in the medical field, especially in electronic health records. Temporal reasoning indeed plays an important role at different stages of patient care: tracking disease status, decision support, prevention of side effects, recognition and discovery of health problems, choice of the appropriate treatment and care quality (Botsis et al., 2011; Chai et al., 2013; Sojic et al., 2016). Because this has yet to be properly implemented in clinical software, it is essential to keep developing NLP techniques and methods that efficiently extract temporal information and medical events found in patient records.

Temporal information extraction has been widely studied. Several methods have been developed to obtain ever more satisfactory results in the extraction of this information, whether by a statistical method (Li and Patrick, 2012) or by a hybrid method combining rule-based and machine-learning pattern (Lin et al., 2013), statistical and symbolic approaches (Tapi Nzali, Tannier and Neveol, 2015a), neural networks and support vector machines (Tourille et al., 2017).

These studies were mainly concentrated on English data, 'due to the lack of publicly available annotated corpora' for other languages, including French (Sun et al., 2013). Recently Campillos et al. (2018) produced a French written clinical corpus with the annotation of temporal entities, attributes, and relations, but it is not yet freely open to the research community.

In this paper, assuming that consideration of aspect could improve the precision of temporal information extraction (see Fig. 1), we undertook to develop an innovative resource which encodes linguistic properties related to the French verbal aspect in medical language. We will test it, within a system of temporal information extraction, in a later paper.

After a brief introduction of the concept of aspect from linguistic and NLP angles and a review of existing resources (section 2), we will define our corpus (section 3) and the method (section 4) used in this research to elaborate this linguistic resource (section 5). We will then assess the coverage of the resource (section 6) and discuss directions for future works (section 7).

2 State of the art

2.1 The aspect, a linguistic category

In linguistics, the grammatical category of

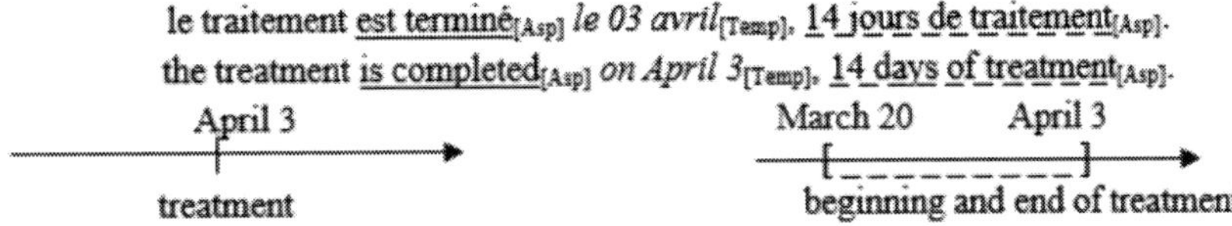

Figure 1. Representation of temporal information extraction *vs.* temporal and aspectual information extraction

Proceedings of the 2nd Clinical Natural Language Processing Workshop, pages 55–64
Minneapolis, Minnesota, June 7, 2019. ©2019 Association for Computational Linguistics

aspect refers to "the representation that the speaker makes of the process expressed by the verb (or by the action name), that is to say, the representation of its duration, its course or its completion (inchoative, progressive, resultant, perfective aspects, etc.)" (Dubois et al., 1994: 53).

Aspect in French refers to three components that should be dissociated: grammatical aspect, Aktionsart (or semantic aspect) and lexical aspect. The grammatical aspect is "a significant variation of the verb related to a choice of the speaker and, in this respect 'subjective'" (Confais, 2002: 202). It is realized morphologically through verbal inflections. Smith (1991) has extensively theorized on the *viewpoint* or grammatical aspect in which she distinguishes the perfective (1), imperfective and neutral aspects; after her, Caudal (2006) adds the resultative aspect.

> (1) J'ai rencontré cette patiente dont <u>j'ai opéré</u> le mari d'une obésité morbide par Sleeve.
> "I met this patient whose husband <u>I performed</u> a sleeve surgery on for morbid obesity." (Perfective)

The Aktionsart (see (2)) describes *eventualities* (Bach, 1986) according to criteria such as telicity, durativity, atomicity or dynamicity (Vendler, 1957; Comrie, 1981; Moens and Steedman, 1988). For the calculation, the verbal diathesis is used, i.e., the verbal kernel extended with its completion and its possible modifiers.

> (2) On <u>a surveillé</u> le patient pendant 48h.
> "We <u>monitored</u> the patient for 48 hours." (Activity)

The lexical aspect is expressed by the very meaning of the verb (Karolak, 2008; Kozareva-Levie, 2011). This aspect "isolates a moment of the process or specifies the place of the said process in an event chain" (Wilmet, 2001: 63) and presents it as "the result of a selection operation of part of the *constituent time* of this process" (Gosselin, 2011: 149). This aspect can be rendered either by the full verb (3) or by a semi-auxiliary, serving as a support verb (e.g. *continuer* 'to continue to').

> (3) J'ai préféré <u>interrompre</u> l'examen au niveau de l'angle droit.
> "I preferred to <u>interrupt</u> the examination at the right angle."

Our objective is not so much to end the aspectual controversy, but rather to identify and select the factual elements from this field that are best suited for operationalization and automatic recognition. In this paper, we focus on the internal lexical aspect (Gosselin, 2011: 149-150). Indeed, it seems particularly relevant to us, in a medical linguistics project, to identify events such as the onset of a disease, the performance of surgery, the resumption of an examination or the end of treatment; all essential aspectual elements to be placed on a patient's timeline.

2.2 What about the aspect in NLP?

NLP researchers have proposed solutions for integrating the aspectual dimension into temporal information extraction system. This integration is made difficult by the complexity of the aspectual phenomenon about which "opinion is often divided as to the appropriate aspectual categories and their realizations" (Bittar, 2010: 33). Among the different methods listed above, we are mainly interested in resources that encode aspectual properties in order to be integrated into information retrieval and information extraction systems. In the late twentieth century, Klavans and Chodorow (1992) developed an aspectual classification system that establishes a distinction between stative and non-stative events using scenario templates. Later, Siegel and McKeown (2001) finalized a statistical method for automatic aspectual classification by prediction on co-occurrence frequencies between verbs and linguistic modifiers.

In 2003, the TimeML specification of event and temporal expressions in natural language text was introduced (TimeML; Pustejovsky et al., 2003). These annotation guidelines include two aspectual levels: i) the aspectual attribute that concerns grammatical aspect; ii) the ALINK that represents the relationship between an aspectual event and its argument event (*initiates, continues, culminates, terminates*).

The following year, the TimeML standard is revised under the name of ISO-TimeML (ISO, 2008) and two aspectual values are added: *imperfective* and *imperfective_progressive*. This new standard is tested in Task B of the Shared Task 'TempEval-2' (Pustejovsky and Verhagen, 2009). In his thesis on the adaptation to French of the ISO-TimeML standard, Bittar (2010) studies the aspectual variants of support verb construction as well as the automatic processing of several aspectual periphrases. He added value to the aspectual attribute, *prospective*, and enriched the ALINK set with the *reinitiates* label.

In the medical field, Styler IV et al. (2014) presented the Thyme-TimeML that integrates contextual aspect attribute – which distinguishes between *intermittent, constant* and *new* events –

and permanence attribute – which differentiates between *chronic* and *acute* illness. Campillos et al. (2018) extended the notion of aspect to all that "encode[s] a change (or lack of change) with regard to an entity: Continue, decrease, Improve, Increase, Reccurrence, Start_Again, Start, Stop, Worsen" (580) when creating an annotated corpus of French medical records.

2.3 Aspectual resources

As far as we know, there are no resources in English or in French that are similar to ours, which is focused on the medical language. However, various resources record some aspectual verbs or constructions and detail their functioning. In this way, FrameNet (Baker et al., 1998) labels semantic roles of verbal arguments for English, in order to show the meaning and usage of verbs senses. FrameNet contains some aspectual nuances for which the possible lexical units are indicated (e.g. *Activity_finish: complete, conclude, finish*), but without any indication of the syntactic construction or type of arguments needed by the verb to take this meaning. The values of *culmination* and *resumption* are not considered here. In the French FrameNet (Candito et al., 2014), no aspectual construction is examined, not even the beginning or the end of an activity.

The lexical resource VerbNet (Kipper-Schuler, 2005) and its French equivalent Verb∃net (Danlos, Nakamura and Pradet, 2014) have a class of aspectual verbs (class 55) in which the verbs expressing the value of beginning, continuation or end could be found. For each of these values, the verbal valency and syntactic constructions of the prototypical verb (e.g. *begin/commencer* in 'begin-55.1') are indicated. We deepen this research in three ways: i) by adding some aspectual subclasses, ii) by describing the lexical units that are synonymous with the verbal prototype and iii) by specifying the semantic class of the arguments.

Two other resources, manually created, exist for French and constitute the theoretical framework of this research: the Lexicon-Grammar (Gross, 1975) and the *Verbes français* (Dubois and Dubois-Charlier, 1997). The first one is based on a descriptive formalism, which we have tried to reproduce to make it automatable; the second one lists a series of aspectual verbs that we have enriched so that it takes into account the medical specificities related to our corpus.

NLP research tackles the notion of aspect. However, there is still a substantial gap to fill, both in French and in the medical field. Our contribution lies in this vast new field of knowledge.

3 Data

It is admitted that the temporal information and how it will be presented will depend on the type of documents analyzed (Tapi Nzali, Tannier, Névéol, 2015b). Clinical documents are very heterogeneous and time references are adapted accordingly. To avoid being restricted to one type of document, we collected a corpus which includes five types of clinical texts in the following proportions (see Table 1):

Operating and Review Protocols	55,174
Letters from Doctor to Patient	3,906
Letters from Doctor to Doctor	70,381
Consultation Notes	49,482
Hospitalization Reports	7,833
Total	**186,776**

Table 1. Types and number of medical texts

These documents (about 54 million tokens), dating from 1996 to 2014, were collected and anonymized as part of a project with six services (abdominal and bariatric surgery, gastroenterology, MRI, scanners, and ultrasound) of a Brussels hospital (iMediate, 2014-2016). We deemed appropriate to use such a considerable amount of data since we focus on a very specific phenomenon, i.e., the lexical aspect conveyed by verbs.

4 Methodology

We created the resource following a 5-step method. Firstly, we established the verbal seed terms list that could evoke a lexical aspect. For this purpose, we started from the definition of aspectual relationship in the ISO-TimeML Standard for annotation (Pustejovsky et al., 2010). Five aspectual relationships are considered, here associated with the prototypical French verb: Initiates (*commencer*), Continues (*continuer*), Terminates (*terminer*), Culminates (*accomplir*) and Reinitiates (*recommencer*) (Bittar, 2010: 80). Ideally, categories of verbs expressing the possible outcome of a hospitalization (*healing, improvement, stability, deterioration,* and *death*; DEFT, 2019) or verbs indicating the *progress* or *decline* of a patient should also be implemented (Elhadad et al., 2015). These new aspectual values require more manual cleaning, which is underway.

Secondly, this list was enriched with the aid of two resources: the consulting of thesauri (TLF*i*, 2012; Crisco, 2019) and an in-depth exploratory analysis of the medical corpus. At the end of this second step, we end up with a total of 142 verbs and verb phrases that can potentially express an aspectual nuance, as follows.

Thirdly, on this basis, extraction grammars were designed in the corpus analysis software Unitex (Paumier, 2016) and applied to the corpus. These grammars enable the creation of a concordance, an 'in context' exploration tool of the aspectual verbs.

Fourthly, using this concordance, we performed a manual vetting which applies three actions on the verbal occurrences: i) the deletion of verbs that never appear (e.g., *to burst into*) or never with an aspectual meaning (e.g., *to break out*) in our clinical language corpus; ii) the removal of non-aspectual verbal constructions (see (4)); iii) the detection of verbs whose aspectual value changes under the negative modality (see (5)).

(4) Par ailleurs, <u>attaque</u> son chir pour abdominoplastie trop serrée.

(5) A <u>arrêté de</u> fumer. > Terminates

"Quit smoking."

Malade <u>n'arrête pas de</u> tousser. > Continues

"Sick person keeps coughing."

Fifthly, we have undertaken a linguistic analysis of this filtered list (Table 2) to establish verb classes characterized by syntactic and semantic properties and to produce the resource described here.

Aspectual type	# verbs before	# verbs after	# constructions
Initiates	59	27	34
Continues	18	16	23
Terminates	35	25	31
Culminates	23	16	23
Reinitiates	10	6	9
Total	**145**	**90**	**120**

Table 2. Number of constructions and verbs by aspectual type before and after automatic vetting

5 Resource

The linguistic resource presented in this paper consists of the description, in tabular form, of 90 verbs and verbal phrases with an aspectual value. After extraction and manual analysis, these 90 verbal expressions lead to 120 different constructions (see Table 2) which are then formally described. For example, the verb *commencer* comes in four forms: *commencer à* (to start doing something), *commencer par* (to start with), *commencer* (+ article) + noun (to start something), *commencer* (to start). Each of these constructions possesses several syntactic and semantic properties. They will, therefore, fall into different descriptive tables.

The ten tables resulting from this study (see Appendix A) allow us to summarize the syntactic and semantic constraints linking some elements of the sentence, frequently medical events.

The structure of the table was determined based on the six following properties: i) aspectual nature; ii) passivization, iii) pronominalization of the complement, iv) number and type of complements; v) nature of the subject and vi) nature of the object. The first binarization of the 120 structures, based on aspectual nature, separates the structures which are always aspectual (6) from those which are only aspectual in certain instances, depending on the transitive or intransitive nature of the verb (7).

(6) Elle <u>se met à</u> lire des notices pharmaceutiques.

"She starts reading pharmaceutical leaflets."

(7) Le Sulpiride <u>coupe</u> les vomissements *vs.* J'<u>ai coupé</u> le fil résorbable.

"Sulpiride stops the vomiting." *vs.* "I cut the absorbable thread."

This first binarization based on the aspectual nature criterion applies to the four tables (tables 2, 3, 5 and 6) that respond identically to classification criteria, but differ in their aspectual dimension.

Tests are then applied to the verbs, in the medical context of the corpus, with regard to certain syntactic and semantic properties. Performing these tests allows us to classify the verbs in the tables according to specific criteria. The tests are called *transformations* (Harris, 1957) and are applied to the simple form of the sentence, i.e., a positive assertion, in the active voice and reduced to the Subject-Verb-Object structure.

In terms of syntax, three properties are evaluated and define the assignment of a verbal structure in one or the other table:

- the existence (8) or the absence (9) of an equivalent form in the passive voice;

  (8) L'examen <u>est abandonné</u> par le médecin.

  "The examination <u>is given up</u> by the doctor."

  (9) *Le malade <u>est prolongé</u> par le médecin.

  *"The patient('s life) <u>is prolonged</u> by the doctor."

- the possibility of pronominalizing the verb complement (10 and 11);

  (10) Le traitement <u>relance</u> le processus d'hépatite colique. → Il le relance.

  "Treatment revives the process of biliary colic." → It revives it.

  (11) Il a cessé toute consommation de bière. → *Il l'a cessée.

"He ceases the whole intake of beer." → *He ceases it.

- the nature of the verb and its complements: verb with a direct object, verb with a prepositional complement, verb with a completive subordinate clause, stative verb and intransitive verb.

Concerning semantic properties, also referred to as *distributional* (Harris, 1954), we essentially examine the subject type (human or thing) and the object type, if relevant. When the subject or the object is an inanimate object, it often corresponds to a medical event. The selection of the type(s) of medical event accepted by the meaning of a verb is indicated in the column corresponding to one of the eleven possible events: administration, restriction or effort (diet, sports, profession, addiction), morphological abnormality, care and treatment, (positive or negative) effect, step, observable entity, findings, surgery, disorder and illness.

Besides, these tables also indicate the aspectual modification of the verb (+) or the permanence of the aspect (-) in the presence of the negative modality. These tables feature two additional columns: the meaning of the verb in this structure and the aspect taken by the structure. Finally, we indicate the presence of an adverbial phrase and its type (of time, of manner, or instrument), when it is recurrent for this meaning.

This resource is available upon request and will shortly be expanded. For an example of the table, see Appendix B.

6   Evaluation

To evaluate our resource, we estimated its coverage on 100 new medical texts that serve as a gold standard. These texts come from a different genre since they are 100 post hospitalization reports written by doctors. This different textual genre, still specific to the medical language, should allow a greater generalization of the resource, in that they convey a greater variety of linguistic phenomena.

In these texts, we have identified and annotated all the verbs, and only the verbs, that correspond to one of the five aspects of our typology. We calculated the coverage in terms of aspectual lemmata (Table 3), occurrences (Table 4) and occurrences by aspectual values (Table 5).

	Absolute number	Coverage Rate
Present	34	0,74
Missing	12	0,26
Total	46	1

Table 3. Coverage for aspectual lemmata

	Absolute number	Coverage Rate
Present	104	0,76
Missing	34	0,24
Total	138	1

Table 4. Coverage for occurrences

	Init.	Cont.	Term.	Culm.	Rein.
Present	8	11	8	3	5
Missing	2	5	3	1	0
Total	10	16	11	4	5
Coverage Rate	0,8	0,69	0,73	0,75	1

Table 5. Coverage for occurrences by aspectual values

Results are satisfactory, but probably insufficient for an industrial exploitation. We, therefore, want to integrate the cases identified as missing in the analysis and do this analysis again until reaching coverage of 0.9 by dragging it on a new corpus of 100 texts.

7   Conclusion

The development of such a linguistic resource, in which the medical language is formalized according to the lexical aspect of certain verbs, serves two purposes in the NLP field. On the one hand, these descriptions make it possible to distinguish the aspectual senses from the other meanings of a verb. They allow, among other things, to make a decision in case of verbal ambiguity. As a result, it is easier to include the aspect into the clinical patient's history, which would then take into account some values that were previously omitted. On the other hand, with the semantic tagging of the agent and patient of these verbal structures, it becomes possible to more accurately identify medical events, be it in a vacuum or with regard to their localization and their evolution on the patient's timeline.

We are now faced with two possible follow-ups. Firstly, an evaluation of the resource efficiency still needs to be done by integrating a temporal information extraction system to see how results can be increased and improved. Secondly, we need to extend the scope of the covered phenomena by listing specific aspectual and medical concepts such as the relapse, the chronicity or the worsening.

Acknowledgments

We would like to express our special thanks and gratitude to our colleague T. François for his help and comments during the redaction of this paper. We would also thank G. Bardiaux, translator and reviewer for the language.

References

Edmond Bach. 1986. The Algebra of Events. *Linguistics and Philosophy*, 9:5-16.

Collin F. Baker, Charles J. Fillmore and John Lowe. 1998. The Berkeley FrameNet project. In *COLINACL '98: Proceedings of the Conference.* Montreal, Canada.

Steven Bethard, Guergana Savova, Martha Palmer and James Pustejovsky. 2017. SemEval-2017 Task12: Clinical TempEval. In *Proceedings of the 11th International Workshop on Semantic Evaluation.* Vancouver, Canada, Aug. 3-4 2017. Association for Computational Linguistics, 1052-1062. http://www.aclweb.org/anthology/S17-2093.

André Bittar. 2010. *Building a TimeBank for French: A Reference Corpus Annotated According to the ISO-TimeML.* Ph.D. Thesis, Prof. Laurence Danlos and Pascal Denis, Université Paris Diderot, Nov. 19 2006.

Taxiarchis Botsis, Michael D. Nguyen, Emily J. Woo, Marianthi Markatou and Robert Ball. 2011. Text mining for the Vaccine Adverse Event Reporting System: medical text classification using informative feature selection. *Journal of the American Medical Informatics Association,* 18(5):631-638.

Leonardo Campillos, Louise Deléger, Cyril Grouin, Thierry Hamon, Anne-Laure Ligozat and Aurélie Névéol. 2018. A French Clinical Corpus with Comprehensive Semantic Annotations: Development of the Medical Entity and Relation LIMSI annotated Text corpus (MERLOT). *Language Resources and Evaluation,* 52(2):571-601.

Marie Candito, Pascal Amsili, Lucie Barque, Farah Benamara, Gaël De Chalendar, Marianne Djemaa, Pauline Haas, Richard Huyghe, Yvette Yannick Mathier, Philippe Muller, Benoît Sagot and Laure Vieu. 2014. Developing a French framenet: Methodology and first results. In *Proceedings of the 9th international conference on Language Resources and Evaluation (LREC 2014).* Reykjavik, Iceland.

Patrick Caudal. 2006. *Aspect.* In Danièle Godard, Laurent Roussarie and Francis Corblin (eds.). *Sémanticlopédie: dictionnaire de sémantique,* GDR Sémantique & Modélisation, CNRS, http://www.semantique-gdr.net/dico/.

Kevin E. K. Chai, Stephen Anthony, Enrico Coiera and Farah Magrabi. 2013. Using statistical text classification to identify health information technology incidents. *Journal of the American Medical Informatics Association,* 20(5):980-985.

Vincent Claveau, Natalia Grabar, Cyril Grouin and Thierry Hamin. 2019 (à par.). DEFT 2019. Défi Fouille de Textes. Recherche et extraction d'information dans des cas cliniques. TALN 2019, Toulouse, France.

Bernard Comrie. 1981. *Language universals and linguistic typology: Syntax and morphology.* University of Chicago Press, Chicago.

Jean-Paul Confais. 2002. *Temps, mode, aspect : les approches des morphèmes verbaux et leurs problèmes à l'exemple du français et de l'allemand.* Presses universitaires du Mirail, Toulouse.

Laurence Danlos, Takuya Nakamura and Quentin Pradet. 2014. Vers la création d'un Verb∃Net du français. In *Atelier FondamenTAL.* TALN 2014, Marseille, France.

Jean Dubois and Françoise Dubois-Charlier. 1997. *Les verbes français.* Larousse-Bordes, Paris.

Jean Dubois, Jean-Baptiste Marcellesi, Jean-Pierre Mével and Mathée Giacomo. 1994. *Dictionnaire de linguistique et des sciences du langage.* Larousse, Paris.

Noémie Elhadad, Sameer Pradhan, Sharon Lipsky Gorman, Suresh Manandhar, Wendy Chapman and Guergana Savova. 2015. SemEval-2015 Task 14: Analysis of Clinical Text. In *Proceedings of the 9th International Workshop on Semantic Evaluation (SemEval 2015).* Denver, Colorado, USA, June 4-5 2015. Association for Computational Linguistics, 303-310. https://www.aclweb.org/anthology/S15-2051.

Laurent Gosselin. 2011. L'aspect de phase en français : le rôle des périphrases verbales. *Journal of French Language Studies,* 21(3):149-171.

Maurice Gross. 1975. *Méthodes en syntaxe. Régime des constructions complétives.* Hermann, Paris.

Zellig Harris. 1954. Distributional Structure. *Word,* 10(2-3):146-162.

Zellig Harris. 1957. Co-occurrence and Transformation in Linguistic Structure. *Language,* 33(3.1):283-340.

Paul Imbs (Ed.). (1971-1994). *Trésor de la langue française. Dictionnaire de la langue du XIXe et du XXe siècle (1789-1960).* Paris : Gallimard. 16 vol. En ligne : http://www.cnrtl.fr/definition.

Innoviris. 2014-2016. *iMediate: Interoperability of Medical Data through Information Extraction and*

Term Encoding. Project under the supervision of Prof. Cédrick Fairon.

ISO. 2008. *ISO DIS 24617-1:2008 Language Resource Management – Semantic Annotation Framework – Part 1: Time and Events*. International Organization for Standardization, ISO Central Secretariat, Geneva, Switzerland.

Stanislaw Karolak. 2008. L'aspect dans une langue : le français. *Études cognitives*, 8:11-51.

Karin Kipper-Schuler. 2005. *VerbNet: A broad-coverage, comprehensive verb lexicon*. Ph.D. Thesis, Prof. Martha S. Palmer, University of Pennsylvania.

Judith Klavans and Martin Chodorow. 1992. Degrees of Stativity: The Lexical Representation of Verb Aspect. In *Proceedings of COLING-1992*. Nantes, France, Aug. 23-28 1992. Association for Computational Linguistics, 1126-1131. http://aclweb.org/anthology/C92-4177.

Yordanka Kozareva-Levie. 2011. *L'aspect grammatical et ses manifestations dans les traductions en français de textes littéraires bulgares*. PhD Thesis, Prof. Jocelyne Fernandez-Vest, Université Paris 3, Feb. 7 2011.

Min Li and Jon Patrick. 2012. Extracting Temporal Information from Electronic Patient Records. In *AMIA Annual Symposium Proceedings*, Chicago, USA, Nov. 3-7 2012. American Medical Informatics Association, 542-541. https://www.ncbi.nlm.nih.gov/pmc/articles/PMC3540436/.

Yu-Kai Lin, Hsinchun Chen and Randall A. Brown. 2013. MedTime. A temporal information extraction system for clinical narratives. *Journal of Biomedical Informatics*, 46: S20-S28.

Marc Moens and Mark Steedman. 1988. Temporal Ontology and Temporal Reference. *Computational Linguistics*, 14(2):15-28.

Sébastien Paumier. 2016. *Unitex 3.1 User Manual*. Electronic version. https://unitexgramlab.org/releases/3.1/man/Unitex-GramLab-3.1-usermanual-fr.pdf.

James Pustejovsky, José Castaño, Robert Ingria, Roser Sauri, Robert Gaizauskas, Andrea Setzer and Graham Katz. 2003. TimeML: Robust Specification of Event and Temporal Expressions in Text. In *Fifth International Workshop on Computational Semantics IWCS-5*, Tilburg, Netherlands, Jan. 15-17 2003. http://www.timeml.org/publications/timeMLpubs/IWCS-v4.pdf.

James Pustejovsky and Marc Verhagen. 2009. SemEval-2010 Task 13: Evaluating Events, Time Expressions, and Temporal Relations (TempEval-2). In *Proceedings of the Workshop on Semantic Evaluations: Recent Achievements and Future Directions (SEW-2009)*, Boulder, USA, June 4 2009. Association for Computational Linguistics, 112-116. http://aclweb.org/anthology/W09-2418.

James Pustejovsky, Kiyong Lee, Harry Bunt and Laurent Romary. 2010. ISO-TimeML: An International Standard for Semantic Annotation. In Proceedings of the 7th International Conference on Language Resources and Evaluation, La Valletta, Malta, May 17-23 2010. European Language Resources Association, 394-397.

Eric Siegel and Kathleen McKeown. 2001. Learning Methods to Combine Linguistic Indicators: Improving Aspectual Classification and Revealing Linguistic Insights. *Computational Linguistics*, 26:595-627.

Carlota S. Smith. 1991. *The Parameter of Aspect*. Springer Netherlands, Amsterdam.

Aleksandra Sojic, Walter Terkaj, Giorgia Contini and Marco Sacco. 2016. Modularising ontology and designing inference patterns to personalize health condition assessment: the case of obesity. *Journal of Biomedical Semantics*, 7(1):12.

Jannik Strötgen and Michael Gertz. 2010. HeidelTime: High-quality rule-based extraction and normalization of temporal expressions. In *Proceedings of the 5th International Workshop on Semantic Evaluation*, Uppsala, Sweden, July 11-16 2010. Association for Computational Linguistics, 321-324.

William F. Styler IV, Steven Bethard, Sean Finan, Martha Palmer, Sameer Pradhan, Piet de Groen, Brad Erickson, Timothy Miller, Chen Lin, Guergana Savova and James Putstejovsky. 2014. Temporal Annotation in the Clinical Domain. *Transactions of the Association for Computational Linguistics*, 2:143-154.

Weiyi Sun, Anna Rumshisky and Ozlem Uzuner. 2013. Evaluating temporal relations in clinical text: 2012 i2b2 Challenge. *Journal of the American Medical Informatics Association*, 20(5):806-813.

Mike D Tapi Nzali, Xavier Tannier and Aurélie Névéol.2015a. Automatic Extraction of Time Expressions Across Domains in French Narratives. In *Proceedings of the 2015 Conference on Empirical Methods in Natural Language Processing*, Lisbon, Portugal, Sep. 17-21 2015. Association for Computational Linguistics, 492-498. http://aclweb.org/anthology/D15-1055.

Mike D Tapi Nzali, Xavier Tannier and Aurélie Névéol. 2015b. *Analyse d'expressions temporelles dans les dossiers électroniques patients*. In 22ème Conférence sur le Traitement Automatique des Langues Naturelles, Caen, France, June 22-25 2015. 144-152.

Julien Tourille, Olivier Ferret, Xavier Tannier and Aurélie Névéol. 2017. LIMSI-COT at SemEval-2017 Task 12: Neural architecture for temporal information extraction from clinical narratives. In *Proceedings of the 11th International Workshop on Semantic Evaluation (SemEval-2017)*. Vancouver, Canada, Aug. 3-4 2017. Association for Computational Linguistics, 595-600. http://www.aclweb.org/ anthology/S17-2098.

Zeno Vendler. 1957. Verbs and Times. *The Philosophical Review*, 66(2):143-60.

Marc Wilmet. 1980. Aspect grammatical, aspect sémantique, aspect lexical : un problème de limites. In Jean David and Robert Martin (eds.). *La notion d'aspect*. Actes du colloque organisé par le Centre d'analyse syntaxique de l'université de Metz. May 18-20. Klincksieck, Paris, 51-68.

Appendices

Appendix A. Synopsis of the ten tables and their features

Table	Aspectual meaning	Features
Table 1	Always	Aspectual auxiliary verbs; Infinitive subordinate clause introduced by a preposition and bearing the meaning of the process
Table 2.1	Always	Auxiliary *avoir*; direct object; passivization and pronominalization
Table 2.2	Occasionally	
Table 3.1	Always	Auxiliary *avoir*; direct object; no passivization and no pronominalization; human subject
Table 3.2	Occasionally	
Table 4	Always	Auxiliary *être*; adjectival predicative complements
Table 5.1	Always	Prepositional complement; no passivization and no pronominalization
Table 5.2	Occasionally	
Table 6.1	Always	Intransitive; no passivization and no pronominalization
Table 6.2	Occasionally	

This very wide table (one logical table, Table 2.1) is split below into column groups, with the **Verbe** column repeated in each group. "+" and "-" are the marks printed in the cells.

Verbe — Sens — Circonstant — Exemples — Aspect

Verbe	Sens	Circonstant	Exemples	Aspect
accomplir	mettre à exécution,	-	jusqu'à accomplir 10 jours de traitement.	Culminatif
achever	finir, parachever	instrumental	qui est tarie spontanément	Culminatif
arrêter	stopper	-	Tabac : arrêté il y a 10 ans.	Terminatif
clore	finir, achever	-	je suppose que l'affaire est close.	Culminatif
clôturer	finir, achever	instrumental	à revoir pour clôturer le traitement.	Culminatif
commencer	débuter	-	elle commence la phase de sucreries.	Initiatif
finir	achever, terminer	instrumental	a fini son traitement	Culminatif
freiner	contenir, retenir	-	une couche de fibrine freinant l'évolution.	Terminatif
inaugurer	commencer	-	gastro entérite inaugurant les plaintes.	Initiatif
incuber	couver	-	On incube une maladie	Initiatif
initier	provoquer le début	-	Un suivi urologique a été initié.	Initiatif
juguler	arrêter	-	l'antibiothérapie a jugulé le problème	Terminatif
mettre en route	mettre en marche, d…	-	Je mets en route ces examens	Initiatif
stopper	arrêter, suspendre	-	elle stoppera d'ici 1 semaine ce traitement.	Terminatif
suspendre	arrêter, interrompre	-	On suspend l'examen.	Terminatif
tarir	amenuiser, dissiper	-	Enterol pour tarir les suites de l'entérite.	Terminatif
terminer	achever, finir	-	Il terminait un traitement antibiotique.	Terminatif

Sujet humain / Sujet chose

Verbe	Sujet humain	Sujet chose: restriction ou effort	Sujet chose: cure/traitement/médicament	Sujet chose: observations cliniques	Sujet chose: procédure/acte chirurgical	Sujet chose: troubles/maladie
accomplir	+	-	-	-	-	-
achever	+	-	-	-	-	-
arrêter	+	-	-	-	-	-
clore	+	-	-	-	-	-
clôturer	+	-	-	-	-	-
commencer	+	-	-	-	-	-
finir	+	-	-	-	-	-
freiner	+	-	+	-	-	-
inaugurer	-	-	-	+	-	+
incuber	+	-	-	-	-	-
initier	+	-	+	-	-	+
juguler	-	-	+	-	+	-
mettre en route	+	-	-	-	-	-
stopper	+	-	-	-	-	-
suspendre	+	-	-	-	-	-
tarir	-	+	+	-	+	-
terminer	+	-	-	-	-	-

Propriétés verbales

Verbe	Auxiliaire *avoir*	Auxiliaire *être*	Attribut	Passivation	Pronominalisation	Négation
accomplir	+	-	-	+	+	-
achever	+	-	-	+	+	-
arrêter	+	-	-	+	+	-
clore	+	-	-	+	+	+
clôturer	+	-	-	+	+	+
commencer	+	-	-	+	+	-
finir	+	-	-	+	+	+
freiner	+	-	-	+	+	-
inaugurer	+	-	-	+	+	-
incuber	+	-	-	+	+	-
initier	+	-	-	+	+	-
juguler	+	-	-	+	+	+
mettre en route	+	-	-	+	+	-
stopper	+	-	-	+	+	+
suspendre	+	-	-	+	+	+
tarir	+	-	-	+	+	-
terminer	+	-	-	+	+	+

Complément

Verbe	administratif	restriction ou effort	anormalité morphologique	cure/traitement/médicament	effet positif/négatif	examen/test/bilan	observations cliniques	procédure/acte chirurgical	troubles/maladie
accomplir	-	+	-	-	-	-	-	-	-
achever	-	-	+	+	-	+	-	+	-
arrêter	-	+	-	+	-	+	+	+	-
clore	+	-	-	-	-	-	-	-	-
clôturer	+	-	-	+	-	+	-	-	-
commencer	-	+	-	+	-	+	-	-	+
finir	-	+	-	+	-	+	-	+	-
freiner	-	+	-	-	+	-	-	+	+
inaugurer	-	-	-	-	+	-	-	+	+
incuber	-	-	-	-	-	-	-	-	+
initier	-	+	-	+	-	+	-	+	-
juguler	-	+	-	-	-	-	+	-	+
mettre en route	-	-	-	+	-	+	-	-	-
stopper	-	-	-	+	-	+	-	-	-
suspendre	-	-	-	+	-	+	-	+	-
tarir	-	-	-	+	-	-	+	-	+
terminer	-	+	-	+	-	+	-	+	-

A BERT-based Universal Model for Both Within- and Cross-sentence Clinical Temporal Relation Extraction

Chen Lin[1], Timothy Miller[1], Dmitriy Dligach[2], Steven Bethard[3] and Guergana Savova[1]

[1]Boston Children's Hospital and Harvard Medical School
[2]Loyola University Chicago
[3]University of Arizona
[1]{first.last}@childrens.harvard.edu
[2]ddligach@luc.edu
[3]bethard@email.arizona.edu

Abstract

Classic methods for clinical temporal relation extraction focus on relational candidates within a sentence. On the other hand, breakthrough Bidirectional Encoder Representations from Transformers (BERT) are trained on large quantities of arbitrary spans of contiguous text instead of sentences. In this study, we aim to build a sentence-agnostic framework for the task of CONTAINS temporal relation extraction. We establish a new state-of-the-art result for the task, 0.684F for in-domain (0.055-point improvement) and 0.565F for cross-domain (0.018-point improvement), by fine-tuning BERT and pre-training domain-specific BERT models on sentence-agnostic temporal relation instances with WordPiece-compatible encodings, and augmenting the labeled data with automatically generated "silver" instances.

1 Introduction

The release of BERT (Devlin et al., 2018) has substantially advanced the state-of-the-art in several sentence-level, inter-sentence-level, and token-level tasks. BERT is trained on very large unlabeled corpora to achieve good generalizability. Instead of relying on a recurrent neural network, BERT uses a transformer architecture to better capture long distance dependencies. BERT is able to make predictions that go beyond natural sentence boundaries, because it is trained on fragments of contiguous text that typically span multiple sentences.

These advantages of BERT motivate us to apply it to a traditionally sentence-level task – temporal relation extraction from clinical text. The identification of temporal relations in the clinical narrative can lead to accurate fine-grained analyses of many medical phenomena (e.g., disease progression, longitudinal effects of medications), with a variety of clinical applications such as question answering (Das and Musen, 1995; Kahn et al.,

1990), clinical outcomes prediction (Schmidt et al., 2005), and recognition of temporal patterns and timelines (Zhou and Hripcsak, 2007; Lin et al., 2014). However, the labeled instances for this clinical information extraction task are limited, so neural models trained from scratch may not be able to learn complex linguistic phenomena. Pre-trained models like BERT could potentially provide rich representations as they are trained on massive data.

Classic models for clinical temporal relation extraction have framed the task within a sentence (Sun et al., 2013; Bethard et al., 2015, 2016, 2017), making them susceptible to sentence detection errors. Using BERT, on the other hand, eliminates this sensitivity to sentence boundary errors. The key contributions of this paper are: (1) introducing BERT to the challenging task of clinical temporal relation extraction and evaluating its performance on a widely used testbed (THYME corpus; Styler IV et al., 2014), (2) developing a universal processing mechanism based on a fixed, sentence-boundary agnostic window of contiguous tokens, (3) pre-training BERT on MIMIC-III (Medical Information Mart for Intensive Care) dataset (Johnson et al., 2016) and comparing its performance to BERT and its biomedical adaptation BioBERT (Lee et al., 2019), (4) augmenting the labeled set with automatically generated instances from unlabeled data, and (5) evaluating models for in- and cross-domain tasks on the THYME corpus.

2 Background

Recently, several pre-trained general-purposed language encoders have been proposed, including CoVe (McCann et al., 2017), ELMo (Peters et al., 2018), Flair (Akbik et al., 2018), GPT (Radford et al., 2018), GPT2 (Radford et al., 2019), and BERT (Devlin et al., 2018). These models are trained on vast amounts of unlabeled text to achieve

Proceedings of the 2nd Clinical Natural Language Processing Workshop, pages 65–71
Minneapolis, Minnesota, June 7, 2019. ©2019 Association for Computational Linguistics

generalizable contextualized word embeddings, and some can be fine-tuned to fit a supervised task.

BERT is trained using a masked language model and the next-sentence objectives. Its architecture consists of stacked multi-layered transformers, each implementing a self-attention mechanism with multiple attention heads. BERT can be further pre-trained for specific domains (Lee et al., 2019) or serve as a backbone model to be fine-tuned with one output layer for a wide range of tasks.

For the task of clinical temporal relation extraction, recent years have seen the rise of neural approaches – structured perceptrons (Leeuwenberg and Moens, 2017), convolutional neural networks (CNNs) (Dligach et al., 2017; Lin et al., 2017), and Long Short-Term memory (LSTM) networks (Tourille et al., 2017; Dligach et al., 2017; Lin et al., 2018) – where minimally-engineered inputs have been adopted over heavily feature-engineered techniques (Sun et al., 2013). The THYME corpus (Styler IV et al., 2014), which is annotated with time expressions (TIMEX3), events (EVENT), and temporal relations (TLINK) using an extension of TimeML (Pustejovsky et al., 2003; Pustejovsky and Stubbs, 2011), is a popular choice for evaluation and was used in the Clinical Temp-Eval series (Bethard et al., 2015, 2016, 2017).

CONTAINS relations are by far the most frequent type of relation in the THYME corpus. They signal that an EVENT occurs entirely within the temporal bounds of a *narrative container* (Pustejovsky and Stubbs, 2011). The THYME corpus is limited in size so models developed on it may suffer from low generalizability. Recent efforts to improve performance have attempted tree-structured models (Galvan et al., 2018) or assistance from unlabeled data (Lin et al., 2018). Years of shared work on this problem and plateauing scores may have suggested that performance on this task is at its peak. However, given the successful application of BERT on many different tasks in the general domain, as well as more recent work in relation extraction tasks (Wang et al., 2019; Lee et al., 2019), we wanted to explore applying this new model to the clinical temporal relation extraction task.

Conventionally, the tasks of within- and cross-sentence relation extraction have been treated separately (Sun et al., 2013; Tourille et al., 2017) as they call for different features. While some methods focus on within-sentence relations (as they are the majority), such methods are susceptible to

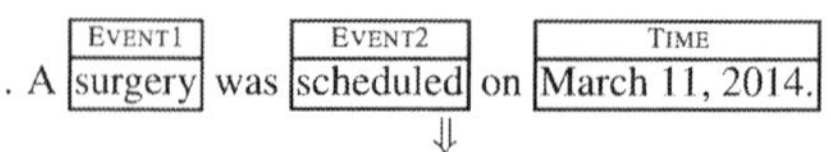

Figure 1: Representations of three candidate relations produced from an example token sequence.

sentence-boundary detection errors. The input sequences of arbitrary lengths that BERT operates on cover both within-sentence and cross-sentence situations, enabling us to design a universal model that is sentence boundary agnostic.

3 Methods

3.1 Task definition

We process the THYME corpus using the segmentation and tokenization modules of Apache cTAKES (http://ctakes.apache.org). We consume gold standard event annotations, gold time expressions and their classes (Styler IV et al., 2014) for generating instances of containment relation candidates. Each instance consists of a pair of event entities, or an event entity and a time expression entity. We preserve the natural order of the two entities in their original context and represent the instance as a sequence of tokens. Depending on the order of the entities, each instance can take one out of three gold standard relational labels, CONTAINS, CONTAINED-BY, and NONE.

The first line of Figure 1 is the token sequence for three gold standard entities, of which two are events, "surgery" and "scheduled", and one is a time expression, "March 11, 2014", whose time class is "date". One can form three candidate relations for these three entities.

3.2 Window-based processing

We aim to build a BERT-based model for both within- and cross-sentence relations. Figure 2 presents the distribution of the distance between the relation arguments in the THYME colon cancer training set expressed as tokens, e.g., 93.07% of the relation arguments are within 50 tokens; 95.14% are 60 tokens apart; 75% are within-sentence.

Thus, instead of looking for candidate pairs within a sentence, we look for pairs within a window of tokens of each other. We test window sizes of 50 or 60 tokens to balance coverage and good positive-to-negative ratio. By using a 60-token window and closure, we derive 413,327 NONE, 10,483

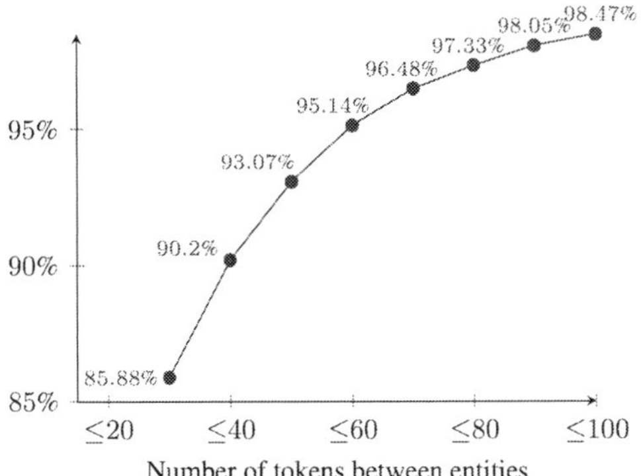

Figure 2: Relation coverage per token distance

CONTAINS, and 2,802 CONTAINS-BY instances from the THYME colon training set. Specifically, for every pair of entities[1] within a section (or if the document is not sectioned, every pair of entities within the document), we generate a relational candidate if the number of base tokens between the entities in the pair is less than the set window size.

XML-tags are often used to mark the position of the entities under consideration in a candidate pair (Dligach et al., 2017), and time expressions with their time class (Lin et al., 2017, 2018) for better generalizability. BERT uses the WordPiece tokenizer which breaks the XML-style tags (especially delimiters like angle brackets and slashes) into subtags. Therefore, we use non-XML tags to mark the positions of the entities and to encode time classes. Such tags should not be actual words and should not be broken into many tokens by WordPiece. Per the case in Figure 1, the event in an event-time relation pair is marked by **es** (event start) and **ee** (event end) and the time expression is represented by non-XML tags (**ts** for time start and **te** for time end) and its time class, for example **ts date te**. Event-event instances are marked with **eas** for event A start, **eae** for event A end, **ebs** for event B start, and **ebe** for event B end, for example . *a eas surgery eae is ebs scheduled ebe on march* 11.

3.3 BioBERT and BERT-MIMIC

A recent publication describes pre-training of BERT on PubMed abstracts (PubMed) and PubMed Central full-text articles (PMC) (BioBERT; Lee et al., 2019).[2] We took this approach a step fur-ther and pre-trained BERT on clinical data from the MIMIC-III (Medical Information Mart for Intensive Care) dataset (Johnson et al., 2016). MIMIC-III contains 879 million words of patients' electronic medical records from Beth Israel Deaconess Medical Center's Intensive Care Unit. The resulting BERT-MIMIC model encapsulates clinical-domain-specific representations.

3.4 Augmenting with "silver" instances

Lin et al. (2018) describe a self-training routing in which they applied a model trained on the labeled THYME data to generate predictions on a set of unlabeled colon cancer data to create "silver" annotations. They demonstrated that adding high confidence positive "silver" relations to the gold training set improves the neural model performance. We apply this technique to our BERT-based models. The differences are 1) our unlabeled colon cancer instances are generated through the window-based mechanism, while their unlabeled instances were sentence-based; 2) we use a fine-tuned BERT model for generating "silver" instances.

3.5 Settings

We use a single NVIDIA GTX Titan Xp GPU to pre-train BERT on MIMIC-III, and fine-tune BERT, BioBERT, and BERT-MIMIC for our task. We use $BERT_{base}$, as the memory requirement of $BERT_{large}$ is too demanding. For fine-tuning, the batch size is selected from (16,32) and the learning rate is selected from (1e-5, 2e-5, 3e-5, 5e-5), using the THYME colon cancer development set. The fine-tuning is done with the Tensorflow-based BERT API, with the hidden state of the "[CLS]" token as the input to the classification layer. Rather than pre-training from scratch, which requires significant computational resources and would remove potentially useful information from the model, we initialize the pre-training on MIMIC data from BERT's final check point, with 10,000 training steps, standard warm up, and takes three hours to finish.

4 Results

All models are evaluated by the standard Clinical TempEval evaluation script so that their performance can be directly compared to published results. Table 1 shows performance on the Clinical TempEval colon cancer test set for the previous best systems, Lin et al. (2018) and Galvan et al. (2018), and window-based universal models.

---

[1] we use the term "entity" to refer to events and time expressions

[2] BioBERT model available at `https://github.com/naver/biobert-pretrained`

Model	P	R	F1
Lin et al. (2018)	0.692	0.576	0.629
Galvan et al. (2018)	**0.983**	0.462	0.629
1. bi-LSTM	0.712	0.490	0.581
2. BERT	0.699	0.625	0.660
3. BERT-T	0.735	0.613	0.669
4. BERT-TS	0.670	**0.697**	0.683
5. BioBERT(pmc)-TS	0.674	0.695	**0.684**
6. BERT-MIMIC-TS	0.673	0.686	0.679

Table 1: Model performance of *CONTAINS* relation on colon cancer test set. T: using non-XML tags; S: adding high confidence positive silver instances.

Model	P	R	F1
Lin et al. (2018)	**0.514**	0.585	0.547
BERT-TS	0.456	0.704	0.553
BioBERT(pmc)-TS	0.473	0.700	**0.565**
BERT-MIMIC-TS	0.457	**0.715**	0.558

Table 2: Model performance of *CONTAINS* relation on brain cancer test set.

We feed the window-based instances with XML-tagged entities to the bidirectional LSTM model without self-training (Lin et al., 2018) (Table 1(1)) as a comparison. Window-based instances with XML-tagged entities (Table 1(2)) and with non-XML tagged entities (Table 1(3)) are fed to BERT to show the difference from tagging. Then, high-confidence positive "silver" instances are added to the training set, fine-tuning is performed for BERT (Table 1(4)), BioBERT(pmc) (Table 1(5)) which showed better results than BioBERT trained on PubMed and PMC+PubMed, and BERT-MIMIC (Table 1(6)) respectively.

To evaluate the generalizability of the models, the best performing models trained on the colon cancer data – BERT (Table 1(4)), Bio-BERT(pmc) (Table 1(5)), and BERT-MIMIC (Table 1(6)) – are directly tested on the Clinical TempEval THYME brain cancer test set. Previous best cross-domain result is reported by Lin et al. (2018) in Table 2.

Thus, we establish a new state-of-the-art result for the task – 0.684F for within-domain (0.055 point improvement) and 0.565F for cross-domain (0.018 point improvement).

5 Discussion

The window-based BERT-fine-tuned model, even with the XML-tags (Table 1(2)), works for both within- and cross-sentence relations. Its perfor-

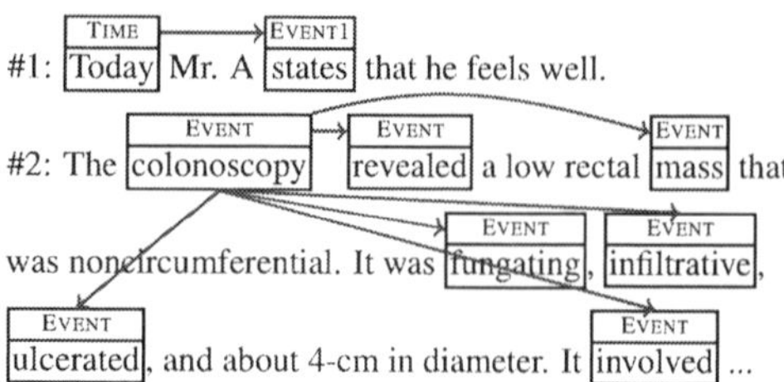

Figure 3: Relations picked up by the universal model.

Category	P	R	F1
within-sentence	0.621	0.712	0.663
cross-sentence	0.359	0.310	0.333

Table 3: Within- vs. cross-sentence results on colon cancer development set.

mance (0.660F) is better than enhanced within-sentence models (Lin et al., 2018; Galvan et al., 2018) (0.629F), and the combination of two separate within- and cross-sentence models (Tourille et al., 2017) (0.613F). The improvement comes from 1) the window-based processing mechanism that bypasses the errors generated by a sentence boundary detector (for example, the sentence splitter creates two sentences for Figure 3(1) by incorrectly disambiguating the period after Mr); 2) the superb long-distance reasoning ability of BERT (Figure 3(2) shows relations we now can pick up from a three-sentence span). As a comparison, the same window-based approach does not work well with bidirectional LSTM model (Table 1(1)). One reason could be that because the bi-LSTM model is not pre-trained on a large corpus, it is likely affected by the limited number of gold annotations especially for large window sizes (like 50 or 60 tokens) which leads to skewing the positive/negative instance ratio further towards the negative labels, thus making fewer positive predictions (0.490 recall). Another explanation could be the different ways the bi-LSTM and BERT implement bidirectionality; each pass of the bi-LSTM is biased towards its nearby information thus favoring short-distance relations within a sentence.

The THYME corpus distribution does not provide gold sentence annotations. The BERT results we present in Table 1 are derived using a 60-token window. This window size produced superior results compared to a 50-token window (0.660F and 0.651F respectively).

Non-XML tags work better with BERT as they

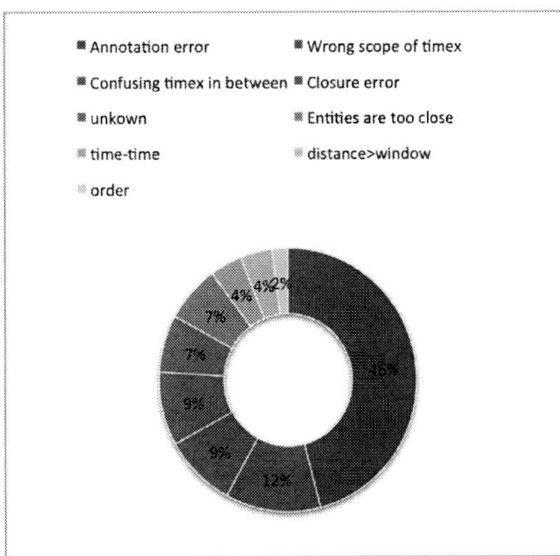

Figure 4: Distribution of 100 Errors

are not split into sub-tags but better preserved (Table 1(2)) vs. (Table 1(3)). We experimented with adding entity tags into BERT's vocabulary, instead of relying on strings (i.e. "es", "ee") that could possibly be confused with real tokens, but did not observe improved performance. We hypothesize that the BERT model needs to be re-trained with the added tags to contextualize their representations. Currently, we are limited by our computational resources to undertake such an endeavor.

Adding high quality silver instances is helpful as they alleviate the skewed positive to negative instance ratio, (Table 1(3)) vs. (Table 1(4)).

BERT-TS and its domain-specific versions (BioBERT(pmc)-TS, BERT-MIMIC-TS) work on par with each other (Table 1(4-5)) for in-domain tasks, and BioBERT(pms)-TS performs better when it is tested for generalizability on the the brain cancer Clinical TempEval test set (Table 2). The clinical-domain specific representation BERT-MIMIC-TS shows slight cross-domain advantage (0.558F) over BERT-TS (0.553F).

We performed error analysis on the output of the best performing model – BioBERT(pmc)-TS – on the THYME colon cancer development set. Applying this model results in 7.0k within-sentence CONTAINS predictions (4.3k correct) and 1.6k cross-sentence predictions (0.6k correct). Table 3 shows the within- and cross-sentence results of the best model on the colon cancer development set. However, these results should not be taken literally but as only an overall trend because closure over the entire set of relations needs to be factored, mak-

ing it hard to isolate the performance of specific subtypes. For that reason, we did not subtype the results into event-event and event-time instances.

We sampled 100 errors evenly distributed over four categories: within-sentence false positives (FP), within-sentence false negatives (FN), cross-sentence FPs, and cross-sentence FNs. The sources of errors are summarized in fig. 4. 1) "Annotation error" (46%) – errors in the gold annotations; 2) "Wrong scope of timex" (12%) – the main reason for FP predictions, especially for cross-sentence ones (10%). The system fails to identify the subtle change of the timex scope and incorrectly links an event to it; 3) "Confusing timex in between" (9%) – there is another time expression occurring between the two arguments, thus the system incorrectly infers the scope of the time expression; 4) "Closure error" (9%); 5) "Unknown" (7%) – errors for which we could not provide a plausable explanation ; 6) "Entities are too close" (7%) – the two entities in question are too close to each other, thus limiting the context for correct reasoning. Prior knowledge would be helpful for these short-distance relations; 7) "Time-time" (4%) – the system generates time-time relations which are oftentimes FPs because gold time-time annotations are scarce ; 8) "Distance > window" (4%) – the distance between the two entities in question is bigger than the window size, resulting in cross-sentence FNs ; 9) "Order" (2%) – the system incorrectly extracts the order of the relation arguments, e.g. predicts CONTAINS instead of CONTAINS-BY .

One path for future research is pre-training BERT on a much larger clinical corpus (for which large scale computational resources are needed). The PMC set may not be clinical enough and the size of MIMIC corpus (0.9B) is too small compared to the other corpora (PubMed 4.5B, PMC 13.5B) to provide sufficient representations.

Acknowledgments

The study was funded by R01LM10090, R01GM114355 and U24CA184407. The content is solely the responsibility of the authors and does not necessarily represent the official views of the National Institutes of Health. We thank Sean Finan for his technical support and the anonymous reviewers for their valuable suggestions and criticism. The Titan Xp GPU used for this research was donated by the NVIDIA Corporation.

References

Alan Akbik, Duncan Blythe, and Roland Vollgraf. 2018. Contextual string embeddings for sequence labeling. In *Proceedings of the 27th International Conference on Computational Linguistics*, pages 1638–1649.

Steven Bethard, Leon Derczynski, Guergana Savova, Guergana Savova, James Pustejovsky, and Marc Verhagen. 2015. Semeval-2015 task 6: Clinical tempeval. In *Proceedings of the 9th International Workshop on Semantic Evaluation (SemEval 2015)*, pages 806–814.

Steven Bethard, Guergana Savova, Wei-Te Chen, Leon Derczynski, James Pustejovsky, and Marc Verhagen. 2016. Semeval-2016 task 12: Clinical tempeval. *Proceedings of SemEval*, pages 1052–1062.

Steven Bethard, Guergana Savova, Martha Palmer, James Pustejovsky, and Marc Verhagen. 2017. Semeval-2017 task 12: Clinical tempeval. *Proceedings of the 11th International Workshop on Semantic Evaluation (SemEval-2017)*, pages 563–570.

Amar K Das and Mark A Musen. 1995. A comparison of the temporal expressiveness of three database query methods. In *Proceedings of the Annual Symposium on Computer Application in Medical Care*, page 331. American Medical Informatics Association.

Jacob Devlin, Ming-Wei Chang, Kenton Lee, and Kristina Toutanova. 2018. Bert: Pre-training of deep bidirectional transformers for language understanding. *arXiv preprint arXiv:1810.04805*.

Dmitriy Dligach, Timothy Miller, Chen Lin, Steven Bethard, and Guergana Savova. 2017. Neural temporal relation extraction. *EACL 2017*, page 746.

Diana Galvan, Naoaki Okazaki, Koji Matsuda, and Kentaro Inui. 2018. Investigating the challenges of temporal relation extraction from clinical text. In *Proceedings of the Ninth International Workshop on Health Text Mining and Information Analysis*, pages 55–64.

Alistair EW Johnson, Tom J Pollard, Lu Shen, Li-wei H Lehman, Mengling Feng, Mohammad Ghassemi, Benjamin Moody, Peter Szolovits, Leo Anthony Celi, and Roger G Mark. 2016. Mimic-iii, a freely accessible critical care database. *Scientific data*, 3.

Michael G Kahn, Larry M Fagan, and Samson Tu. 1990. Extensions to the time-oriented database model to support temporal reasoning in medical expert systems. *Methods of information in medicine*, 30(1):4–14.

Jinhyuk Lee, Wonjin Yoon, Sungdong Kim, Donghyeon Kim, Sunkyu Kim, Chan Ho So, and Jaewoo Kang. 2019. Biobert: a pre-trained biomedical language representation model for biomedical text mining. *arXiv preprint arXiv:1901.08746*.

Tuur Leeuwenberg and Marie-Francine Moens. 2017. Structured learning for temporal relation extraction from clinical records. In *Proceedings of the 15th Conference of the European Chapter of the Association for Computational Linguistics*.

Chen Lin, Elizabeth W Karlson, Dmitriy Dligach, Monica P Ramirez, Timothy A Miller, Huan Mo, Natalie S Braggs, Andrew Cagan, Vivian Gainer, Joshua C Denny, and Guergana K Savova. 2014. Automatic identification of methotrexate-induced liver toxicity in patients with rheumatoid arthritis from the electronic medical record. *Journal of the American Medical Informatics Association*.

Chen Lin, Timothy Miller, Dmitriy Dligach, Hadi Amiri, Steven Bethard, and Guergana Savova. 2018. Self-training improves recurrent neural networks performance for temporal relation extraction. In *Proceedings of the Ninth International Workshop on Health Text Mining and Information Analysis*, pages 165–176.

Chen Lin, Timothy Miller, Dmitriy Dligach, Steven Bethard, and Guergana Savova. 2017. Representations of time expressions for temporal relation extraction with convolutional neural networks. *BioNLP 2017*, pages 322–327.

Bryan McCann, James Bradbury, Caiming Xiong, and Richard Socher. 2017. Learned in translation: Contextualized word vectors. In *Advances in Neural Information Processing Systems*, pages 6294–6305.

Matthew E Peters, Mark Neumann, Mohit Iyyer, Matt Gardner, Christopher Clark, Kenton Lee, and Luke Zettlemoyer. 2018. Deep contextualized word representations. *arXiv preprint arXiv:1802.05365*.

James Pustejovsky, José M Castano, Robert Ingria, Roser Sauri, Robert J Gaizauskas, Andrea Setzer, Graham Katz, and Dragomir R Radev. 2003. Timeml: Robust specification of event and temporal expressions in text. *New directions in question answering*, 3:28–34.

James Pustejovsky and Amber Stubbs. 2011. Increasing informativeness in temporal annotation. In *Proceedings of the 5th Linguistic Annotation Workshop*, pages 152–160. Association for Computational Linguistics.

Alec Radford, Karthik Narasimhan, Tim Salimans, and Ilya Sutskever. 2018. Improving language understanding by generative pre-training. *URL https://s3-us-west-2. amazonaws. com/openai-assets/research-covers/languageunsupervised/language understanding paper. pdf*.

Alec Radford, Jeffrey Wu, Rewon Child, David Luan, Dario Amodei, and Ilya Sutskever. 2019. Language models are unsupervised multitask learners. *URL https://d4mucfpksywv.cloudfront.net/better-language-models/language-models.pdf*.

Reinhold Schmidt, Stefan Ropele, Christian Enzinger, Katja Petrovic, Stephen Smith, Helena Schmidt, Paul M Matthews, and Franz Fazekas. 2005. White matter lesion progression, brain atrophy, and cognitive decline: the austrian stroke prevention study. *Annals of neurology*, 58(4):610–616.

William F Styler IV, Steven Bethard, Sean Finan, Martha Palmer, Sameer Pradhan, Piet C de Groen, Brad Erickson, Timothy Miller, Chen Lin, Guergana Savova, et al. 2014. Temporal annotation in the clinical domain. *Transactions of the Association for Computational Linguistics*, 2:143–154.

Weiyi Sun, Anna Rumshisky, and Ozlem Uzuner. 2013. Evaluating temporal relations in clinical text: 2012 i2b2 challenge. *Journal of the American Medical Informatics Association*, 20(5):806–813.

Julien Tourille, Olivier Ferret, Aurelie Neveol, and Xavier Tannier. 2017. Neural architecture for temporal relation extraction: A bi-lstm approach for detecting narrative containers. In *Proceedings of the 55th Annual Meeting of the Association for Computational Linguistics (Volume 2: Short Papers)*, volume 2, pages 224–230.

Haoyu Wang, Ming Tan, Mo Yu, Shiyu Chang, Dakuo Wang, Kun Xu, Xiaoxiao Guo, and Saloni Potdar. 2019. Extracting multiple-relations in one-pass with pre-trained transformers. *arXiv preprint arXiv:1902.01030*.

Li Zhou and George Hripcsak. 2007. Temporal reasoning with medical dataa review with emphasis on medical natural language processing. *Journal of biomedical informatics*, 40(2):183–202.

Publicly Available Clinical BERT Embeddings

Emily Alsentzer
Harvard-MIT
Cambridge, MA
emilya@mit.edu

John R. Murphy
MIT CSAIL
Cambridge, MA
jrmurphy@mit.edu

Willie Boag
MIT CSAIL
Cambridge, MA
wboag@mit.edu

Wei-Hung Weng
MIT CSAIL
Cambridge, MA
ckbjimmy@mit.edu

Di Jin
MIT CSAIL
Cambridge, MA
jindi15@mit.edu

Tristan Naumann
Microsoft Research
Redmond, WA
tristan@microsoft.com

Matthew B. A. McDermott
MIT CSAIL
Cambridge, MA
mmd@mit.edu

Abstract

Contextual word embedding models such as ELMo (Peters et al., 2018) and BERT (Devlin et al., 2018) have dramatically improved performance for many natural language processing (NLP) tasks in recent months. However, these models have been minimally explored on specialty corpora, such as clinical text; moreover, in the clinical domain, no publicly-available pre-trained BERT models yet exist. In this work, we address this need by exploring and releasing BERT models for clinical text: one for generic clinical text and another for discharge summaries specifically. We demonstrate that using a domain-specific model yields performance improvements on three common clinical NLP tasks as compared to nonspecific embeddings. These domain-specific models are not as performant on two clinical de-identification tasks, and argue that this is a natural consequence of the differences between de-identified source text and synthetically non de-identified task text.

1 Introduction

Natural language processing (NLP) has been shaken in recent months with the dramatic successes enabled by transfer learning and contextual word embedding models, such as ELMo (Peters et al., 2018), ULMFiT (Howard and Ruder, 2018), and BERT (Devlin et al., 2018).

These models have been primarily explored for general domain text, and, recently, biomedical text with BioBERT (Lee et al., 2019). However, clinical narratives (e.g., physician notes) have known differences in linguistic characteristics from both general text and non-clinical biomedical text, motivating the need for specialized clinical BERT models.

In this work, we build and publicly release exactly such an embedding model.[1] Furthermore, we demonstrate on several clinical NLP tasks the improvements this system offers over traditional BERT and BioBERT alike.

In particular, we make the following contributions:

1. We train and publicly release BERT-Base and BioBERT-finetuned models trained on both all clinical notes and only discharge summaries.[2]

2. We demonstrate that using clinical specific contextual embeddings improves both upon general domain results and BioBERT results across 2 well established clinical NER tasks and one medical natural language inference task (i2b2 2010 (Uzuner et al., 2011), i2b2 2012 (Sun et al., 2013a,b), and MedNLI (Romanov and Shivade, 2018)). On 2 de-identification (de-ID) tasks, i2b2 2006 (Uzuner et al., 2007) and i2b2 2014 (Stubbs et al., 2015; Stubbs and Uzuner, 2015), general BERT and BioBERT outperform clinical BERT and we argue that fundamental facets of the de-ID context motivate this lack of performance.

2 Related Work

Contextual Embeddings in General Traditional word-level vector representations, such as word2vec (Mikolov et al., 2013), GloVe (Pennington et al., 2014), and fastText (Bojanowski et al.,

---

[1] github.com/EmilyAlsentzer/clinicalBERT
[2] Discharge summaries are commonly used in downstream tasks.

Proceedings of the 2nd Clinical Natural Language Processing Workshop, pages 72–78
Minneapolis, Minnesota, June 7, 2019. ©2019 Association for Computational Linguistics

2017), express all possible meanings of a word as a single vector representation and cannot disambiguate the word senses based on the surrounding context. Over the last two years, ELMo (Peters et al., 2018) and BERT (Devlin et al., 2018) present strong solutions that can provide contextualized word representations. By pre-training on a large text corpus as a language model, ELMo can create a context-sensitive embedding for each word in a given sentence, which will be fed into downstream tasks. Compared to ELMo, BERT is deeper and contains much more parameters, thus possessing greater representation power. More importantly, rather than simply providing word embeddings as features, BERT can be incorporated into a downstream task and gets fine-tuned as an integrated task-specific architecture.

BERT has, in general, been found to be superior to ELMo and far superior to non-contextual embeddings on a variety of tasks, including those in the clinical domain (Si et al., 2019). For this reason, we only examine BERT here, rather than including ELMo or non-contextual embedding methods.

Contextual Clinical & Biomedical Embeddings
Several works have explored the utility of contextual models in the clinical and biomedical domains. BioBERT (Lee et al., 2019) trains a BERT model over a corpus of biomedical research articles sourced from PubMed[3] article abstracts and PubMed Central[4] article full texts. They find the specificity offered by biomedical texts translated to improved performance on several biomedical NLP tasks, and fully release their pre-trained BERT model.

On clinical text, (Khin et al., 2018) uses a general-domain pretrained ELMo model towards the task of clinical text de-identification, reporting near state-of-the-art performance on the i2b2 2014 task (Stubbs and Uzuner, 2015; Stubbs et al., 2015) and state of the art performance on several axes of the HIPAA PHI dataset.

Two works that we know of train contextual embedding models on clinical corpora.

(Zhu et al., 2018) trains an ELMo model over a corpus of mixed clinical discharge summaries, clinical radiology notes and medically oriented wikipedia articles, then demonstrates improved performance on the i2b2 2010 task (Uzuner et al.,

2011). They release a pre-trained ELMo model along with their work, enabling further clinical NLP research to work with these powerful contextual embeddings.

(Si et al., 2019), released in late February 2019, train a clinical note corpus BERT language model and uses complex task-specific models to yield improvements over both traditional embeddings and ELMo embeddings on the i2b2 2010 and 2012 tasks (Sun et al., 2013b,a) and the SemEval 2014 task 7 (Pradhan et al., 2014) and 2015 task 14 (Elhadad et al.) tasks, establishing new state-of-the-art results on all four corpora. However, this work neither releases their embeddings for the larger community nor examines the performance opportunities offered by fine-tuning BioBERT with clinical text or by training note-type specific embedding models, as we do.

3 Methods

In this section, we first describe our clinical text dataset, the details of the BERT training procedure, and finally the specific tasks we examine.

3.1 Data

We use clinical text from the approximately 2 million notes in the MIMIC-III v1.4 database (Johnson et al., 2016). Details of our text pre-processing procedure can be found in Appendix A. Note that while some of our tasks use a small subset of MIMIC notes in their corpora, we do not try to filter these notes out of our BERT pre-training procedure. We expect the bias this induces is negligible given the relative sizes of the two corpora.

We train two varieties of BERT on MIMIC notes: Clinical BERT, which uses text from all note types, and Discharge Summary BERT, which uses only discharge summaries in an effort to tailor the corpus to downstream tasks (which often largely use discharge summaries).

Note that we train our clinical BERT instantiations on all notes of the appropriate type(s), without regard for whether or not any individual note appeared in any of the train/test sets for the various tasks we use (two of which use a small subset of MIMIC notes either partially or completely as their backing corpora). We feel this has a negligible impact given the dramatically larger size of the entire MIMIC corpus relative to the various task corpora.

---

[3]https://www.ncbi.nlm.nih.gov/pubmed/
[4]https://www.ncbi.nlm.nih.gov/pmc/

3.2 BERT Training

In this work, we aim to provide the pre-trained embeddings as a community resource, rather than demonstrate technical novelty in the training procedure, and accordingly our BERT training procedure is completely standard. As such, we have relegated specifics of the training procedure to Appendix B.

We trained two BERT models on clinical text: 1) Clinical BERT, initialized from BERT-Base, and 2) Clinical BioBERT, initialized from BioBERT. For all downstream tasks, BERT models were allowed to be fine-tuned, then the output BERT embedding was passed through a single linear layer for classification, either at a per-token level for NER or de-ID tasks or applied to the sentinel "begin sentence" token for MedNLI. Note that this is a substantially lower capacity model than, for example, the Bi-LSTM layer used in (Si et al., 2019). This reduced capacity potentially limits performance on downstream tasks, but is in line with our goal of demonstrating the efficacy of clinical-specific embeddings and releasing a pre-trained BERT model for these embeddings. We did not experiment with more complex representations as our goal is not to necessarily surpass state-of-the-art performances on these tasks.

Computational Cost Pre-processing and training BERT on MIMIC notes took significant computational resources. We estimate that our entire embedding model procedure took roughly 17 - 18 days of computational runtime using a single GeForce GTX TITAN X 12 GB GPU (and significant CPU power and memory for pre-processing tasks). This is not including any time required to download or setup MIMIC or to train any final downstream tasks. 18 days of continuous runtime is a significant investment and may be beyond the reach of some labs or institutions. This is precisely why we believe that releasing our pre-trained model will be useful to the community.

3.3 Tasks

The Clinical BERT and Clinical BioBERT models were applied to the MedNLI natural language inference task (Romanov and Shivade, 2018) and four i2b2 named entity recognition (NER) tasks, all in IOB format (Ramshaw and Marcus, 1995): i2b2 2006 1B de-identification (Uzuner et al., 2007), i2b2 2010 concept extraction (Uzuner et al., 2011), i2b2 2012 entity extrac-

Dataset	Metric	Dim	# Sentences		
			Train	Dev	Test
MedNLI	Accuracy	3	11232	1395	1422
i2b2 2006	Exact F1	17	44392	5547	18095
i2b2 2010	Exact F1	7	14504	1809	27624
i2b2 2012	Exact F1	13	6624	820	5664
i2b2 2014	Exact F1	43	45232	5648	32586

Table 1: Task dataset evaluation metrics, output dimensionality, and train/dev/test dataset sizes (in number of sentences). Exact F1 requires that the text span and label be an exact match to be considered correct.

tion challenge (Sun et al., 2013a,b), i2b2 2014 7A de-identification challenge (Stubbs and Uzuner, 2015; Stubbs et al., 2015). Details of the IOB format can be seen in the appendix, section C. All task dataset sizes, evaluation metrics, and number of classes are shown in Table 1.

Note that our two de-identification (de-ID) datasets present synthetically-masked PHI in their texts—e.g., they replace instances of real names, hospitals, etc., with synthetic, but consistent and realistic, names, hospitals, etc. As a result, they present significantly different text distributions than traditionally de-identified text (such as MIMIC notes) which will instead present sentinel "PHI" symbols at locations where PHI was removed.

4   Results & Discussions

In this section, we will first describe quantitative comparisons of the various BERT models on the clinical NLP tasks we considered, and second describe qualitative evaluations of the differences between Clinical- and Bio- BERT.

Clinical NLP Tasks Full results are shown in Table 2. On three of the five tasks (MedNLI, i2b2 2010, and i2b2 2012), clinically fine-tuned BioBERT shows improvements over BioBERT or general BERT. Notably, on MedNLI, clinical BERT actually yields a new state of the art, yielding a performance of 85.4% accuracy as compared to the prior state of the art of 73.5% (Romanov and Shivade, 2018) obtained via the InferSent model (Conneau et al., 2017). However, on our two de-ID tasks, i2b2 2006 and i2b2 2014, clinical BERT offers no improvements over Bio- or general BERT. This is actually not surprising, and is instead, we argue, a direct consequence of the na-

Model	MedNLI	i2b2 2006	i2b2 2010	i2b2 2012	i2b2 2014
BERT	77.6%	93.9	83.5	75.9	92.8
BioBERT	80.8%	**94.8**	86.5	78.9	**93.0**
Clinical BERT	80.8%	91.5	86.4	78.5	92.6
Discharge Summary BERT	80.6%	91.9	86.4	78.4	92.8
Bio+Clinical BERT	**82.7%**	94.7	87.2	**78.9**	92.5
Bio+Discharge Summary BERT	**82.7%**	94.8	**87.8**	78.9	92.7

Table 2: Accuracy (MedNLI) and Exact F1 score (i2b2) across various clinical NLP tasks.

Model	Glucose	Disease Seizure	Pneumonia	Transfer	Operations Admitted	Discharge	Beach	Generic Newspaper	Table
BioBERT	insulin exhaustion dioxide	episode appetite attack	vaccine infection plague	drainage division transplant	admission sinking hospital	admission wave sight	coast rock reef	news official industry	tables row dinner
Clinical	potassium sodium sugar	headache stroke agitation	consolidation tuberculosis infection	transferred admitted arrival	admission transferred admit	disposition transfer transferred	shore ocean land	publication organization publicity	scenario compilation technology

Table 3: Nearest neighbors for 3 sentinel words for each of 3 categories. In the Disease and operations categories, clinical BERT appears to show greater cohesion within the clinical domain than BioBERT, whereas for generic words, the methods do not differ much, as expected.

ture of de-ID challenges.

De-ID challenge data presents a different data distribution than MIMIC text. In MIMIC, PHI is identified and replaced with sentinel PHI markers, whereas in the de-ID task, PHI is masked with synthetic, but realistic PHI. This data drift would be problematic for any embedding model, but will be especially damaging to contextual embedding models like BERT because the underlying sentence structure will have changed: in raw MIMIC, sentences with PHI will *universally* have a sentinel PHI token. In contrast, in the de-ID corpus, all such sentences will have different synthetic masks, meaning that a canonical, nearly constant sentence structure present during BERT's training will be non-existent at task-time. For these reasons, we think it is sensible that clinical BERT is not successful on the de-ID corpora. Furthermore, this is a good example for the community given how prevalent the assumption is that contextual embedding models trained on task-like corpora will offer dramatic improvements.

Overall, we feel our results demonstrates the utility of using domain-specific contextual embeddings for non de-ID clinical NLP tasks. Additionally, on one task Discharge Summary BERT offers performance improvements over Clinical BERT, so it may be that adding greater specificity to the underlying corpus is helpful in some cases. We release both models with this work for public use.

Qualitative Embedding Comparisons   Table 3 shows the nearest neighbors for 3 words each from 3 categories under BioBERT and Clinical BERT. These lists suggest that Clinical BERT retains greater cohesion around medical or clinic-operations relevant terms than does BioBERT. For example, the word "Discharge" is most closely associated with "admission," "wave," and "sight" under BioBERT, yet only the former seems relevant to clinical operations. In contrast, under Clinical BERT, the associated words all are meaningful in a clinical operations context.

Limitations & Future Work   This work has several notable limitations. First, we do not experiment with any more advanced model architectures atop our embeddings. This likely hurts our performance. Second, MIMIC only contains notes from the intensive care unit of a single healthcare institution (BIDMC). Differences in care practices across institutions are significant, and using notes from multiple institutions could offer significant gains. Lastly, our model shows no improvements for either de-ID task we explored. If our hypothesis is correct as to its cause, a possible solution could entail introducing synthetic de-ID into the source clinical text and using that as the source for de-ID tasks going forward.

5 Conclusion

In this work, we pretrain and release clinically oriented BERT models, some trained solely on clinical text, and others fine-tuned atop BioBERT. We find robust evidence that our clinical embeddings are superior to general domain or BioBERT specific embeddings for non de-ID tasks, and that using note-type specific corpora can induce further selective performance benefits. To the best of our knowledge, our work is the first to release clinically trained BERT models. Our hope is that all clinical NLP researchers will be able to benefit from these embeddings without the necessity of the significant computational resources required to train these models over the MIMIC corpus.

6 Acknowledgements

This research was funded in part by grants from the National Institutes of Health (NIH): Harvard Medical School Biomedical Informatics and Data Science Research Training Grant T15LM007092 (Co-PIs: Alexa T. McCray, PhD and Nils Gehlenborg, PhD), National Institute of Mental Health (NIMH) grant P50-MH106933, National Human Genome Research Institute (NHGRI) grant U54-HG007963, and National Science Foundation Graduate Research Fellowship Program (NSF GRFP) under Grant No. 1122374. Additional funding was received from the MIT UROP program.

References

Piotr Bojanowski, Edouard Grave, Armand Joulin, and Tomas Mikolov. 2017. Enriching word vectors with subword information. *Transactions of the Association for Computational Linguistics*, 5:135–146.

Alexis Conneau, Douwe Kiela, Holger Schwenk, Loic Barrault, and Antoine Bordes. 2017. Supervised Learning of Universal Sentence Representations from Natural Language Inference Data. *arXiv:1705.02364 [cs]*. ArXiv: 1705.02364.

Jacob Devlin, Ming-Wei Chang, Kenton Lee, and Kristina Toutanova. 2018. BERT: Pre-training of Deep Bidirectional Transformers for Language Understanding. *arXiv:1810.04805 [cs]*. ArXiv: 1810.04805.

Noemie Elhadad, Sameer Pradhan, Sharon Gorman, Suresh Manandhar, Wendy Chapman, and Guergana Savova. SemEval-2015 Task 14: Analysis of Clinical Text. page 8.

Jeremy Howard and Sebastian Ruder. 2018. Universal Language Model Fine-tuning for Text Classification. *arXiv:1801.06146 [cs, stat]*. ArXiv: 1801.06146.

Alistair E. W. Johnson, Tom J. Pollard, Lu Shen, Liwei H. Lehman, Mengling Feng, Mohammad Ghassemi, Benjamin Moody, Peter Szolovits, Leo Anthony Celi, and Roger G. Mark. 2016. MIMIC-III, a freely accessible critical care database. *Scientific Data*, 3:160035.

Kaung Khin, Philipp Burckhardt, and Rema Padman. 2018. A Deep Learning Architecture for De-identification of Patient Notes: Implementation and Evaluation. *arXiv:1810.01570 [cs]*. ArXiv: 1810.01570.

Jinhyuk Lee, Wonjin Yoon, Sungdong Kim, Donghyeon Kim, Sunkyu Kim, Chan Ho So, and Jaewoo Kang. 2019. BioBERT: a pre-trained biomedical language representation model for biomedical text mining. *arXiv:1901.08746 [cs]*. ArXiv: 1901.08746.

Tomas Mikolov, Ilya Sutskever, Kai Chen, Greg S Corrado, and Jeff Dean. 2013. Distributed representations of words and phrases and their compositionality. In *Advances in neural information processing systems*, pages 3111–3119.

Mark Neumann, Daniel King, Iz Beltagy, and Waleed Ammar. 2019. ScispaCy: Fast and Robust Models for Biomedical Natural Language Processing. *arXiv:1902.07669 [cs]*. ArXiv: 1902.07669.

Jeffrey Pennington, Richard Socher, and Christopher Manning. 2014. Glove: Global vectors for word representation. In *Proceedings of the 2014 conference on empirical methods in natural language processing (EMNLP)*, pages 1532–1543.

Matthew E. Peters, Mark Neumann, Mohit Iyyer, Matt Gardner, Christopher Clark, Kenton Lee, and Luke Zettlemoyer. 2018. Deep contextualized word representations. *arXiv:1802.05365 [cs]*. ArXiv: 1802.05365.

Sameer Pradhan, Nomie Elhadad, Wendy Chapman, Suresh Manandhar, and Guergana Savova. 2014. SemEval-2014 Task 7: Analysis of Clinical Text. In *Proceedings of the 8th International Workshop on Semantic Evaluation (SemEval 2014)*, pages 54–62, Dublin, Ireland. Association for Computational Linguistics and Dublin City University.

Lance A. Ramshaw and Mitchell P. Marcus. 1995. Text Chunking using Transformation-Based Learning. *arXiv:cmp-lg/9505040*. ArXiv: cmp-lg/9505040.

Alexey Romanov and Chaitanya Shivade. 2018. Lessons from Natural Language Inference in the Clinical Domain. *arXiv:1808.06752 [cs]*. ArXiv: 1808.06752.

Yuqi Si, Jingqi Wang, Hua Xu, and Kirk Roberts. 2019. Enhancing Clinical Concept Extraction with Contextual Embedding. *arXiv:1902.08691 [cs]*. ArXiv: 1902.08691.

Amber Stubbs, Christopher Kotfila, and zlem Uzuner. 2015. Automated systems for the de-identification of longitudinal clinical narratives: Overview of 2014 i2b2/UTHealth shared task Track 1. *Journal of Biomedical Informatics*, 58 Suppl:S11–19.

Amber Stubbs and zlem Uzuner. 2015. Annotating longitudinal clinical narratives for de-identification: The 2014 i2b2/UTHealth corpus. *Journal of Biomedical Informatics*, 58 Suppl:S20–29.

Weiyi Sun, Anna Rumshisky, and Ozlem Uzuner. 2013a. Annotating temporal information in clinical narratives. *Journal of Biomedical Informatics*, 46 Suppl:S5–12.

Weiyi Sun, Anna Rumshisky, and Ozlem Uzuner. 2013b. Evaluating temporal relations in clinical text: 2012 i2b2 Challenge. *Journal of the American Medical Informatics Association: JAMIA*, 20(5):806–813.

Ozlem Uzuner, Yuan Luo, and Peter Szolovits. 2007. Evaluating the state-of-the-art in automatic de-identification. *Journal of the American Medical Informatics Association: JAMIA*, 14(5):550–563.

zlem Uzuner, Brett R South, Shuying Shen, and Scott L DuVall. 2011. 2010 i2b2/VA challenge on concepts, assertions, and relations in clinical text. *Journal of the American Medical Informatics Association : JAMIA*, 18(5):552–556.

Henghui Zhu, Ioannis Ch Paschalidis, and Amir Tahmasebi. 2018. Clinical Concept Extraction with Contextual Word Embedding. *arXiv:1810.10566 [cs]*. ArXiv: 1810.10566.

A   MIMIC Notes

MIMIC notes are distributed among 15 note types (Figure 1). Many note types are semi-structured, with section headers separating free text paragraphs. To process these notes, we split all notes into sections, then used Scispacy (Neumann et al., 2019) (specifically, the `en_core_sci_md` tokenizer) to perform sentence extraction. The sentences are input into the BERT-Base and BioBERT models for additional pre-training on clinical text.

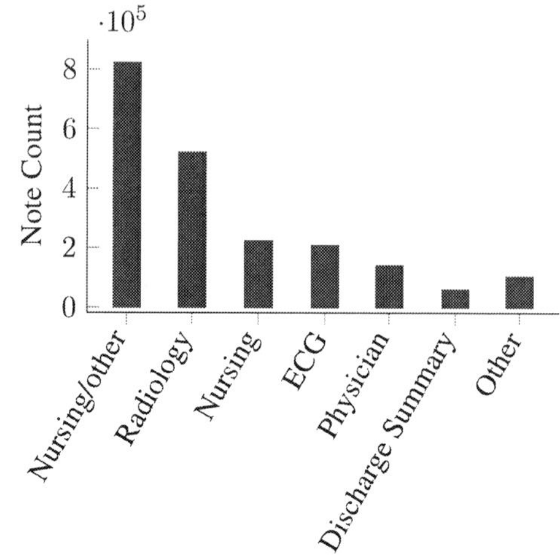

Figure 1: Relative prevalence of MIMIC notes types.

B   BERT Training Details

For all pre-training experiments, we leverage the tensorflow implementation of BERT (Devlin et al., 2018).[5]

B.1   Pre-training

We used a batch size of 32, a maximum sequence length of 128, and a learning rate of $5 \cdot 10^{-5}$ for pre-training our models. Models were trained for 150,000 steps. We experimented with models pre-trained for 300,000 steps, but we found no significant differences in downstream task performance with these models. The dup factor for duplicating input data with different masks was set to 5. All other default parameters were used (specifically, masked language model probability = 0.15 and max predictions per sequence = 20).

B.2   Fine-tuning

For all downstream tasks, we explored the following hyperparameters: learning rate $\in \{2 \cdot 10^{-5}, 3 \cdot 10^{-5}, 5 \cdot 10^{-5}\}$, batch size $\in \{16, 32\}$, and epochs $\in \{3, 4\}$. For the NER tasks, we also tried epoch $\in \{2\}$. The maximum sequence length was 150 across all tasks. Due to time constraints, only 2 epochs were run for the i2b2 2014 task.

C   IOB Format

The IOB (Inside-Outside-Beginning) format (Ramshaw and Marcus, 1995) is a method of encoding span-based NER tasks to add more granularity to the label space over span positions, specifically re-classifying each class as having three subclasses:

Inside (I-) This label is used to specify words *within a span* for this class.

Outside (O) This label is used to specify words *outside any span* for this class. This label will be shared across all classes and will replace the "no class" label applied to extraneous words.

Beginning (B-) This label is used to specify words at the *beginning of a span* for this class.

For example, if the input text, with span labels is given as
"The patient is very sick."
with NER labels
"Null Null Null Problem Problem"
we could convert this into IOB format via
"O O O B-Problem I-Problem"

---

[5]https://github.com/google-research/bert

A General-Purpose Annotation Model for Knowledge Discovery: Case Study in Spanish Clinical Text

Alejandro Piad-Morffis[1], **Yoan Gutiérrez**[2], **Suilan Estevez-Velarde**[1], **Rafael Muñoz**[2]

[1]School of Math and Computer Science, University of Havana
{apiad, sestevez}@matcom.uh.cu
[2]Deparment of Software and Computing Systems, University of Alicante
{ygutierrez, rafael}@dlsi.ua.es

Abstract

Knowledge discovery from text in natural language is a task usually aided by the manual construction of annotated corpora. Specifically in the clinical domain, several annotation models are used depending on the characteristics of the task to solve (e.g., named entity recognition, relation extraction, etc.). However, few general-purpose annotation models exist, that can support a broad range of knowledge extraction tasks. This paper presents an annotation model designed to capture a large portion of the semantics of natural language text. The structure of the annotation model is presented, with examples of annotated sentences and a brief description of each semantic role and relation defined. This research focuses on an application to clinical texts in the Spanish language. Nevertheless, the presented annotation model is extensible to other domains and languages. An example of annotated sentences, guidelines, and suitable configuration files for an annotation tool are also provided for the research community.

1 Introduction

Knowledge discovery is a field of computer science that shows an accelerated growth in the past three decades. Advances in this area have been applied in many domains, from databases (Fayyad et al., 1996; Stahl et al.) to images (Lu et al., 2016) and natural language text (Carlson et al., 2010). Specifically in natural language text, this field is highly relevant in the biomedical and health domains, where it is used for performing tasks such as Named Entity Recognition (NER), Relationship Extraction and Hypothesis Generation, among others. (Simpson and Demner-Fushman, 2012). These tasks generally use annotated corpora for learning the characteristics that appear in the text and mapping them to knowledge structures. For each task, specific annotation models

have been designed that focus on specific elements of the text. For example, in NER tasks is more important to focus on nominal phrases than other grammatical constructions.

Despite that these domain-specific tasks are different, most of them share common characteristics. For example, most tasks deal with the detection of relevant entities and their relations. Hence, promoting general-purpose annotation models would allow the design of reusable and cross-domain knowledge discovery techniques. In this line, several domain-independent semantic representations have been developed (e.g., AMR (Banarescu et al., 2013), PropBank (Palmer et al., 2005), FrameNet (Baker et al., 1998)). However, these representations rely heavily on fine-grained lexicons that define specific semantic roles for each word meaning. Therefore, developing knowledge discovery systems with this level of detail supposes great challenges. Using more coarse-grained semantic representation, even with the loss of some representational capacity, would simplify the creation of automatic techniques based on machine learning. This representation could also be used as the first stage in a pipeline for a domain-specific task, thus reusing resources and techniques in domains with few available resources.

This paper presents a general-purpose annotation model specifically designed to enable knowledge discovery techniques in biomedical text. This model represents the most relevant aspects of the semantic meaning of sentences in natural language, that allows the representation of the basic knowledge contained in a sentence. Even though this model is language-agnostic, we focus on Spanish text because is a less pervasive language than English in terms of computational resources available. However, this model can be applied to several western languages (e.g., English, French, Spanish, Portuguese) without change, be-

79

Proceedings of the 2nd Clinical Natural Language Processing Workshop, pages 79–88
Minneapolis, Minnesota, June 7, 2019. ©2019 Association for Computational Linguistics

cause it doesn't rely heavily on the grammatical structure of the sentence. At the moment of writing, this model is being used to annotate a Spanish corpus of clinical text for a shared evaluation task[1]. Relevant configuration files and example annotated sentences are also published online[2].

The remainder of the paper is organized as follows: Section 2 presents a brief review of annotation models and related corpora in the health domain. Section 3 describes our proposal for a general-purpose annotation model with examples and highlights its key design decisions. Section 4 proposes a methodology for the annotation, normalization, agreement and evaluation of a corpus based on this annotation model. Finally, Section 5 provides preliminary conclusions and prospects of our proposal.

2 Annotation models for knowledge discovery

In this section we present a review of relevant annotation models from which we draw inspiration. We focus general-purpose annotation models 2.1 as well as on annotation models that have been applied to the health domain 2.2.

2.1 General-purpose annotation models

Several general-purpose semantic annotation models have been developed, that attempt to represent the semantics of a sentence beyond the syntactic structure. These models are loosely based on the Subject-Verb-Object grammatical structure that is pervasive in human language.

PropBank (Palmer et al., 2005) proposes a general purpose annotation schema, based on annotating predicates (verbs) as the main semantic constituents of a sentence. ProbBank's annotation schema is able to represent several semantic relations, including the agent that causes an action, the receiver of the effects of an action, time and location modifiers, and causal relationships. One key characteristic of PropBank is that every predicate defines custom semantic roles, i.e., the predicate "*accept*" defines roles for the agent who accepts (ARG0), the object that is accepted (ARG1), and the agent from whom that object is accepted.

FrameNet (Baker et al., 1998) is a lexical database and an annotated corpus that models the semantic roles and relations in a natural language sentence through conceptual structures named *frames*. Frames represent general-purpose concepts, or events, that define the possible semantic relations in which those concepts can be realized in natural language.

VerbNet (Schuler, 2005) is a verb lexicon that also defines specific semantic roles for each verb. In VerbNet, verbs are organized in a hierarchy, and linked through different thematic roles, such as agents, cause, source, or topic. These elements allow to capture the semantic representation of sentences.

PropBank semantic roles are similar to the thematic roles defined in VerbNet and frame elements in FrameNet. As such, there are resources that link these semantic structures (Palmer, 2009).

A more recent proposal is Abstract Meaning Representation (Banarescu et al., 2013, ARM). AMR constitutes a semantic representation schema for English sentences that also attempts to cover a wide range of semantic relations with a general-purpose model. AMR includes PropBank semantic roles, as well as coreference resolution within the same sentence, named entities and types, negation, and other modifiers in a graph structure that represents the meaning of a natural language sentence. However, even though AMR captures the full semantic meaning of a sentence, for the purpose of knowledge discovery it is still considerably abstract, and additional processing is necessary to extract concrete structures of knowledge (Rao et al., 2017).

The annotation model proposed in this research shares similarities from general-purpose semantic annotation models such as AMR and PropBank. In contrast to these resources, our model makes no distinction between different types of actions, which are loosely related to verbs, as explained in Section 3. Instead, we define two general-purpose roles, the agent that performs and action, and the receiver of the effects of the action. These roles roughly correspond to ARG0 and ARG1 respectively in PropBank, although in specific cases their semantic meaning might differ. This simplification is directed towards enabling the automation of the annotation process with the use of machine learning techniques. Another key difference of our model is the inclusion of general-purpose taxonomic relations (e.g, *hypernomy/hyponomy* and *meronym/holonym*) that are inferred from the sen-

---

[1]https://knowledge-learning.github.io/ehealthkd-2019/

[2]https://github.com/knowledge-learning/satr-ann

tence. These relations are directed towards easing the automatic construction of knowledge bases.

2.2 Annotations models in the health domain

Knowledge discovery tasks in the health domain are often supported by the construction of manually-annotated corpora. Several task-specific annotation models have been developed for this purpose. One example is the DrugSemantics corpus (Moreno et al., 2017) where product characteristics are annotated, and BARR2 (Intxaurrondo et al., 2018) which is concerned with biomedical abbreviations. Many corpora include specific types of named entities relevant to the medical domain, such as DDI (Herrero-Zazo et al., 2013) which annotates drugs and other substances. Other examples include i2b2 (Uzuner et al., 2010) which annotates medications, dosages and other details of drug administration and CLEF (Roberts et al., 2009) which annotate different types of conditions, devices and their results in specific clinical cases. Given the specificity of the annotated concepts, most of these resources are built by biomedical experts.

The previous examples are corpora helpful in designing techniques oriented towards narrow tasks, where the annotation model is specifically designed to only consider portions of the text relevant to the concepts of interests (i.e., medical entities, genes, etc.). An alternative approach that attempts to model a wide range of the semantics of a document is Bio-AMR (May and Priyadarshi, 2017). This corpus contains health-related sentences annotated with their AMR structure, a general-purpose semantic representation of natural text. Another relevant resource is BioFrameNet (Dolbey et al., 2006), an extension to FrameNet with specific semantic roles for the biomedical domain. A positive consequence of using general-purpose semantic annotations is that it doesn't necessarily require experts in biomedical areas to participate in the annotation process.

The eHealth-KD corpus (Martínez Cámara et al., 2018) attempts to achieve a middle ground by representing a broad range of knowledge with a simple annotation model based on Subject-Action-Target triplets and 4 additional semantic relations. However, after the annotation process several shortcomings were identified. One example is the necessity for including causality and entailment as explicit relations, rather than representing

them through actions, given the importance of this type of assertions in medical texts. Likewise, the annotation lacks the ability to represent coreferences ("*this*", "*that*"), and for this reason many sentences cannot be fully annotated. Also, complex linguistic constructions that represent composite concepts (e.g., "*the patients that received treatment*") are difficult to annotate, especially when they participate in other relations. This paper extends the annotation model used by the eHealth-KD corpus with semantic elements used in general-purpose annotation models, such as AMR and PropBank. This extension allows solving the aforementioned issues and increases its representational power without adding an overly complex set of new semantic roles and relations.

3 Annotation model

In this section, we define an annotation model that attempts to represent the most relevant semantic relations in a natural language sentence. This model should avoid ambiguities as much as possible, such that different human annotators can agree with a high probability. The model needs to be expressive enough to capture relevant domain concepts and their interactions. It must also be able to represent complex concepts that are built by the combination of simpler concepts. This model is designed to aid in the construction of knowledge discovery systems. For this reason, it is necessary to detach the model representation as much as possible from the grammatical structure of sentences, and instead attempt to represent its semantic meaning.

With these objectives in mind, the annotation model proposed in this research is based on the Subject-Verb-Object grammatical structure present in western languages. However, since we are interested in annotating fragments of knowledge, the semantic role of annotated entities does not necessarily match the grammatical role. The main semantic roles of this model are `Concept` and `Action`, which are used to represent factual information about what is being done, by who, to whom. These structures can be contextualized with time, location, and other general circumstances. An additional semantic role named `Predicate` is used to build more complex conceptualizations from simpler ones. Finally, 6 specific semantic relations are used to represent general-purpose knowledge. The relations `is-a`,

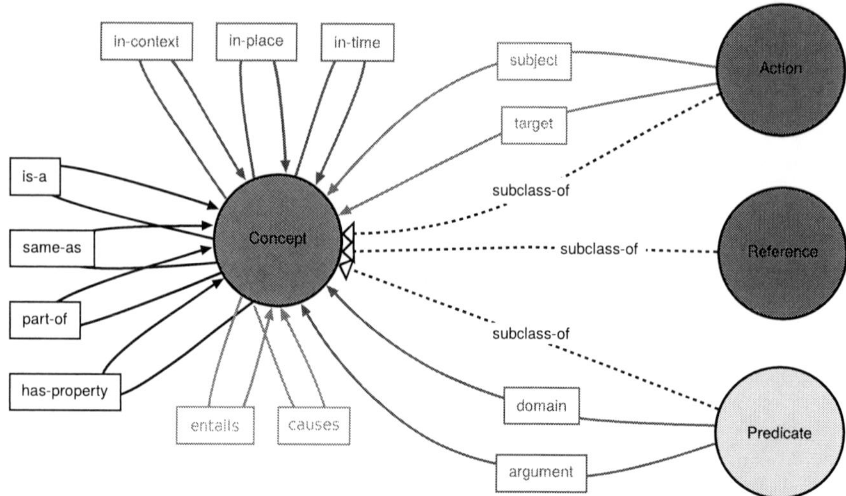

Figure 1: Conceptual schema for the annotation model. Each of the semantic roles defined in the annotation model are represented as circles. The possible relations defined between each pair of roles are represented in rectangles.

`same-as`, `has-property` and `part-of` are taken from taxonomic and ontologic representations, while the relations `causes` and `entails` are taken from the domain of text comprehension.

In contrast with AMR and PropBank, our annotation model does not yet specifies the semantic meaning of each `Concept` and `Action`. The actual meaning must be inferred from the text of the annotated entities. Likewise, the exact meaning of each semantic role (e.g, the receiver in "*accept*") is also inferred from the text, and must be resolver in a later stage. The taxonomic relations allow the capture of domain-specific definitions, that more in fine-grained task would be represented with specific entity types and relations. The domain-specific knowledge is thus represented by the semantic meaning of the annotated words, and not explicitly represented by specific entity types or relations.

The following sections explain each semantic role and relation in details and provide examples of its use in natural text sentences. Figure 1 shows a graphic representation of our annotation model.

3.1 Concepts

A `Concept` role is used to annotate fragments of text that represent a single unit of information in the domain. It can be a named entity, or a common noun, adjective or verb, that represents a concept relevant in the textual domain. Hence, almost every word or phrase that carries a singular meaning is annotated as `Concept` (or one of its derivatives, as explained next). Tokens such as articles, prepositions and conjunctions which only carry a grammatical function but not a semantic meaning are not annotated.

As an example, consider the sentence: "*El asma afecta las vías respiratorias*"[3]. In this sentence, the word *asma* is a clearly distinguishable concept in the health domain, whose meaning is independent of its grammatical role in the sentence. Some concepts such as *vías respiratorias* are multi-word, either because the single words that compose it are meaningless by themselves, or because the concept formed by their union is different from the individual meanings. In this case, even though *vías* and *respiratorias* by themselves have individual well-defined meanings, the concept *vías respiratorias* has a very definite meaning in the health domain that makes it a single unit of information, i.e., an specialist in the domain can clearly identify it.

3.2 Actions

An `Action` is a specific type of `Concept` which indicates a process or event, that some other concept can perform or receive the effects of, or an interaction between concepts. In the previous example, *afecta* is an action. An `Action` can be linked to relevant concepts by two semantic roles: `subject` and `target`. The `subject` is the concept that produces the action, while the `target` is the concept that receives the ef-

---

[3]In English: *Asthma affects the respiratory tract.*

fect of the action. In the previous example, the `subject` of *afecta* is *asma*, and the `target` is *vías respiratorias*. An `Action` can have zero or more `subjects` and/or `targets`. Figure 2 shows a graphical representation of the previous sentence with the corresponding `Concepts` and `Actions`, and the respective `subject` and `target` annotations.

Figure 2: Annotation of `Concepts` and `Actions` in an example sentence.

In the previous example the `Action` is indicated by a word with the grammatical role of verb, which is intuitively the most common case. However, an action can also be indicated by a word with another grammatical role, such as nouns. For example, in the phrase "...*el empeoramiento de los síntomas...*"[4], the word *empeoramiento* is still considered an action even though it is not a verb, since it describes a process or event that happens to some other concept. Thus, the semantic role `Action` describes the intended meaning of a concept in the semantic domain, rather than its grammatical function in any specific sentence. If a domain concept expresses a process or event that produces effects on other `Concepts`, then it is an `Action`, even if it can be used in different grammatical functions.

3.3 References

A `Reference` is a type of `Concept` that has no specific semantic meaning, but it is necessary for grammatical reasons. It is used to annotate pronouns (e.g., *este*, *aquel*, etc.) and other referential elements when necessary, such as when they play the role of `subject` or `target`.

3.4 Predicates

A `Predicate` is used to form more complex concepts by combining, filtering or modifying other `Concepts` in a sentence. A common use case is for defining a subset of a `Concept` given some properties. For example, in the phrase "...*afecta a las personas mayores de 60 años...*"[5], the word *mayores* is annotated as a `Predicate`

that filters some of the people. In conjunction with `Predicates`, any concept can play two additional roles: the `domain` or an `argument` of the predicate. In the previous example the `domain` is played with the `Concept` *personas*, and the only `argument` is *60 años*.

This construction gives rise to a new concept, that of people older than 60 years, which can be understood as the application of the filter *mayores* on a set of elements defined by the `Concept` *personas*, of whom those with the argument *60 años* are selected. The new complex concept built this way is represented in the sentence by the `Predicate` itself. Hence, to continue with the previous example, if we want these "older people" to play the `target` role then the corresponding annotation goes from the `Action` to the `Predicate`, as shown in Figure 3. It would be a mistake to say the `subject` of *afecta* is *personas* because this concept represents all people. Hence, the `Predicate` is used to represented not the filtering operation itself, but actually the filtered concept.

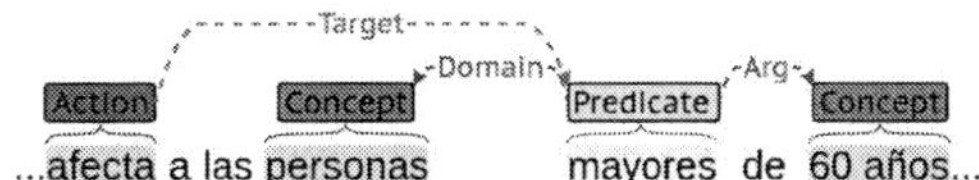

Figure 3: Annotation of `Predicates` and `Actions` in an example sentence.

3.5 Composing concepts

Just as `Predicates` can be used to define composite concepts, this can also be accomplished by considering an `Action` as the `subject` or `target` of another. For example, in the sentence "*Los empleados dedicados al cuidado de la salud están expuestos a riesgos laborales*"[6], there is complex concept involving *empleados*, *cuidado* and *salud*. This concept then acts as the `target` of *expuestos*, since it is not all employees that are exposed to hazards, but only those dedicated to health care (see Figure 4). This strategy can also be used to represent nominalizations, where the nominalized verb can be annotated as an `Action` and the corresponding `subject` and `target` construct the complex concept.

---

[4]In English: *... the worsening of symptoms...*

[5]In English: *...affects people older than 60 years...*

[6]In English: *Employees dedicated to health care are exposed to occupational hazards.*

Figure 4: Annotation of composite concepts formed when an `Action` is `subject` of another.

3.6 Taxonomic relations

`Actions` and `Concepts` allow the capture of a large part of the semantic meaning of a sentence, by annotating as actions all the concepts that indicate any interaction between other concepts. However, some specific types of interactions are so common, that they are considered in many knowledge domains as building blocks for ontological of taxonomic representations. Such is the case of *hypernymy/hyonymy* pairs (i.e., `is-a` relations) and *meronym/holonym* pairs (e.g. *part-of* relations), which form the core of several knowledge bases.

These two types of relations are very common in most knowledge domains, and there many different textual variants to express these ideas. Arguably, it is better to explicitly represent them as relations between concepts, rather than resorting to annotate as an `Action` forms of the verb *to be*. Furthermore, an explicit annotation of these relations enables automatic knowledge discovery systems trained on these annotations to extract more compact and concise structures of knowledge, since there is no additional interpretation necessary.

The relations *is-a* and *part-of* can be explicitly indicated in the text by the appereance of common textual patterns (e.g., Hearst patterns (Hearst, 1992)). However, we also consider their annotation even when no explicit textual cues appear. For example, in the phrase "*...el corazón y otros órganos...*"[7] it is implicitly begin stated that *corazón* `is-a` *órganos*. A similar case is the example "*...el corazón y otras partes del cuerpo...*"[8] that implicitly indicates that the heart is a part of the body.

The relation `same-as` is used to indicate synonyms, or concepts that are considered equal in the document's domain. It can also be used when some simple concept is defined by describing it as another more complex concept, such as in the following example: "*Una ampolla es la piel que cubre una herida*"[9]. In this example,

the `Concept` *ampolla* is being defined as another complex concept, formed by the `Action` *cubre* with `subject` *piel* and `target` *herida*. Hence, in this example the sentence is annotated as shown in Figure 5.

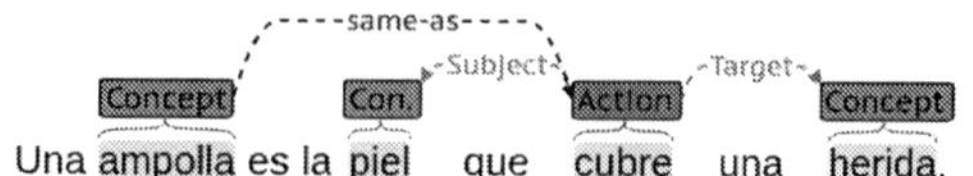

Figure 5: Annotation of a `same-as` relation in a definition.

The relation `has-property` is used to specify that a concept has a property or characteristic, or can be described by another concept. The simplest example is "*...el asma es peligrosa...*"[10], in which the `Concept` *asma* is related by `has-property` to the `Concept` *peligrosa*.

For all the taxonomic relations, we only consider the annotation when the sentence actually implies the existence of such relation, even if the implication is implicit. In no case we consider their annotation based solely on external or domain knowledge.

3.7 Causation and entailment

The previous 4 semantic relations are useful for capturing the taxonomic structure of the knowledge expressed in natural text. Two additional relations are defined for capturing logical connections between concepts: `causes` and `entails`. The relation `causes` is used to express that some event (identified in general as a `Concept`) is a possible cause for another event. An example is "*El asma provoca que las vías respiratorias se inflamen*"[11], annotated as shown in Figure 6. This relation indicates causation, not correlation or logical implication. Hence, it must be clearly stated in a sentence that there is a direct causation link between events. There is also a degree of uncertainty implied in the causation, which means that if *A* causes *B*, it doesn't necessarily imply that

---

[7]In English: *...the heart and other organs...*

[8]In English: *...the heart and other parts of the body...*

[9]In English: *A blister is the skin that covers a wound.*

[10]In English: *...asthma is dangerous...*

[11]In English: *Asthma causes the respiratory tract to become inflamed.*

every time *A* happens *B* will follow, or that anytime *B* happens, is due to *A*.

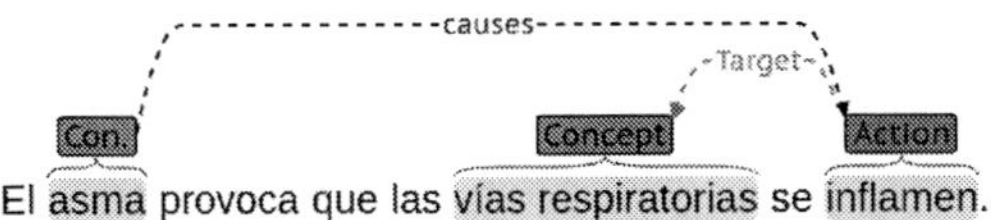

Figure 6: Annotation of the relation `causes`.

In contrast, the relation `entails` is used to denote a logical implication. In this case, it is not necessary for events to be related by causation at all; what must hold is that when some assertion *A* is true then it is always the case that assertion *B* is true. The annotation of causation and entailment avoids annotating several words and phrases that share the same semantic meaning. For example, in Figure 6 we refrain from annotating "*provoca*", since the actual meaning is already represented by `causes`.

3.8 Contextualization

Sometimes concepts only participate in certain relations with a precondition, such as during a specific period of time, in a specific location, or with some additional properties. An example is the sentence "*El dengue en estado avanzado es peligroso*"[12]. In this sentence the annotation *dengue* `has-property` *peligroso* fails to capture the whole semantic of the message, since dengue is not necessarily always dangerous (according to the sentence), but only in the specific situation when it is in advanced stage. For these situations, our model includes three contextual relations: `in-time`, `in-place` and the more general `in-context`. The previous sentence is annotated as shown in Figure 7.

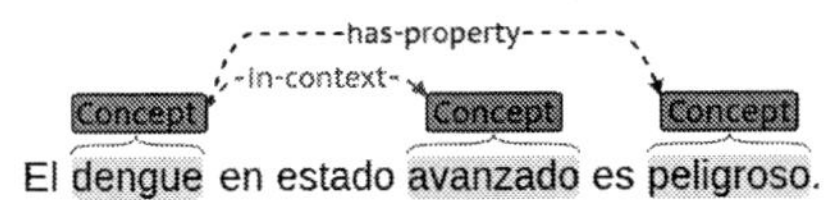

Figure 7: Annotation of the relation `in-context`.

The difference between contextual relations and the rest is that they do not define an assertion, but are only useful for building more complex concepts. For example, the annotation *dengue* `in-context` *avanzado* does not say that dengue always has the quality of being advanced. It is only when linked by `has-property` (or another

---

[12]In English: *Dengue in advanced stage is dangerous.*

relation) to other concepts, that this construction is meaningful. For this reason it is not correct to interchange `in-context` with `has-property`, since a `has-property` relation does state a specific assertion by its own.

3.9 Attributes

Four additional Boolean attributes can be attached to any concept to further qualify or describe it: `negated`, `uncertain`, `diminished` and `emphasized`. These attributes are used to avoid annotating stopwords such as *no*, *mucho*, *poco*, *puede*, and instead directly attaching the corresponding qualifier to the concept itself. These attributes also capture the intended negation, uncertainty or emphasis even when it is implied and not explicitly indicated by another word. An example is the phrase: "*...en ocasiones cura...*"[13] in which there is an implied uncertainty in the `Action` *cura*.

4 Annotation methodology

In this section, we briefly describe a methodology for creating a corpus based in this annotation model. At the moment of writing this process is being applied to the annotation of a corpus of 1000 Spanish sentences in the clinical text domain. This corpus is the main evaluation scenario for the eHealth-KD challenge to be hosted at IberLEF 2019[14]. The partial annotations and corpus statistics are available online[15].

The annotation process begins with the creation of a small collection of annotated sentences (i.e., a trial corpus) by a group of expert annotators. The selected sentences should cover all the important annotation patterns, and ideally, the most significant sources of ambiguity. From this trial corpus, an annotation guide can be constructed, that contains example annotations of all the semantic roles and relations defined. This guide defines the annotation protocol and also how to disambiguate conflicting patterns. The annotation guide is used as reference by the rest of the annotators during the whole process. For the annotation process we propose the following stages:

1. Manually tagging a set sentences independently by different non-biomedical experts.

---

[13]In English: *...ocassionally it heals...*

[14]`https://knowledge-learning.github.io/ehealthkd-2019`

[15]`https://github.com/knowledge-learning/satr-ann`

Each sentence is tagged by two different annotators. Annotators are allowed to discuss general strategies, but should not discuss the specific sentences they are assigned. When in doubt, they will refer to the annotation guide and the trial examples.

2. Merging and normalization of tagging sentences between two annotators. In this case, another annotator selects the best annotations when contradictions exist. This stage can be aided by merging scripts that automatically detect and highlight conflicts.

3. The normalized sentences are verified and agreed upon by a committee of expert researchers in natural language processing, that decide which sentences are finally included in the corpus. Alternatively, if all members of the committee agree than a different annotation improves a specific sentence, it can be changed, but this situation should be the exception rather than the norm.

After the three stages, the set of manually annotated and revised sentences constitute the new corpus. These sentences should be then evaluated as described in Section 4.1.

4.1 Annotation evaluation

To evaluate the manual annotation agreement in the corpus, we propose to compute a micro-average of all the matches between every pair of annotations of the same sentences. This comparison can be performed in two stages. First, when the non-expert annotators label all the original sentences, each sentence receives annotations from two different people. Second, after the sentences are combined and revised by the expert committee, they can be compared to the original sentences, to understand how much the corpus changed between non-expert annotations in the review process. Since the annotation task involves selecting subsets of text and labelling them with different tags, we propose to use an F_1 metric (as opposed to the most common Kappa metric), such as the one used by Moreno et al. (2017) for the DrugSemantics corpus. Since the annotation involves fragments of text, it is important to consider partial agreement between annotators. For this purpose, we propose to score partially matching spans of texts proportionally to the length of their intersection.

Another important evaluation metric is the human performance in this task, since corpora created with this annotation models are frequently used for machine learning tasks. We propose that after the corpus is built an additional annotator performs a manual labelling of a predefined subset of the sentences. This annotator can be trained with the same annotation guidelines, but should not have been exposed to this specific subset of sentences before. This can be used as a baseline for human performance and can be compared to the performance of different algorithms trained in the corpus. In the eHealth-KD challenge, this strategy will be applied to provide a human performance metric for comparative purposes.

4.2 Annotation guidelines

The most relevant characteristic of the annotation model presented in this research is that it intends to represent the semantic, rather than the syntax of sentences. For this purpose, it is necessary to avoid in annotators incorrect mindsets that fix semantic roles to grammatical functions (e.g., considering that verbs are almost always actions). The correct process is understanding the semantic meaning of a sentence first, and then representing it using the annotations. A useful heuristic is to attempt to reconstruct a sentence from the annotations, possibly with a different wording than the original, but with the same meaning. It is also important to annotate all the concepts that appear in the sentence even if they cannot be eventually interrelated. Finally, we prefer annotating the most explicit relation possible; for example, using `cause` instead of using an Action such as "*produce*" or "*provoca*", if `cause` accurately captures the semantic meaning of the corresponding phrase.

4.3 Annotation tools

The tool proposed for all the manual annotation process is BRAT (Stenetorp et al., 2012). This tool makes it possible to visually select text portions, assign labels and connect them by relations, through a simple web interface that requires little to no previous training. Even though BRAT allows a limited form of collaborative annotation, we actually prefer that different annotators work in different copies of the text (Stage 1), and afterwards perform an automatic merging process using custom scripts that output a BRAT-compatible result. Then, in Stage 2, the expert who performs the normalization can continue to use BRAT to correct mistakes. Furthermore, the web interface of BRAT enables online collaboration between annotators that are not physically close. For our model, we provide relevant configuration files for BRAT and 50 annotated examples sentences online[16].

5 Conclusions and future work

This research proposes a general-purpose annotation model that captures a broad range of semantic information from textual content, based on Subject-Action-Target triplets plus additional semantic relations. This model extends the annotation model used by the eHealth-KD corpus, with the addition of two semantic roles (`Predicate` and `Reference`), the representation of causation and entailment, and the possibility of identifying contextual qualifiers. Theses additions allow capturing more complex semantic information than the previous model. Our ongoing efforts focus on annotating a large corpus of clinical text in Spanish for supporting shared evaluation campaigns.

The semantic roles and relations defined map to common concepts and relations used in knowledge bases and ontologies, which simplifies the task of building semantic networks from the annotated text. In the future we will focus on this mapping stage, which will also require linking these concepts to entities hosted at shared knowledge bases, such as DBpedia (Auer et al., 2007) and UMLS (Bodenreider, 2004). In addition, we also plan to pursue the annotation of clinical text, and extending to additional languages and other domains, such as news, scientific papers, encyclopedic articles and others.

Acknowledgments

Funding: This research has been supported by a Carolina Foundation grant in agreement with University of Alicante and University of Havana. Moreover, it has also been partially funded by both aforementioned universities and the Generalitat Valenciana (Conselleria d'Educació, Investigació, Cultura i Esport) through the projects PROMETEO/2018/089, PROMETEU/2018/089; Social-Univ 2.0 (ENCARGO-INTERNOOMNI-1); and PINGVALUE3-18Y.

The authors would like to thank the team of annotators from the School of Math and Computer Science, at the University of Havana.

This version of the paper takes into account helpful comments provided by the anonymous reviewers.

References

Sören Auer, Christian Bizer, Georgi Kobilarov, Jens Lehmann, Richard Cyganiak, and Zachary Ives. 2007. Dbpedia: A nucleus for a web of open data. In *The semantic web*, pages 722–735. Springer.

Collin F Baker, Charles J Fillmore, and John B Lowe. 1998. The berkeley framenet project. In *Proceedings of the 17th international conference on Computational linguistics-Volume 1*, pages 86–90. Association for Computational Linguistics.

Laura Banarescu, Claire Bonial, Shu Cai, Madalina Georgescu, Kira Griffitt, Ulf Hermjakob, Kevin Knight, Philipp Koehn, Martha Palmer, and Nathan Schneider. 2013. Abstract meaning representation for sembanking. In *Proceedings of the 7th Linguistic Annotation Workshop and Interoperability with Discourse*, pages 178–186, Sofia, Bulgaria. Association for Computational Linguistics.

Olivier Bodenreider. 2004. The unified medical language system (umls): integrating biomedical terminology. *Nucleic acids research*, 32(suppl_1):D267–D270.

Andrew Carlson, Justin Betteridge, Bryan Kisiel, Burr Settles, Estevam R. Hruschka, Jr., and Tom M. Mitchell. 2010. Toward an architecture for never-ending language learning. In *Proceedings of the Twenty-Fourth AAAI Conference on Artificial Intelligence*, AAAI'10, pages 1306–1313. AAAI Press.

Andrew Dolbey, Michael Ellsworth, and Jan Scheffczyk. 2006. Bioframenet: A domain-specific framenet extension with links to biomedical ontologies. *KR-MED 2006*, page 87.

Usama Fayyad, Gregory Piatetsky-Shapiro, and Padhraic Smyth. 1996. From data mining to knowledge discovery in databases. *AI magazine*, 17(3):37.

Marti A Hearst. 1992. Automatic acquisition of hyponyms from large text corpora. In *Proceedings of the 14th conference on Computational linguistics-Volume 2*, pages 539–545. Association for Computational Linguistics.

María Herrero-Zazo, Isabel Segura-Bedmar, Paloma Martínez, and Thierry Declerck. 2013. The ddi corpus: An annotated corpus with pharmacological substances and drug–drug interactions. *Journal of biomedical informatics*, 46(5):914–920.

A Intxaurrondo, JC de la Torre, H Rodriguez Betanco, M Marimon, JA Lopez-Martin, A Gonzalez-Agirre, J Santamaria, M Villegas, and M Krallinger. 2018.

---

[16]`https://github.com/knowledge-learning/satr-ann/tree/master/data/v1`

Resources, guidelines and annotations for the recognition, definition resolution and concept normalization of spanish clinical abbreviations: the barr2 corpus. SEPLN.

Cewu Lu, Ranjay Krishna, Michael Bernstein, and Li Fei-Fei. 2016. Visual relationship detection with language priors. In *Computer Vision – ECCV 2016*, pages 852–869. Springer International Publishing.

Eugenio Martínez Cámara, Yudivian Almeida Cruz, Manuel Carlos Díaz Galiano, Suilan Estévez-Velarde, Miguel Ángel García Cumbreras, Manuel García Vega, Yoan Gutiérrez, Arturo Montejo Ráez, Andres Montoyo, Rafael Muñoz, et al. 2018. Overview of tass 2018: Opinions, health and emotions.

Jonathan May and Jay Priyadarshi. 2017. Semeval-2017 task 9: Abstract meaning representation parsing and generation. In *Proceedings of the 11th International Workshop on Semantic Evaluation (SemEval-2017)*, pages 536–545.

Isabel Moreno, Ester Boldrini, Paloma Moreda, and M Teresa Romá-Ferri. 2017. Drugsemantics: a corpus for named entity recognition in spanish summaries of product characteristics. *Journal of biomedical informatics*, 72:8–22.

Martha Palmer. 2009. Semlink: Linking propbank, verbnet and framenet. In *Proceedings of the generative lexicon conference*, pages 9–15. GenLex-09, Pisa, Italy.

Martha Palmer, Daniel Gildea, and Paul Kingsbury. 2005. The proposition bank: An annotated corpus of semantic roles. *Computational linguistics*, 31(1):71–106.

Sudha Rao, Daniel Marcu, Kevin Knight, and Hal Daumé III. 2017. Biomedical event extraction using abstract meaning representation. *BioNLP 2017*, pages 126–135.

Angus Roberts, Robert Gaizauskas, Mark Hepple, George Demetriou, Yikun Guo, Ian Roberts, and Andrea Setzer. 2009. Building a semantically annotated corpus of clinical texts. *Journal of biomedical informatics*, 42(5):950–966.

Karin Kipper Schuler. 2005. *Verbnet: A Broad-coverage, Comprehensive Verb Lexicon*. Ph.D. thesis, Philadelphia, PA, USA. AAI3179808.

Matthew S. Simpson and Dina Demner-Fushman. 2012. *Biomedical Text Mining: A Survey of Recent Progress*, pages 465–517. Springer US, Boston, MA.

Frederic Stahl, Bogdan Gabrys, Mohamed Medhat Gaber, and Monika Berendsen. An overview of interactive visual data mining techniques for knowledge discovery. *Wiley Interdisciplinary Reviews: Data Mining and Knowledge Discovery*, 3(4):239–256.

Pontus Stenetorp, Sampo Pyysalo, Goran Topić, Tomoko Ohta, Sophia Ananiadou, and Jun'ichi Tsujii. 2012. Brat: A web-based tool for nlp-assisted text annotation. In *Proceedings of the Demonstrations at the 13th Conference of the European Chapter of the Association for Computational Linguistics*, EACL '12, pages 102–107, Stroudsburg, PA, USA. Association for Computational Linguistics.

Özlem Uzuner, Imre Solti, and Eithon Cadag. 2010. Extracting medication information from clinical text. *Journal of the American Medical Informatics Association*, 17(5):514–518.

Predicting ICU transfers using text messages between nurses and doctors

Faiza Khan Khattak[1,2,3]**, Chloé Pou-Prom**[2]**, Robert Wu**[4]**, Frank Rudzicz**[1,2,3,5]

[1]Department of Computer Science, University of Toronto
[2]St. Michael's Hospital
[3]Vector Institute for Artificial Intelligence
[4]Toronto General Hospital
[5]Surgical Safety Technologies
`faizakk@cs.toronto.edu, poupromc@smh.ca,`
`robert.wu@uhn.ca, frank@cs.toronto.edu`

Abstract

We explore the use of real-time clinical information, i.e., text messages sent between nurses and doctors regarding patient conditions in order to predict transfer to the intensive care unit (ICU). Preliminary results, in data from five hospitals, indicate that, despite being short and full of noise, text messages can augment other visit information to improve the performance of ICU transfer prediction.

1 Introduction

'Failure to rescue' is an important aspect of patient safety and can be caused by poor communication, or a lack of situational awareness, in the care team (Brady and Goldenhar, 2014). There has been increased recognition of the importance of acting on deteriorating patients by escalating their care via rapid response and emergency medical teams (De-Vita et al., 2006). Established criteria, such as the Modified Early Warning Score (MEWS) (Subbe et al., 2001), identify patients at risk of deterioration. Recently, machine learning approaches have employed electronic patient record data, vital signs, and laboratory results (Zhou et al., 2016; Futoma et al., 2015; Che et al., 2016; Frost et al., 2017), and have typically performed better than MEWS (Churpek et al., 2016; Zhai et al., 2014).

Related work in intensive care unit (ICU) transfer prediction often relies on structured data (i.e., lab results and vitals) taken from the patient's electronic health record. For instance, Tabak et al. (2017) developed a measure that relied on both clinical and administrative data (e.g., diagnosis, length of stay, number of previous discharges) and predicted hospital readmission with c-statistics up to 0.722. Similarly, Genevès et al. (2018) focused on drug prescription data on the day of admission, and predicted various forms of risk, including ICU admissions ($\geq$65% AUC). By contrast,

Escudié et al. (2018) represented the *text* of electronic health records based on the Fast Healthcare Interoperability Resources format[1] and used word embedding and random forests to predict disease codes at the time of discharge, with a wide range in accuracies. Miotto et al. (2016) embedded medications, diagnoses, procedures, lab tests, and other structured information in a deep neural net and were able to predict various diseases with an average AUC-ROC of 0.773. Crucially, none of these systems used dynamic real-time data on a patient.

Real-time clinical information, especially communication between nurses and doctors, may be useful in improving the accuracy of detecting deteriorating patients (Rajkomar et al., 2018). In particular, this information may hold vital data not included in other fields, including changes in consciousness, pain, and other symptoms. Often, urgent communication in the hospital still occurs through pagers, limiting analysis of this communication (De Meester et al., 2013; Wu et al., 2013; Johnston et al., 2014). In some hospitals, however, communication occurs through text messaging. This transition from unrecorded messages to text allows for deeper analysis of these potentially crucial information. In this work, we evaluate the impact of using text messages between physicians and nurses to predict ICU transfer.

2 Data

Our data consist of 38,373 patients across 49,224 visits, between 2011 and 2017, divided into five groups according to different institutional codes. Messages from 2011 to 2015 are in a different format (from an older system), so we focus our analysis on messages from 2015 to 2017. We also exclude all patients who have missing institutional

---

[1]`https://www.hl7.org/fhir/overview.html`

Proceedings of the 2nd Clinical Natural Language Processing Workshop, pages 89–94
Minneapolis, Minnesota, June 7, 2019. ©2019 Association for Computational Linguistics

	Group A	Group B	Group C	Group D	Group E
Patient info.					
# Patients (M/F)	4,536 / 4,031	3488 / 3363	206 / 202	21 / 19	17 / 10
Age at admission	63.45 (18.55)	70.01 (18.86)	72.75 (14.45)	72.59 (17.35)	72.66 (12.07)
# mheaders/patient	13.86 (23.07)	15.54 (24.96)	21.81 (38.58)	15.07 (19.68)	11.82 (9.17)
# mreplies/patient	14.27 (23.52)	16.46 (26.49)	22.68 (40.86)	21.61 (23.39)	12.32 (8.74)
Visit info.					
# Visits	10,001	8,586	527	57	30
# visits/patient	1.35 (0.89)	1.41 (1.02)	1.37 (0.86)	1.48 (0.85)	1.29 (0.60)
# days/visit	9.80 (19.01)	9.91 (21.47)	15.22 (19.87)	12.76 (14.75)	9.22 (6.47)
# mheaders/visit	9.85 (16.58)	10.64 (17.84)	15.48 (27.02)	14.40 (18.14)	8.67 (7.97)
# mreplies/visit	10.18 (16.98)	11.31 (18.95)	16.18 (28.46)	15.07 (19.68)	9.03 (7.99)
Messages info.					
# mheaders	98,468	91,330	8,159	821	260
# mreply	99,456	95,654	8,395	844	271
ICU%	16.75%	0.36%	35.86%	22.12%	2.01%
# tokens/mheader	22.31 (14.22)	22.90 (14.28)	22.68 (14.62)	22.38 (13.47)	23.70 (13.84)
# tokens/mreply	7.34 (7.97)	7.55 (8.07)	7.47 (7.89)	7.05 (7.22)	7.42 (7.17)

Table 1: Patient, visit, and messages information of data between years 2015 and 2017 used to train models for predicting ICU transfer. We indicate standard deviation in parentheses. ICU % is the ratio of mheaders resulting in ICU transfer within 3 days of the message send date.

code in their record. Data include patient and visit information, and text messages.

Patient information includes patient ID, date of birth, gender, date admitted, most recent medication, and most recent diagnosis.

Visit information includes visit number, discharge date time, diagnosis made during the visit[2], visit type ("Emergency" or "Inpatient"), doctors' notes, lab results, institutional code, and an Admission/Discharge/Transfer (ADT) code indicating to where the patient was admitted, discharged, or transferred to. Of the 539 ADT values, 19 correspond to an ICU transfer.

Text messages are collected from the hospital network system and split into *message headers* and *message replies*. *Message headers* consist of text messages sent from nurses to physicians. These messages include information such as medication and status of patient. Some message headers have a corresponding *message reply*, which consists of text responses from doctors. The database system in which these text messages are stored only allows for replies from doctor but not a reply back from nurse. If a nurse replies back, it is considered a new message header, making it difficult to track a "conversation thread". Sometimes the message

reply gets sent more than one time and many other times it is empty. In our experiments, we only look at the *message header*, as most *message replies* are short and uninformative. The top most frequent replies are: *"thanks"*, *"ok"* and *"noted"* across all groups. We split the data by institutional code and report a summary of the demographics, visits, and messages in Table 1.

mheader: *"hb=65, cr=123 & more lab res up from last nights bldwork. Ping if anything you want me to follow up."*   **mreply:** *"informed."*
mheader: *"dc hep drip on epr. Pls see chart order. Thnx."*   **mreply:** *"done thanks"*
mheader: *"hey are icu recommends to be cosigned. thx."*   **mreply:** *"Ok. Pls run one l of ringers wide & then one more"*

Table 2: Examples of *message header* (mheader) and *message reply* (mreply) pairs. Modified for anonymity.

Text messages can be challenging to analyze, given spelling mistakes, abbreviations specific to the medical domain, missing punctuation, and other challenges. Open-source spelling correction

---

[2]This is not the same as the diagnosis in the patient information.

	Group A		Group C	
	$--$	$+Ling$	$--$	$+Ling$
$Visit$	$0.47 \pm (0.01)$	$0.50 \pm (0.01)$	$0.44 \pm (0.02)$	$0.53 \pm (0.02)$
$Visit + TFIDF$	$\mathbf{0.51 \pm (0.01)}$	$0.48 \pm (0.01)$	$0.56 \pm (0.04)$	$0.56 \pm (0.04)$
$Visit + w2v_{SMS}$	$\mathbf{0.51 \pm (0.02)}$	$0.48 \pm (0.01)$	$\mathbf{0.57 \pm (0.05)}$	$\mathbf{0.57 \pm (0.04)}$
$Visit + w2v_{Pubmed}$	$\mathbf{0.51 \pm (0.01)}$	$0.49\pm (0.01)$	$0.54 \pm (0.04)$	$0.54 \pm (0.04)$
$Visit + TFIDF + w2v_{SMS}$	$\mathbf{0.51\pm (0.01)}$	$0.48 \pm (0.01)$	$0.56 \pm (0.04)$	$0.56 \pm (0.04)$
$Visit + TFIDF + w2v_{Pubmed}$	$0.49\pm (0.01)$	$0.47\pm (0.01)$	$0.54\pm (0.03)$	$0.51 \pm (0.04)$

Table 3: Macro F_1- scores on the logistic regression model for Group A and C. We report the macro F_1 metric averaged over 5-fold cross-validation (with standard deviations in parentheses).

software[3] provides little improvement, due to the domain-specific nature of the words. E.g., the message *'pls add prn pain med, not PO. thx'* gets corrected to *'ls add pr pain mod, not PO. tax'*. We provide examples of message header and message reply pairs in Table 2.

We focus our experiments on Group A since it has the most amount of data, and on Group C since it has the most number of messages per visit and the longest messages. We use the ADT (Admission/Discharge/Transfer) code in the patients' records to determine transfer to the ICU. A *mheader* is determined to have the outcome if an ICU transfer occurs within the next 3 days of the message send date (Table 1).

3 Methods

For each text message, we include the patient's age and gender, the total number of days spent in hospital at the time the message is sent[4], their prescribed medication at the time of the message, and their diagnosis. The medication and diagnosis are encoded with one-word TF-IDF.

We then look at the following representations of text messages. For each representation, we use at most 20 words and zero-pad if necessary:

TF-IDF: We represent each text message with its TF-IDF representation. We experiment with word, n-gram, and character-level TF-IDF, as well as combinations. We use n-gram TF-IDF ($n = 1, 2, 3$) in our final models.

Word2Vec: We use 1) pre-trained word embeddings (Mikolov et al., 2013) trained on publicly available PubMed articles (Moen and Ananiadou, 2013), as well as 2) our own word embeddings, trained on the text messages data. We train word

embeddings of dimension size 100, with a context window equal to 5 for training (Bojanowski et al., 2017). We explore different combinations of the text message word embeddings through concatenation, summing, and averaging. We report results using a combination of all three types. More specifically, we concatenate twenty 100-dimensional word embeddings (2000 dimensions), a sum of the word embeddings (100 dimensions), and an average of the 20 words (100 dimensions), for a total of 2200-dimensional feature vector.

Linguistic features: We represent each text message as a vector containing 9 linguistic features. We compute lexical features (character and word count, word density[5]), syntactic features (counts of nouns, verbs, adjectives, and adverbs), and positive and negative polarity extracted from `nltk`'s sentiment analyzer (Loper and Bird, 2002).

We use an ANOVA-based feature selection (Pedregosa et al., 2011), and we train a logistic regression model. We report the macro F_1 metric averaged across 5-fold cross-validation.

4 Results

We experiment with *Visit* (i.e., age, gender, total number of days spend in hospital, medication, and diagnosis), *TFIDF*, *Ling* (i.e., linguistic), $w2v_{SMS}$ (i.e., word vectors trained on text messages), and $w2v_{Pubmed}$ (i.e., pre-trained word vectors from PubMed) features. When multiple text representations are used (e.g., TF-IDF and w2v), we concatenate them together. Typically, the addition of linguistic features does not seem to improve performance.

We then look at performance across data and report results in Table 4 on the logistic regression model using visit information only, visit fea-

---

[3] `https://github.com/rfk/pyenchant`

[4] this includes the number of days spent in the hospital from *previous* visits

[5] *Word density* is the number of words in a message divided by the number of characters in a message.

tures augmented with text message representations ($w2v_{SMS}$, and $TFIDF$).

	visit	visit + $\mathbf{w_{sms}}$	visit + tfidf
A	0.47 (0.01)	**0.51 (0.02)**	**0.51 (0.01)**
B	0.48 (0.01)	0.46 (0.07)	**0.50 (0.01)**
C	0.44 (0.02)	**0.57 (0.05)**	**0.56 (0.04)**
D	0.44 (0.03)	**0.46 (0.07)**	0.44 (0.04)
E	0.69 (0.28)	0.69 (0.28)	0.69 (0.28)

Table 4: Model performance across the different data. F_1 macro results on a logistic regression model using 1) visit features only, and 2) visit features, word2vec embeddings (i.e., $w2v_{SMS}$) and 3) visit features, TF-IDF features.

Our results indicate that the addition of information from text messages improves results in ICU transfer prediction three days before the event happens. Our best results are in the model consisting of visit and word2vec features trained on our data (i.e., $w2v_{SMS}$). We look more closely at the performance of this model with this subset of features in Table 5. As expected, the model does better on messages that don't result in ICU transfer. We obtain recall of 0.22 and 0.43 in ICU transfer messages for Groups *A* and *C*, respectively.

		Group A	**Group C**
No ICU transfer	**P**	0.86 (0.01)	0.78 (0.05)
	R	0.80 (0.05)	0.73 (0.07)
ICU transfer	**P**	0.16 (0.02)	0.36 (0.06)
	R	0.22 (0.06)	0.43 (0.13)
Micro F$_1$		0.72 (0.04)	0.65 (0.05)
Macro F$_1$		0.51 (0.02)	0.57 (0.05)
Weighted F$_1$		0.74 (0.03)	0.66 (0.05)

Table 5: Results for logistic regression model using Visit and $w2v_{SMS}$.

5 Discussion

Table 4 shows that the addition of text message representations yields to improvements in Groups *A*, *B*, *C*, and *D*. The greatest improvement in in Group *C*. The proportion of messages which are followed by an ICU transfer three days later is much higher in Group *C*, which could reasonably explain the difference in performance. However, we also note that text messages in Group *C* tend to be longer than other data, and that nurses in Group *C* send more messages per visit. Across all data, the best model performance is for Group

E but no improvement after adding text messages. However, it consists of the smallest number of messages and the highest variance in performance across validation folds. The ratio of messages which are followed by an ICU transfer in the next 3 days are 16.75%, 0.36%, 35.86%, 22.12% and 2.01% for Groups *A*, *B*, *C*, *D*, and *E*, respectively (Table 2). The differences in performance could be attributed to the number of messages.

Word	**w2v$_{SMS}$**	**w2v$_{Pubmed}$**
dr	dr., doctor, md, resident, oncologist	99:1, diastereos-electivities, ee, =98:2, 98:2
bld	blood, bloood, blod , frozen, pt.iv	whi, bldB, EPS-deficient, transposon-generated, A-factor-deficient
med	medication, pill, lactulose, risperidone, hypoglycemics	Nicolae, Delores, Dres, habil., CSc.
bp	b/p, bp=, bp-, bpm, pulse	nt, bps, nts, bp-long, bp-long
icu	msicu, emerg, er, cvicu, gim	bag/mask, Patient-initiated, extra-hospital, patient-cycled, airway-management

Table 6: Comparison of word embeddings. Top five similar words for common abbreviated medical terms. **w2v$_{SMS}$** denotes the word embeddings trained on our text message data and **w2v$_{Pubmed}$** denotes the word embeddings trained on publicly available PubMed articles.

Using word embeddings trained on our data performs better than the pre-trained ones. We dig deeper and report the top 5 similar words of some common medical terms in Table 6. Word embeddings trained on text messages do a much better job of capturing different spellings (e.g., *"bp"* and *"b/p"*) as well as common misspellings (e.g., *"blood"* and *"blod"*). These results further highlight the need for context-specific word embeddings (Chiu et al., 2016).

6 Conclusion & Future Work

In this work, we look at the added value of text messages sent from nurses to doctors in predicting transfer to the ICU within three days of the message send date. We find that including messages from information - through linguistic features, TF-IDF features, and word vector representations - improves performance. This finding is consistent in 4 of the 5 datasets divided by institutional codes. The best performance was observed in the data with the most ICU transfers, the longest text messages and the most text messages per visit and per patient. We find that using word vectors trained on the text messages results in the best model performance, and a closer look shows that the embeddings do a better job at capturing misspellings and abbreviations unique to text messages.

In future work, we want to investigate differences across the data, and hope to identify key features of the text messages that are relevant in identifying ICU transfer. Other than that, we will also investigate the utility of adding the message replies, along with the message headers, as features. In this work, we have only looked at predictions for a given text message. Exploring how the prediction probabilities change over time would also be of interest. We will also consider different word embeddings (Peters et al., 2018), as we hypothesize that character-level word embeddings could better capture the unique vocabulary of text messages. To address class imbalance, we will explore undersampling/oversampling methods such as SMOTE (Chawla et al., 2002). Furthermore, we want to look at the added value of text messages in a more complex set of features (i.e., lab results and vitals), as we believe that this would provide a complete picture of the patient's visit profile.

Acknowledgments

Rudzicz is an Inaugural CIFAR Chair in Artificial Intelligence.

References

Piotr Bojanowski, Edouard Grave, Armand Joulin, and Tomas Mikolov. 2017. Enriching word vectors with subword information. *TACL*, 5:135–146.

Patrick W. Brady and Linda M. Goldenhar. 2014. A qualitative study examining the influences on situation awareness and the identification, mitigation and escalation of recognised patient risk. *BMJ Qual Saf*, 23(2):153–161.

Nitesh V. Chawla, Kevin W. Bowyer, Lawrence O. Hall, and W. Philip Kegelmeyer. 2002. Smote: synthetic minority over-sampling technique. *Journal of artificial intelligence research*, 16:321–357.

Zhengping Che, Sanjay Purushotham, Robinder Khemani, and Yan Liu. 2016. Interpretable deep models for icu outcome prediction. In *AMIA Annual Symposium Proceedings*, volume 2016, page 371. American Medical Informatics Association.

Billy Chiu, Gamal Crichton, Anna Korhonen, and Sampo Pyysalo. 2016. How to train good word embeddings for biomedical nlp. In *Proceedings of the 15th Workshop on Biomedical Natural Language Processing*, pages 166–174.

Matthew M. Churpek, Trevor C. Yuen, Christopher Winslow, David O. Meltzer, Michael W. Kattan, and Dana P. Edelson. 2016. Multicenter comparison of machine learning methods and conventional regression for predicting clinical deterioration on the wards. *Critical care medicine*, 44(2):368.

Koen De Meester, M. Verspuy, Koen G. Monsieurs, and Peter Van Bogaert. 2013. Sbar improves nurse–physician communication and reduces unexpected death: A pre and post intervention study. *Resuscitation*, 84(9):1192–1196.

Michael A. DeVita, Rinaldo Bellomo, Kenneth Hillman, John Kellum, Armando Rotondi, Dan Teres, Andrew Auerbach, Wen-Jon Chen, Kathy Duncan, Gary Kenward, et al. 2006. Findings of the first consensus conference on medical emergency teams. *Critical care medicine*, 34(9):2463–2478.

Jean-Baptiste Escudié, Alaa Saade, Alice Coucke, and Marc Lelarge. 2018. Deep representation for patient visits from electronic health records. *arXiv preprint arXiv:1803.09533*.

David W. Frost, Shankar Vembu, Jiayi Wang, Karen Tu, Quaid Morris, and Howard B. Abrams. 2017. Using the electronic medical record to identify patients at high risk for frequent emergency department visits and high system costs. *The American journal of medicine*, 130(5):601–e17.

Joseph Futoma, Jonathan Morris, and Joseph Lucas. 2015. A comparison of models for predicting early hospital readmissions. *Journal of biomedical informatics*, 56:229–238.

Pierre Genevès, Thomas Calmant, Nabil Layaïda, Marion Lepelley, Svetlana Artemova, and Jean-Luc Bosson. 2018. Scalable machine learning for predicting at-risk profiles upon hospital admission. 12:23–34.

Maximilian Johnston, Sonal Arora, Dominic King, Luke Stroman, and Ara Darzi. 2014. Escalation of care and failure to rescue: a multicenter, multiprofessional qualitative study. *Surgery*, 155(6):989–994.

Edward Loper and Steven Bird. 2002. Nltk: The natural language toolkit. In *In Proceedings of the ACL Workshop on Effective Tools and Methodologies for Teaching Natural Language Processing and Computational Linguistics. Philadelphia: Association for Computational Linguistics.*

Tomas Mikolov, Ilya Sutskever, Kai Chen, Greg S Corrado, and Jeff Dean. 2013. Distributed representations of words and phrases and their compositionality. In *Advances in neural information processing systems*, pages 3111–3119.

Riccardo Miotto, Li Li, Brian A. Kidd, and Joel T Dudley. 2016. Deep patient: an unsupervised representation to predict the future of patients from the electronic health records. *Scientific reports*, 6:26094.

SPFGH Moen and Tapio Salakoski2 Sophia Ananiadou. 2013. Distributional semantics resources for biomedical text processing. In *Proceedings of the 5th International Symposium on Languages in Biology and Medicine, Tokyo, Japan*, pages 39–43.

Fabian Pedregosa, Gael Varoquaux, Alexandre Gramfort, Vincent Michel, Bertrand Thirion, O. Grisel, M. Blondel, P. Prettenhofer, R. Weiss, V. Dubourg, J. Vanderplas, A. Passos, D. Cournapeau, M. Brucher, M. Perrot, and E. Duchesnay. 2011. Scikit-learn: Machine learning in Python. *Journal of Machine Learning Research*, 12:2825–2830.

Matthew E. Peters, Mark Neumann, Mohit Iyyer, Matt Gardner, Christopher Clark, Kenton Lee, and Luke Zettlemoyer. 2018. Deep contextualized word representations. *CoRR*, abs/1802.05365.

Alvin Rajkomar, Eyal Oren, Kai Chen, Andrew M Dai, Nissan Hajaj, Michaela Hardt, Peter J Liu, Xiaobing Liu, Jake Marcus, Mimi Sun, et al. 2018. Scalable and accurate deep learning with electronic health records. *npj Digital Medicine*, 1(1):18.

C.P. Subbe, M. Kruger, P. Rutherford, and L. Gemmel. 2001. Validation of a modified early warning score in medical admissions. *Qjm*, 94(10):521–526.

Ying P. Tabak, Xiaowu Sun, Carlos M. Nunez, Vikas Gupta, and Richard S. Johannes. 2017. Predicting readmission at early hospitalization using electronic clinical data: an early readmission risk score. *Medical care*, 55(3):267.

Robert C Wu, Vivian Lo, Dante Morra, Brian M Wong, Robert Sargeant, Ken Locke, Rodrigo Cavalcanti, Sherman D. Quan, Peter Rossos, Kim Tran, et al. 2013. The intended and unintended consequences of communication systems on general internal medicine inpatient care delivery: a prospective observational case study of five teaching hospitals. *Journal of the American Medical Informatics Association*, 20(4):766–777.

Haijun Zhai, Patrick Brady, Qi Li, Todd Lingren, Yizhao Ni, Derek S Wheeler, and Imre Solti. 2014. Developing and evaluating a machine learning based algorithm to predict the need of pediatric intensive care unit transfer for newly hospitalized children. *Resuscitation*, 85(8):1065–1071.

Huaqiong Zhou, Phillip R. Della, Pamela Roberts, Louise Goh, and Satvinder S. Dhaliwal. 2016. Utility of models to predict 28-day or 30-day unplanned hospital readmissions: an updated systematic review. *BMJ open*, 6(6):e011060.

Medical Entity Linking using Triplet Network

[1]Ishani Mondal   [1]Sukannya Purkayastha   [1]Sudeshna Sarkar   [1]Pawan Goyal
[2]Jitesh K Pillai   [2]Amitava Bhattacharyya   [2]Mahanandeeshwar Gattu
[1]Department of Computer Science and Engineering, IIT Kharagpur
[2]Excelra Knowledge Solutions Pvt Ltd, Hyderabad, India

Abstract

Entity linking (or Normalization) is an essential task in text mining that maps the entity mentions in the medical text to standard entities in a given Knowledge Base (KB). This task is of great importance in the medical domain. It can also be used for merging different medical and clinical ontologies. In this paper, we center around the problem of disease linking or normalization. This task is executed in two phases: candidate generation and candidate scoring. In this paper, we present an approach to rank the candidate Knowledge Base entries based on their similarity with disease mention. We make use of the Triplet Network for candidate ranking. While the existing methods have used carefully generated sieves and external resources for candidate generation, we introduce a robust and portable candidate generation scheme that does not make use of the hand-crafted rules. Experimental results on the standard benchmark NCBI disease dataset demonstrate that our system outperforms the prior methods by a significant margin.

1 Introduction

A disease is an abnormal medical condition that poses a negative impact on the organisms and enabling access to disease information is the goal of various information extraction as well as text mining tasks. The task of disease normalization consists of assigning a unique concept identifier to the disease names occurring in the clinical text. However, this task is challenging as the diseases mentioned in the text may display morphological or orthographical variations, may utilize different word orderings or equivalent words. Consider the following examples:

> **Example 1**: "..characteristics of the disorder include a **short trunk and extremities**..."
> **Source** : (PMID:7874117)
> **Example 2**: "**Renal amyloidosis**, prevented by colchicine, is the most severe complication of FMF ..." **Source** : (PMID:10364520)

In Example 1, the disease mention **short trunk and extremities** should be mapped to a candidate Knowledge Base entry(D006130) containing synonyms like **Growth Disorder**. In Example 2, **Renal amyloidosis** should be assigned to Knowledge Base ID (C538249) which has synonyms such as, **Amyloidosis 8**.

Based on our studies and analysis of the medical literature, it has been observed that the same disease name may occur in multiple variant forms such as. synonyms replacement (e.g.*"lung cancer"*, *"lung carcinoma"*), spelling variation (*"Acetolysis"*, *"acetolisis"*), a short description modifier precedes the disease name (e.g. *"massive heart attack"*), different word orderings (eg. *"alpha-galactosidase deficiency"*, *"deficiency of alpha-galactosidase"*).

In this paper, we have formulated the task of learning mention-candidate pair similarity using Triplet Networks (Hoffer and Ailon, 2015). Furthermore, we have explored in-domain word[1] and subword embeddings (Bojanowski et al., 2017) as input representations. We find that sub-word information boosts up the performance due to gained information for out-of-vocabulary terms and word compositionality of the disease mentions.

The primary contributions of this paper are three-fold: 1) By identifying positive and negative candidates concerning a disease mention, we optimize the Triplet Network with a loss function that influences the relative distance constraint 2) We have explored the capability of in-

---

[1]http://evexdb.org/pmresources/vec-space-models/

Proceedings of the 2nd Clinical Natural Language Processing Workshop, pages 95–100
Minneapolis, Minnesota, June 7, 2019. ©2019 Association for Computational Linguistics

Dataset	Abstracts	Total	Unique
Training set	692	5932	1538
Test set	100	960	427
Total	792	6892	1965

Table 1: NCBI Disease Corpus Statistics

domain sub-word level information[2] in solving the task of disease normalization. 3) Unlike existing systems (D'Souza and Ng, 2015), (Li et al., 2017), we present a robust and portable candidate generation approach without making use of external resources or hand-engineered sieves to deal with morphological variations. Our system achieves state-of-the-art performance on NCBI disease dataset (Dogan et al., 2014)

2 Dataset

The NCBI disease corpus (Dogan et al., 2014) contains 792 Pubmed abstracts with disorder concepts manually annotated. In this dataset, disorder mentions in each abstract are manually annotated with the identifier of the concept in the reference ontology to which it refers. It uses MEDIC lexicon (Davis et al., 2012) as the reference ontology. (See Table 1 for dataset statistics)

3 Methodology

The dataset consists of a certain number of abbreviations, in order to identify these cases, we have considered the mentions composed of all uppercase letters as abbreviations. We find the disease mentions immediately preceding the abbreviated terms and substitute all the occurrences of the abbreviated words in that document with the corresponding expanded disease mentions. Our system primarily consists of two modules: 1) **Candidate generation**: (See section 3.1) Generate potential candidates from the Knowledge Base corresponding to a disease mention. 2) **Candidate ranking**: (See section 3.2) Rank those potential candidates corresponding to a disease mention.

3.1 Candidate generation

In this section, we discuss the algorithm which generates the potential candidates to which the disease mentions might be referring. In this study, the Knowledge Base entries were sampled from

the entire MEDIC Lexicon, but not limited to only annotations in the NCBI Disease Corpus.

For a given disease mention, the candidate generation algorithm generates candidates from the Knowledge Base entries. Suppose, the Knowledge Base consists of k entries, each having a certain number of synonyms. Each multi-word synonym represented by the sum of its word embeddings. For a given mention m consisting of l words represented by $\{m_1, m_2, \ldots, m_l\}$, we represent m as the sum of its word embeddings. The steps for the candidate generation algorithm are as follows:

- **Step 1**: Candidate Set 1, $\{C_1\}$: Calculate the cosine similarity between vector representation of each synonym (candidate) of the KBIDs and the mention. Identify the top k_1 ids whose candidates have cosine similarity greater than or equal to threshold t_1.

- **Step 2**: Candidate Set 2, $\{C_2\}$: Calculate the Jaccard overlap of the mention and the candidates of each KBID. Identify the top k_2 ids having Jaccard overlap score greater than or equal to threshold t_2.

Note: $\min(\mid C_1 \mid, \mid C_2 \mid) \leq \mid C_1 \cup C_2 \mid \leq (k_1 + k_2)$ In our experiments, we choose $t_1 = 0.7$, $t_2 = 0.1$, $k_1 = 3$ and $k_2 = 7$.

We provide examples of candidates generated from our proposed algorithm below.

> **Mention**: "bacteremic infections due to Neisseria"
> **Candidate Set 1, $\{C_1\}$** = {"bacterial neisseria infections"}
> **Candidate Set 2, $\{C_2\}$** = {"bacterial neisseria infections" , "DNA-virus infections" , "Screw-Worm Infections" }

3.2 Candidate Ranking

Assume that there are n candidates represented by $\{c_1, c_2, \ldots, c_n\}$ for an entity mention m, we use a Triplet Network which has proven to perform well in many Computer Vision (Hoffer and Ailon, 2015) as well as Natural Language Processing tasks (Clark and Manning, 2016) . As such given a triplet, the idea is to leverage the notion of reducing the distance between the mention and its positive candidate while increasing the distance between the mention and its negative candidate.

---

[2]https://github.com/ncbi-nlp/BioSentVec.git

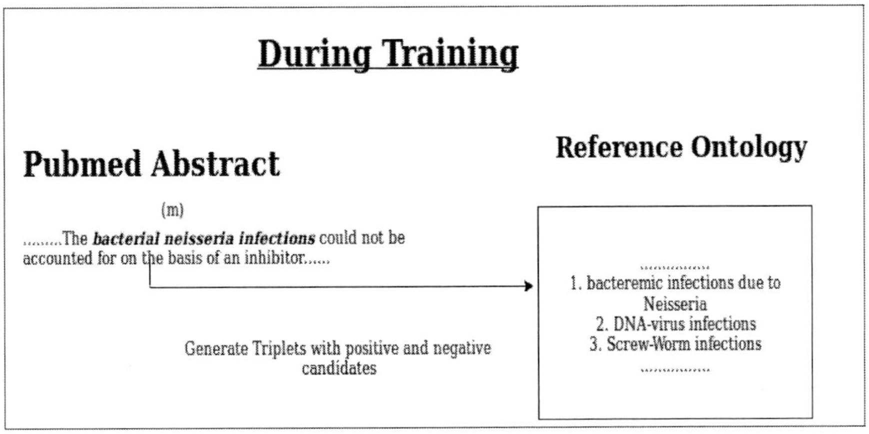

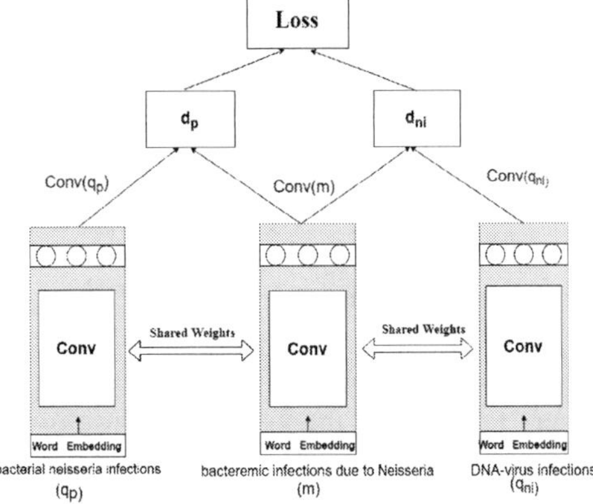

Figure 1: Pictorial Representation of the training Data Generation Process

3.2.1 Triplet data generation

In order to learn better semantic representations between a disease mention and its corresponding candidates, we have generated training data in the form of triplets consisting of disease mention m, positive candidate q_p, negative candidate q_n. The triplet is represented as (q_p, m, q_{n_i}) where $i \in \{1 \ldots [|k_1 \cup k_2| - 1]\}$.

An example of the triplet data is given below:

> **Disease Mention**: "bacteremic infections due to Neisseria"
> **Positive Candidate**: "bacterial neisseria infections"
> **Negative Candidates**: "DNA-virus infections", "Screw-Worm Infections".
> The triplets are as follows:
>
> - ("bacterial neisseria infections", "bacteremic infections due to Neisseria", "DNA-virus infections")
>
> - ("bacterial neisseria infections", "bacteremic infections due to Neisseria", "Screw-Worm Infections")

3.2.2 Model Architecture

The Triplet Network architecture as proposed by (Hoffer and Ailon, 2015) has been adopted for the task of entity normalization. To train the model, each triplet consisting of mentions and its candidates are fed into the parameter-shared network ($Conv$), as a sequence of word embeddings. For a triplet, (q_p, m, q_{n_i}) the layer outputs their representations $Conv(q_p)$, $Conv(m)$ and $Conv(q_{n_i})$ respectively. Our objective is to make the repre-

Figure 2: The word and sub-word embeddings of triplet ('bacterial neisseria infections', 'bacteremic infections due to Neisseria', 'Screw-Worm Infections') are fed as batches into the Triplet Network.

sentations of m and q_p closer than the representations of m and q_{n_i}. Thus the next layer uses a distance function, denoted by dis, to compute the distances as follows:

$$d_p = dis(Conv(m), Conv(q_p))$$

$$d_{n_i} = dis(Conv(m), Conv(q_{n_i}))$$

Here d_p specifies the distance between target disease mention m and q_p while d_{n_i} specifies the distance between target disease mention m and q_{n_i}. The triplet loss function (L) used for achieving this goal has been formulated as follows:

$$L = \max(d_p - d_{n_i} + \alpha, 0)$$

Another variable α, a hyperparameter is added to the loss equation which defines how far away the dissimilarities should be. Thereafter, by using this loss function, we calculate the gradients and update the parameters of the network based on these gradient values. For training the network, we take mention m and randomly sample q_p and q_{n_i} and compute their loss function and update their gradients.

We use 200-dimensional word2vec (Mikolov et al., 2013) embeddings trained on Wikipedia and Pubmed PMC-Corpus (Pyysalo et al., 2013) as input to $Conv$. To deal with the huge number of out-of- vocabulary terms in the medical domain, we have used the $fastText$ based sub-word embeddings (Galea et al., 2018). $fastText$ (Bojanowski et al., 2017) has been applied on PubMed and MIMIC-III (Johnson et al., 2016) to generate 200- dimensional word embeddings, the window size being 20, learning rate 0.05, sampling threshold 1e-4, and negative examples 10 (yijia zhang et al., 2018).

3.2.3 Training Details

$Conv$ is composed of one convolutional and max-pooling layer. ReLU non-linearity (Maas, 2013) is applied between two consecutive layers. The final embedding of $Conv$ is a fixed-length(128) vector. For dis and the loss function we use the L2 distance (Danielsson, 1980). The triplet loss has been applied. For training we use Adam Optimizer (Kingma and Ba, 2015) with an initial learning rate of 0.001. Training has been done for 50 epochs, and early stopping has been employed on the basis of the accuracy of the validation set. After hyperparameter tuning, several experiments have been performed, and the results on the best hyperparameter settings have been reported.

3.2.4 Evaluation

After the model has been trained, we evaluate the rank of each of the disease mentions in the test set. For each of the disease mention m in the test set, we run the candidate generation algorithm to find out the maximum cosine similar candidates for the potential KnowledgeBaseIDs. The positive candidate is labelled as 1 while the rest has been labelled as 0. During the process of evaluation, we calculate the similarity score between the disease mention and its candidates. The similarity scores are then sorted in descending manner in order to rank the candidates based on its similarity. We choose the candidate with the maximum similarity score for each of the disease mentions.

Model Name	Accuracy
(D'Souza and Ng, 2015)	84.65
(Li et al., 2017)	86.10
Triplet CNN + static word2vec	86.09
Triplet CNN + dynamic word2vec	87.85
Triplet CNN + subword	89.65
Triplet CNN + subword + abb	**90.01**

Table 2: The table shows the accuracy of our system in comparison with the baseline systems.

We choose the evaluation measure as accuracy. Since, the highest similar candidate is of primary interest in the task of entity linking, so we choose the top-K (Where $K = 1$).

TP = It signifies that the highest ranked candidate for disease mention m is the actual referent KnowledgebaseID.

FP = It signifies that the highest ranked candidate for disease mention m is not the actual referent KnowledgebaseID.

$$Accuracy = \frac{TP}{TP + FP}$$

4 Results

We report accuracy for our system in finding the correct Knowledge Base ID corresponding to a disease mention in the text. **Table 2** shows that in comparison with the existing baseline systems, **Subword information** as input to the Triplet Network and abbreviation expansion from the document context (Triplet CNN+subword+abb) performs the best. From the feature ablation, it is clear that the in-domain word embeddings((Triplet CNN + dynamic word2vec) and (Triplet CNN + static word2vec)) are essential for capturing better semantic representations.

5 Analysis

In this section, we throw some light on both the merits and demerits of the proposed system with respect to the baseline models.

5.1 Merit Analysis

We compare our results with other rule-based and neural network based methods known to perform well on this standard dataset. To gain more insights into our proposed model, in particular, the importance of the domain-specific word and subword representation to capture the semantic and syntactic similarity using Triplet Network, we select some examples from the labeled test set. In figure 2, two different cases have been shown which demonstrate the performance gap between our and the existing baseline systems.

In Example 1, the disease mention *"inherited neurodegeneration"* was not mapped with *"heredodegenerative disorders"* (D020271) by the existing methods, because of their incapability to capture the semantic similarity. In contrast to this, our system obtains additional semantic and syntactic information from the domain-specific subword embeddings and thereby maps to the correct concept ID.

In Example 2, the abbreviation *"AS"* is polysemous in nature as it can either be mapped to the concepts like *"Angelman Syndrome"* (PMID : 9585605) and *"Ankolysing Spondylitis"* (PMID : 9336417). Due to the lack of contextual information in the existing models, they were not able to handle the polysemous nature of the abbreviations; but abbreviation expansion from the document level context in our system handles this scenario.

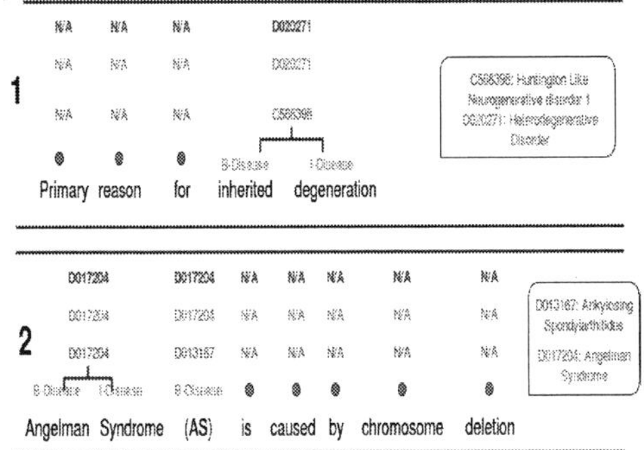

Figure 3: The NER tags as input are shown in purple, the gold standard conceptID is shown in green, the predictions from the baseline systems are shown in red, whereas the prediction from the proposed system is shown in blue.

5.2 Demerit Analysis

The error types incurred by the proposed system have been explained in detail as follows:

1) **Ambiguous distribution of importance to the disease name**: The system fails to understand which part of disease mention to provide more attention while performing normalization. Suppose the disease mention is **"colorectal adenoma"**, during normalization, the system mistakenly normalizes the disease to the concept ID predominated by **"colorectal"**. Automatic identification of such semantic attention is challenging and deserves a significant spot in the future research.

2) **Incorrect mapping of certain ambiguous disease names**: Suppose the disease mention dysmorphic features in "..loss of MAGEL2 may be critical to abnormalities in brain development and **dysmorphic features** in individuals with PWS.." (PMID: 10915770) has been mapped to D057215 whereas the same disease mention in "..She had minor **dysmorphic features** consistent with those of.." (PMID: 8071957) has been assigned to D000013. Since, in these two examples, the disease mention in these two examples have been assigned as "diseaseClass" and "Modifier" features respectively. It happens due to different NER features of the mention annotated in the dataset. But incorporating this NER feature in our proposed model unnecessarily generates huge number of false positives.

6 Conclusion

In this paper, we have formulated the task of entity linking as a candidate ranking approach. Using a Triplet Network, we learn high-quality representations of candidates, tailored to reveal relative distances between the disease mention and its positive and negative candidates. Furthermore, we take a step towards eliminating the need to generate candidates based on hand-crafted rules and external knowledge resources. Though our method outperforms the existing systems by a strong margin, there is a scope for improvement in terms of attention-based disease similarity (viz, "Neisseric infections" imply the importance of "Neisseric" during its similarity computation with the "bacterial neisseria infections"). An intriguing course for future work is to further explore the robustness and scalability of this approach to other clinical datasets for entity normalization.

Acknowledgments

This work has been supported by the project "Effective Drug Repurposing through literature and patent mining, data integration and development of systems pharmacology platform" sponsored by MHRD, India and Excelra Knowledge Solutions, Hyderabad. Besides, the authors would like to thank the anonymous reviewers for their valuable comments and feedback.

References

Piotr Bojanowski, Edouard Grave, Armand Joulin, and Tomas Mikolov. 2017. Enriching word vectors with subword information. *Transactions of the Association for Computational Linguistics*, 5:135–146.

Kevin Clark and Christopher D. Manning. 2016. Deep reinforcement learning for mention-ranking coreference models. In *Proceedings of the 2016 Conference on Empirical Methods in Natural Language Processing*, pages 2256–2262. Association for Computational Linguistics.

Per-Erik Danielsson. 1980. Euclidean distance mapping. *Computer Graphics and Image Processing*, 14(3):227 – 248.

Allan Peter Davis, Thomas C. Wiegers, Michael C. Rosenstein, and Carolyn J. Mattingly. 2012. Medic: a practical disease vocabulary used at the comparative toxicogenomics database. *Database (Oxford)*, 2012:bar065–bar065. 22434833[pmid].

Rezarta Islamaj Dogan, Robert Leaman, and Zhiyong Lu. 2014. Ncbi disease corpus: a resource for disease name recognition and concept normalization. *J Biomed Inform*, 47:1–10. 24393765[pmid].

Jennifer D'Souza and Vincent Ng. 2015. Sieve-based entity linking for the biomedical domain. In *Proceedings of the 53rd Annual Meeting of the Association for Computational Linguistics and the 7th International Joint Conference on Natural Language Processing (Volume 2: Short Papers)*, pages 297–302.

Dieter Galea, Ivan Laponogov, and Kirill A. Veselkov. 2018. Sub-word information in pre-trained biomedical word representations: evaluation and hyperparameter optimization. In *BioNLP*.

Elad Hoffer and Nir Ailon. 2015. Deep metric learning using triplet network. In *SIMBAD*.

Alistair E. W. Johnson, Tom J. Pollard, Lu Shen, Liwei H. Lehman, Mengling Feng, Mohammad Ghassemi, Benjamin Moody, Peter Szolovits, Leo Anthony Celi, and Roger G. Mark. 2016. Mimic-iii, a freely accessible critical care database. *Scientific Data*, 3:160035 EP –. Data Descriptor.

Diederik P. Kingma and Jimmy Ba. 2015. Adam: A method for stochastic optimization. *CoRR*, abs/1412.6980.

Haodi Li, Qingcai Chen, Buzhou Tang, Xiaolong Wang, Hua Xu, Baohua Wang, and Dong Huang. 2017. Cnn-based ranking for biomedical entity normalization. *BMC Bioinformatics*, 18(Suppl 11):385–385. 28984180[pmid].

Andrew L. Maas. 2013. Rectifier nonlinearities improve neural network acoustic models.

Tomas Mikolov, Ilya Sutskever, Kai Chen, Greg S Corrado, and Jeff Dean. 2013. Distributed representations of words and phrases and their compositionality. In C. J. C. Burges, L. Bottou, M. Welling, Z. Ghahramani, and K. Q. Weinberger, editors, *Advances in Neural Information Processing Systems 26*, pages 3111–3119. Curran Associates, Inc.

Sampo Pyysalo, F Ginter, Hans Moen, T Salakoski, and Sophia Ananiadou. 2013. Distributional semantics resources for biomedical text processing. *Proceedings of Languages in Biology and Medicine*.

yijia zhang, qingyu chen, zhihao yang, hongfei lin, and Zhiyong Lu. 2018. BioWordVec: Improving Biomedical Word Embeddings with Subword Information and MeSH Ontology.

Annotating and Characterizing Clinical Sentences
with Explicit Why-QA Cues

Jungwei Fan

Division of Digital Health Sciences, Mayo Clinic

200 1st Street SW, RO-HA-2-CSHCD, Rochester, MN 55905

fan.jung-wei@mayo.edu

Abstract

Many clinical information needs can be stated as why-questions. The answers to them represent important clinical reasoning and justification. Clinical notes are a rich source for such why-question answering (why-QA). However, there are few dedicated corpora, and little is known about the characteristics of clinical why-QA narratives. To address this gap, the study performed manual annotation of 277 sentences containing explicit why-QA cues and summarized their quantitative and qualitative properties. The contributions are: 1) sharing a seed corpus that can be used for various QA-related training purposes, 2) adding to our knowledge about the diversity and distribution of clinical why-QA contents.

1 Introduction

The thought process involved in clinical reasoning and decision-making can be naturally framed into a series of questions and answers. In addition to the tangible value as handy assistance, making computers handle question-answering (QA) is considered a remarkable achievement in artificial intelligence. Accordingly, there has been vital interest in developing clinical QA systems, e.g., AskHERMES (Cao et al., 2011), MiPACQ (Cairns et al., 2011), and MEANS (Abacha & Zweigenbaum, 2015). Among the targets, why-QA represents a special category that deals with cause, motivation, circumstance, and purpose (Verberne, 2006). Within the top ten question types asked by family doctors (Ely et al., 1999), 20% of them can actually be paraphrased into a why-question. Besides the sizable presence, clinical why-QA is both semantically and pragmatically rich because: 1) toward the deep explanatory end the task almost resembles expert-level synthesis and inference, 2) toward the shallower end it usually involves identifying the documented reason that a decision was made.

It is worth clarifying here two different scenarios that QA tasks are defined. The first aligns more along consulting knowledge sources to answer a question that is not patient-specific, e.g., *Why do phenobarbital and Dilantin counteract each other?* This is also the scenario that most of the existing clinical QA systems handle. The second scenario (focus of this study) is to find the answer within a given document (a.k.a. reading comprehension), which can especially benefit patient-specific QA based on information mentioned in clinical notes. In the general domain such reading comprehension QA has more than a decade of research, with widely used corpora such as the SQuAD (Rajpurkar, Zhang, Lopyrev, & Liang, 2016) and that by Verberne, Boves, Oostdijk, & Coppen (2006). There have not been comparable resources in the clinical domain until a couple of works in 2018 (see Related work section).

The recently developed corpora in clinical reading comprehension QA are extremely valuable, but also limited with regard to why-QA research because 1) their coverage and analysis did not emphasize on why-questions, 2) the annotation methods could have missed many representative why-QA targets. Therefore, the current study aims to compensate for these oversights through systematic inspection into clinical sentences that contain the intuitive cues "because" and "due to". The rationale is: we might never know what can be missed by diving right into complex cases, unless the low-hanging offers are well understood first. In fact, the results revealed many informative clinical topics and patterns involved in why-QA. Along with the diverse topics, the well-formed linguistic constructs based on the two unambiguous cues make this small corpus an ideal seed training set to stabilize models or to bootstrap other solutions.

101

Proceedings of the 2nd Clinical Natural Language Processing Workshop, pages 101–106
Minneapolis, Minnesota, June 7, 2019. ©2019 Association for Computational Linguistics

2   Related work

There has been considerable annotation research for why-QA in non-medical domains. As part of developing a why-QA system, Higashinaka & Isozaki (2008) used information retrieval to search documents possibly relevant to each why-question, followed by manual validation of qualified QA pairs. Mrozinski, Whittaker, & Furui (2008) used Mechanical Turk to recruit annotators for reading Wikipedia articles and generating why-questions based on the contents. Dulceanu et al. (2018) applied web scraping over community forums to collect why-QAs about Adobe Photoshop usage. The answer quality was backed either by questioner feedback or by community votes. Prasad & Joshi (2008) proposed leveraging causal relations in the richly annotated Penn Discourse Treebank to derive why-QAs.

In the clinical domain there were two corpora developed for reading comprehension QA based on electronic medical records (EMR), and both had broad coverage not limited to only why-QAs. In Raghavan, Patwardhan, Liang, & Devarakonda (2018), medical students were presented with structured and unstructured EMR information of each patient and were instructed to come up with realistic questions for a hypothetical office encounter. The patient's notes were then loaded into an annotation tool for them to mark answer text spans. Pampari, Raghavan, Liang, & Peng (2018) developed emrQA, a large clinical QA corpus generated through template-based semantic extraction from the i2b2 NLP challenge datasets.[*] The emrQA contains 7.5% of why-QAs, but they mainly ask about why the patient received a test or treatment, due to the partial interest of the original challenge annotations.

3   Methods

The study notes were from the 2010 i2b2/VA NLP challenge (Uzuner, South, Shen, & DuVall, 2011), obtained through an academic data use agreement.[†] The corpus consists of 426 discharge summaries from Partners Healthcare and Beth Israel Deaconess Medical Center. The two considerations in choosing this dataset were: 1) the sentences were pre-chunked that made the

downstream analysis easier, 2) it overlapped with the emrQA corpus and thus allowed comparison of coverage, etc.

Case-insensitive word search was performed using "because" and "due to" into the 426 notes. To avoid massive false positives, highly ambiguous cues such as "for" were avoided in this pilot study. The author then manually reviewed the 280 hit sentences, of which 79 were from "because" and 201 from "due to". The review involved two tasks: 1) generate a QA pair from the sentence, and 2) categorize the question anchor and the answer. Using the following sentence as an example:

The patient had urinary tract infection and received Bactrim, which was stopped later because of diarrhea.

The generated QA pair was:

Q: Why was the Bactrim for urinary tract infection stopped?
A: diarrhea

It was required that each answer must come from a substring of the source sentence. For each annotation, the line number and character offset of the answer were preserved so as to facilitate computable reuses. The types of question anchors and their answers were induced and consolidated throughout the entire review process. For example, the categorization for the specific QA pair above was:

Question anchor: medication avoidance
Answer reason: adverse effect

Upon completing the annotation, descriptive statistics were derived to show notable properties:

- Sentence coverage of the annotated why-QAs as compared to that of emrQA (Figure 1).
- Distribution of clinical notes with respect to the number of sentences that contain either of the why-cues (Table 1).
- Distribution of the categorized why-question anchors and answer types (Tables 2, 3, and 4).

4   Results

As a simple comparison of the question sources, sentence coverage of the annotated why-QAs versus the emrQA why-associated entries is

---

[*] https://www.i2b2.org/NLP/DataSets/
[†] Complying with the i2b2 NLP data use agreement, examples in this paper have been modified and differ from the original text.

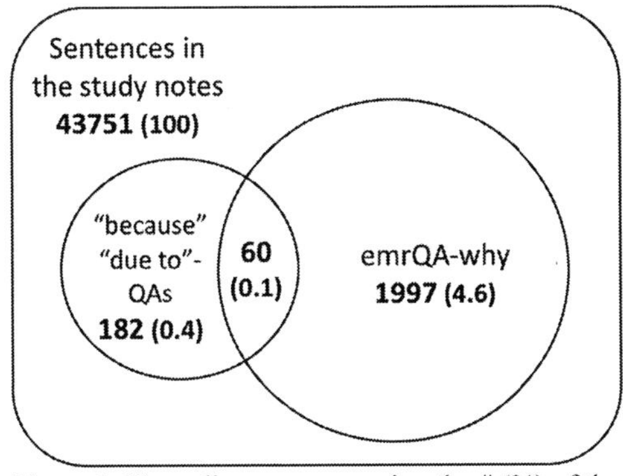

Figure 1: Venn diagram comparing the # (%) of the
annotated sentences to that of emrQA

# of cue-containing sentences in the note	# (%) of notes
0	280 (65.7)
1	74 (17.4)
2	39 (9.2)
3	16 (3.8)
4	12 (2.8)
5	2 (0.5)
6	2 (0.5)
7	1 (0.2)

Table 1: Distribution of notes containing the
"because" or "due to" cue

Why-question anchor	Answer reason type	# of QAs (%)
abnormal manifestation	disease-caused	51 (20.8)
abnormal manifestation	adverse effect	19 (7.8)
abnormal manifestation	manifestation elaborated	6 (2.4)
abnormal manifestation	disease interaction	3 (1.2)
abnormal manifestation	environment factor	2 (0.8)
procedure disposition	clinical indication	39 (15.9)
procedure disposition	patient preference	1 (0.4)
consultation, admission, discharge, or transfer event	clinical indication	34 (13.9)
consultation, admission, discharge, or transfer event	patient preference	2 (0.8)
consultation, admission, discharge, or transfer event	environment factor	1 (0.4)
medication avoidance	adverse effect	14 (5.7)
medication avoidance	disease interaction	8 (3.3)
medication avoidance	patient preference	2 (0.8)
medication avoidance	disease attribute	1 (0.4)
medication avoidance	procedure interaction	1 (0.4)
procedure avoidance	disease interaction	12 (4.9)
procedure avoidance	patient preference	3 (1.2)
procedure avoidance	procedure interaction	3 (1.2)
procedure avoidance	adverse effect	2 (0.8)
procedure avoidance	disease attribute	2 (0.8)
procedure avoidance	patient attribute	2 (0.8)
procedure unsuccessful	patient attribute	9 (3.7)
procedure unsuccessful	disease interaction	6 (2.4)
procedure unsuccessful	environment factor	2 (0.8)
procedure unsuccessful	disease attribute	1 (0.4)
procedure unsuccessful	disease-caused	1 (0.4)
procedure unsuccessful	procedure interaction	1 (0.4)
medication administered	clinical indication	12 (4.9)
medication administered	patient attribute	1 (0.4)
patient interpretation	patient assessment	1 (0.4)
procedure effective	patient attribute	1 (0.4)
social background	family factor	1 (0.4)
nonmedical treat	patient preference	1 (0.4)

Table 2: Detailed distribution of QA pairs by type

illustrated in Figure 1. There were a total of 43,751 sentences (including those short section headers) in the study corpus of 426 clinical notes. The emrQA used 2,057 sentences in generating its QA pairs, which were basically all about reasons for ordering a test or treatment. The cue-based annotation used 242 sentences, yet the derived why-QAs were much more diverse (see Table 2). There were 60 sentences used by both.

Two reasons that the original 280 hit sentences dropped to the 242 distinct annotated sentences were: 1) there were 3 sentences actually containing both cues, 2) 35 of the sentences were not usable to generate a QA pair because of anaphora. Note that it is possible for a double-cue sentence to generate two separate questions because of different why-anchors. As for the prevalence of the two cues, Table 1 shows that more than 30% (100% − 65.7%) of the study notes had at least one cue, with as many as 7 cue-containing sentences within one note.

The full categorization and distribution of the annotated why-QAs are shown in Table 2, while the distributions aggregated by the question anchors and answer reason types are in Table 3 and Table 4 respectively.

Example contexts of some noteworthy why-QA categories as follows:
[abnormal manifestation → disease-caused]
>> Why did his arm show poor motor movement? → loss of sensation
[procedure disposition → clinical indication]
>> Why was ultrafiltration fluid removal done at each dialysis session? → volume overload
[medication administered → clinical indication]
>> Why was he given levofloxacin? → gram-positive cocci
[consultation/admission, discharge, or transfer event → clinical indication]
>> Why was she admitted? → cholangitis
[procedure avoidance → disease interaction]
>> Why was the dobutamine stress test deferred? → patient having fever and hypotension
[procedure unsuccessful → patient attribute]
>> Why the GI PEG placement failed? → difficult anatomy
[procedure avoidance → patient preference]
>> Why the patient refused transesophageal echo? → did not want to swallow the probe
[medication avoidance → procedure interaction]
>> Why was metformin held temporarily? → CT with contrast

Why-question anchor	# of QAs (%)
abnormal manifestation	81 (33.1)
procedure disposition	40 (16.3)
consultation, admission, discharge, or transfer event	37 (15.1)
medication avoidance	26 (10.6)
procedure avoidance	24 (9.8)
procedure unsuccessful	20 (8.2)
medication administered	13 (5.3)
patient interpretation	1 (0.4)
procedure effective	1 (0.4)
social background	1 (0.4)
nonmedical treat	1 (0.4)

Table 3: Distribution of QA pairs aggregated by the why-question anchor types

Answer reason type	# of QAs (%)
clinical indication	85 (34.7)
disease-caused	52 (21.2)
adverse effect	35 (14.3)
disease interaction	29 (11.8)
patient attribute	13 (5.3)
patient preference	9 (3.7)
manifestation elaborated	6 (2.4)
environment factor	5 (2.0)
procedure interaction	5 (2.0)
disease attribute	4 (1.6)
patient assessment	1 (0.4)
family factor	1 (0.4)

Table 4: Distribution of QA pairs aggregated by the answer reason types

5 Discussion

Although the explicit cues contributed a relatively small set of why-QAs, they exhibit a wealth of subject contours for further investigation. The majority of the emrQA why-questions correspond to the two anchor categories procedure disposition and medication administered, together covering only 21.6% among the various anchors in Table 3. Notably, the top anchor category abnormal manifestation (33.1%) concurs with the most commonly asked why-equivalent questions surveyed by (Ely et al., 1999), i.e., *What is the cause of a symptom or finding?* This concordance implies clinicians tend to explicitly document reasons on certain topics they feel like inquiring in practice as well. Moreover, annotations of medication avoidance and procedure avoidance (together making 20.4% of the anchors) host rich knowledge that is worth capturing systematically.

For example, procedure interaction and disease interaction (e.g., risk from comorbidity) are typical reasons in avoiding certain intervention.

Even though the annotations involve only simple cues and single-sentence contexts, they should benefit the training of QA systems. It is known that such instances of atomic and regular structure can help stabilize/smooth the behavior of statistical models. The other possible route is to use the annotations as seed examples and train a question-generation model that automatically asks why-questions as additional training data. Although the study was short of resource to include experimental validation, it is hoped that at least as a self-contained descriptive analysis the results can be informative to the clinical NLP community.

The representativeness of the study was limited by using only discharge summaries and the two specific cues. The annotations with the complete answer available within one sentence do not touch upon complex scenarios that require synthesizing cross-sentence information. The questions from rephrasing sentences may lack natural intent and diversity, which was a limitation likely shared by repurposing NLP challenge annotations as done in emrQA. This study used only one annotator, which would introduce subjectivity especially in categorizing the QAs.

The annotations by this study are available at https://github.com/Jung-wei/ClinicalWhyQA

Acknowledgments

Deidentified clinical records used in this research were provided by the i2b2 National Center for Biomedical Computing funded by U54LM008748 and were originally prepared for the Shared Tasks for Challenges in NLP for Clinical Data organized by Dr. Ozlem Uzuner, i2b2 and SUNY.

I would like to thank the anonymous reviewers for their constructive feedback.

References

Abacha, A. B., & Zweigenbaum, P. (2015). MEANS: A medical question-answering system combining NLP techniques and semantic Web technologies. *Information processing & management, 51*(5), 570-594.

Cairns, B. L., Nielsen, R. D., Masanz, J. J., Martin, J. H., Palmer, M. S., Ward, W. H., & Savova, G. K. (2011). The MiPACQ clinical question answering system. *AMIA Annu Symp Proc, 2011*, 171-180.

Cao, Y., Liu, F., Simpson, P., Antieau, L., Bennett, A., Cimino, J. J., . . . Yu, H. (2011). AskHERMES: An online question answering system for complex clinical questions. *J Biomed Inform, 44*(2), 277-288. doi:10.1016/j.jbi.2011.01.004

Dulceanu, A., Le Dinh, T., Chang, W., Bui, T., Kim, D. S., Vu, M. C., & Kim, S. (2018). PhotoshopQuiA: A corpus of non-factoid questions and answers for why-question answering. *Proceedings of the 11th International Conference on Language Resources and Evaluation (LREC 2018)*.

Ely, J. W., Osheroff, J. A., Ebell, M. H., Bergus, G. R., Levy, B. T., Chambliss, M. L., & Evans, E. R. (1999). Analysis of questions asked by family doctors regarding patient care. *BMJ, 319*(7206), 358-361.

Higashinaka, R., & Isozaki, H. (2008). Corpus-based question answering for why-questions. *Proceedings of the Third International Joint Conference on Natural Language Processing: Volume-I.*

Mrozinski, J., Whittaker, E., & Furui, S. (2008). Collecting a why-question corpus for development and evaluation of an automatic QA-system. *Proceedings of ACL-08: HLT*, 443-451.

Pampari, A., Raghavan, P., Liang, J., & Peng, J. (2018). emrQA: A large corpus for question answering on electronic medical records. *arXiv preprint arXiv:1809.00732.*

Prasad, R., & Joshi, A. (2008). A discourse-based approach to generating why-questions from texts. *Proceedings of the Workshop on the Question Generation Shared Task and Evaluation Challenge*, 1-3.

Raghavan, P., Patwardhan, S., Liang, J. J., & Devarakonda, M. V. (2018). Annotating electronic medical records for question answering. *arXiv preprint arXiv:1805.06816.*

Rajpurkar, P., Zhang, J., Lopyrev, K., & Liang, P. (2016). SQuAD: 100,000+ questions for machine comprehension of text. *Proceedings of the Conference on Empirical Methods in Natural Language Processing (EMNLP).*

Uzuner, O., South, B. R., Shen, S., & DuVall, S. L. (2011). 2010 i2b2/VA challenge on concepts, assertions, and relations in clinical text. *J Am Med Inform Assoc, 18*(5), 552-556. doi:10.1136/amiajnl-2011-000203

Verberne, S. (2006). Developing an approach for why-question answering. *Proceedings of the 11th*

Conference of the European Chapter of the Association for Computational Linguistics: Student Research Workshop, 39-46.

Verberne, S., Boves, L., Oostdijk, N., & Coppen, P. (2006). Data for question answering: the case of why. *Proceedings of the 5th International Conference on Language Resources and Evaluation (LREC 2006)*.

Extracting Factual Min/Max Age Information from Clinical Trial Studies

Yufang Hou[1], Debasis Ganguly[1], Léa A. Deleris[2], Francesca Bonin[1]
[1]IBM Research, Ireland
{yhou,debasga1,fbonin}@ie.ibm.com
[2]BNP Paribas
lea.deleris@bnpparibas.com

Abstract

Population age information is an essential characteristic of clinical trials. In this paper, we focus on extracting minimum and maximum (min/max) age values for the study samples from clinical research articles. Specifically, we investigate the use of a neural network model for question answering to address this information extraction task. The min/max age QA model is trained on the massive structured clinical study records from *ClinicalTrials.gov*. For each article, based on multiple min and max age values extracted from the QA model, we predict both actual min/max age values for the study samples and filter out non-factual age expressions. Our system improves the results over (i) a passage retrieval based IE system and (ii) a CRF-based system by a large margin when evaluated on an annotated dataset consisting of 50 research papers on smoking cessation.

1 Introduction

Clinical trials are an important source of scientific evidence for guiding the practice of evidence-based medicine. However, many characteristics of clinical trials are only reported in the published research articles. The health service community could benefit from knowledge bases populated with detailed information from clinical trials reported in research articles. With this in mind, clinical information extraction aims to extract such information from journal articles that report randomized controlled trials (Kiritchenko et al., 2010; Wallace et al., 2016).

Relevant information about clinical trials can be categorised along: *(i)* trial's population characteristics (e.g. minimum and maximum age of the participants, education level, marital status, health status), *(ii)* intervention methods, both what is being done (e.g. specific drug and dosage, planning sessions, use of an app for daily reporting) and how it is being administered (e.g., where, how often and by whom), and *(iii)* outcome of the study (e.g., *30% of the population stopped smoking after 6 months*).

In this paper, we focus on extracting population characteristics and in particular minimum and maximum (min/max) age values associated with the study samples from clinical trials research articles.

Unlike (Summerscales, 2013), our aim is to extract information from the full article, rather than only from the abstract, as we have observed that age information is not always described in the abstracts. In our testing dataset consisting of 50 research papers, only nine papers describe the min/max age information in their abstracts.

Naturally, analysing the entire article presents many challenges. Our goal is to identify the factual min/max age value information for the persons who actually participated in the clinical trial (see Example 1 and Example 2 below). This should be distinguished from non-factual min/max age information (Example 3 and Example 4) and also from min/max age information which is not related to the participants in the study (Example 5 and Example 6).

(1) Participants were 83 smokers, who were **18-23** years old and undergraduate students ...

(2) participants aged **18-24** years were randomized to a brief office intervention (n=99) or to an expressive writing plus brief office intervention (n=97).

(3) To be included in the study, smokers had to be between the ages of **18** and **60** years ...

(4) The subjects were eligible for inclusion if they were at least **18** years of age, reported smoking 10 or more cigarettes per day, ...

Proceedings of the 2nd Clinical Natural Language Processing Workshop, pages 107–116
Minneapolis, Minnesota, June 7, 2019. ©2019 Association for Computational Linguistics

(5) An estimated 23.6% of young adults aged **18-24** years are current smokers.

(6) Smoking Dutch youths had in many cases tried their first cigarette at the age of **11-12** years.

Our proposed system extracts factual min/max age values of the study samples directly from research articles in PDF format. We leverage the massive structured clinical study records from *ClinicalTrials.gov* to provide distant supervision for min/max age value extraction. Furthermore, inspired by the work on hedging detection on Bioscience domain (Light et al., 2004; Kilicoglu and Bergler, 2008; Farkas et al., 2010), we explore a list of "speculation cues" to filter out non-factual min/max age expressions. Our system improves the results over *(i)* a passage retrieval based IE system and *(ii)* a CRF-based system by a large margin when evaluated on an annotated dataset consisting of 50 research papers on smoking cessation.

2 Related Work

2.1 Clinical Information Extraction

In general, research on information extraction from medical literature is still in its infancy involving a number of limitations, such as lack of common benchmarking datasets, and a lack of general consensus on the class of approaches that are reported to work well on such benchmarks.

Some work has been conducted on supervised approaches for medical information extraction. Multiple studies have concentrated their efforts on medical abstract. In (Kim et al., 2011), the authors propose a conditional random filed (CRF) classification method for labelling medical abstract sentences according to medical categories, such as outcome, intervention, population. Hansen et al., 2008 (Hansen et al., 2008) developed a Support Vector Machine algorithm for extracting the number of trials participants from medical abstracts, while in (Hassanzadeh et al., 2014), the authors use a machine learning approach for classifying abstract sentences according to the PICO (Population, Intervention, Comparison, Outcome) scheme.

Other studies have exploited the entire article, for the extraction of papers' metadata as (Lin et al., 2010): the authors propose a preliminary system based on CRF for extracting formulaic text (authors names, email and institution) as well as some key study parameters as free text, from PubMed-Central articles. They reach promising results for the formulaic text, but only moderate success for the free text attributes. The study in (Luan et al., 2017) involves finding key-phrases from scientific articles and then classifying them. However, these categories are much broader (coarse-grained), e.g. 'process', 'task' etc., than the fine-grained categories in our task (min/max age).

A few studies have tackled the min/max age extraction problem. Most research work on extracting information from clinical trial literature considers "eligibility criteria" as a target element, which often contains min/max age information (de Bruijn et al., 2008; Kiritchenko et al., 2010).

However, min/max age information contained in the eligibility criteria refers to the planned min/max age and may be different from the actual min/max age values of the study samples (for example: the researchers could decide to test a population of women between 20-30 years, but realistically they could gather participants only between 22 and 28 years old). (Summerscales, 2013) carefully designed a number of heuristic rules to extract min/max age values of the study population from the abstracts. We differ from this latter work as we (a) extract such information from the full articles and (b) use a machine learning approach. In addition, we integrate the rules designed by (Summerscales, 2013) into our passage retrieval based IE system as a baseline.

Generally, in contrast to previous work, in this paper we a) concentrate on the extraction of population characteristics, b) use the entire article for detecting the min/max age and c) compare an unsupervised approach with a QA-based approach.

2.2 Question Answering

Most recently, *reading comprehension* or *question answering based on context* has gained popularity within the NLP community, in particular since (Rajpurkar et al., 2016) released a large-scale dataset (SQuAD) consisting of 100,000+ questions on a set of Wikipedia articles. In the medical domain, (Šuster and Daelemans, 2018) created a dataset of clinical case reports for machine reading comprehension (CliCR). The dataset contains around 100,000 gap-filling queries on 12,000 case reports. These queries are created by blanking out medical entities in the *learning points* sections using some heuristics.

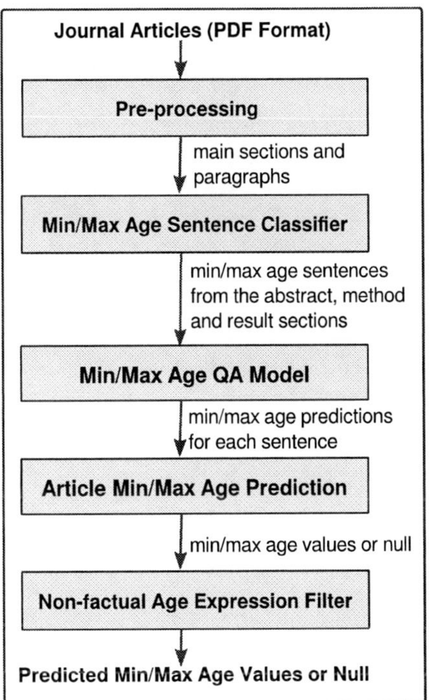

Figure 1: Proposed QA based factual min/max age value extraction framework.

We explore the QA framework for min/max age value extraction. Various neural network models have been proposed for question answering but these models trained on SQuAD or CliCR do not work well in our scenario because these datasets do not contain the queries targeting the specific min/max age values expressed in the text. Therefore, we leverage instead the massive structured clinical study records on *ClinicalTrials.gov* and create the training data for our min/max age value extraction component.

2.3 Non-factual Information Detection

There has been a significant amount of research in detecting speculative language in scientific research articles (Hyland, 1998; Light et al., 2004; Kilicoglu and Bergler, 2008; Medlock and Briscoe, 2007; Farkas et al., 2010; Morante and Sporleder, 2012). Our task requires to extract information from definite statements, therefore we use a list of speculation cues to filter out sentences where min/max age information are expressed speculatively.

3 Approach

We develop a pipeline to extract factual min/max age information from clinical trial studies. We divide the task in two steps: 1) finding sentences containing min/max age information; 2) extracting the value from those sentences. For the first we develop **Min/Max age Sentence Classifier** and for the second we propose a QA approach and develop the module **Min/Max Age QA Model**.

Figure 1 illustrated the process associated with our proposed system. In the following sections, we describe how we create training data from *ClinicalTrials.gov* as well as each component of our system in detail.

3.1 Creating Training Data Using Clinical Study Records

We leverage the massive structured clinical study records on *ClinicalTrials.gov* to create training data for *Min/Max Age Sentence classifier* and *Min/Max Age QA Model*. *ClinicalTrials.gov* is one of the largest database of clinical studies conducted around the world. It currently holds registrations around 273,000 trials from 204 countries. Each trial registration record contains a column called "Eligibility Criteria", additionally min and/or max age values are indicated if they are present in the description text of the eligibility criteria. Figure 2 shows an example of a clinical study record from *ClinicalTrials.gov*.

Note that most min/age expressions in eligibility criteria are speculative (e.g., *at least 21 years of age*, or *child must be ages 6-12 years old*), nevertheless they are still reflective of various linguistic forms for factual min/max age (e.g., *aged 6-12 years old* or *age* $\geq$ *18 years*). Therefore we expect that the models trained on this "noisy" dataset can still (1) identify sentences containing min/max age information and (2) predict the min/max age values.

3.2 Pre-processing

Given a research article in PDF format, we first extract clean text from the PDF file using GRO-BID (Lopez, 2009). We associate each paragraph to one of the five main sections: *abstract, introduction, method, result* and *discussion*. This step may introduce some noise (e.g., including the content from the table as the main body text) because parsing PDF file in different styles is a challenging task in itself.

The Symptom Experience Study in Persons With Non-Small Cell Lung Cancer (SES)	
Recruitment Information	
Recruitment Status	Completed
Actual Enrollment	74
Original Estimated Enrollment	86
Eligibility Criteria	Inclusion Criteria: - Women and men at least 21 years of age with suspected NSCLC to be confirmed after surgery. - Planned surgical resection, not diagnostics alone, for treatment of suspected non-small cell lung cancer (NSCLC) to include such surgical approaches as open thoracotomy, video assisted thoracic surgery (VATS), and Robotic procedures. - Karnofsky Performance Status score of at least 70%. - Thoracic surgeon approval pre- and post-surgery. - Medically stable co-morbid conditions including cardiovascular disease such as post-myocardial infarction, stable coronary bypass graft surgery, and stable percutaneous transluminal coronary angioplasty; and mild to moderate cardiopulmonary obstructive disease. - Has phone access capability. - Able to speak and write English. - Able to hear and speak for phone interviews. - Owns a television. - Lives within 1.5 hours driving distance of recruitment site.
Mininum Age	21
Maximum Age	null

Figure 2: An example of a clinical study record from *ClinicalTrials.gov*.

3.3 Identifying Sentences Containing Min/Max Age Information:Min/Max age Sentence Classifier

After pre-processing, we identify sentences that contain min/max age information. At the inference stage, we first split paragraphs to sentences using Stanford CoreNLP Toolkit (Manning et al., 2014), then apply a classifier (*Min-MaxAgeSentFinder*) to predict sentences containing min/max age information among all sentences containing the word "age/ages/aged" or "year/years".

To train our *MinMaxAgeSentFinder* classifier, we create the training data using the eligibility criteria of the structured clinical study records from *ClinicalTrials.gov*. Text in eligibility criteria can be quite long (for instance, some criteria contain more than 10 clauses/sentences), so we only keep the clause/sentence which contains the annotated min/max age value(s). More specifically, we first split the eligibility criteria into sentences/clauses using the delimiter "-", then choose the clauses/sentences which contain the annotated min/max age values as well as the word "age/ages/aged" or "year/years". For instance, in the example shown in Figure 2, we will keep the sentence *"Women and men at least 21 years of age with suspected NSCLC to be confirmed after surgery."* as the positive training instance and filter out other sentences/clauses.

We randomly choose 20,000 such sentences/clauses (10,000 for min age and 10,000 for max age) as positive training instances. Negative training instances are sentences which do not contain the word "age/ages/aged" or "year/years" from 60 clinical research articles. Note that these articles are different from the articles in the testing dataset. We use MaxEnt classifier to train *MinMaxAgeSentFinder* with the following features: adjacent word n-grams (n=1-4) and adjacent letter n-grams within words.

3.4 Predicting Min/Max Age Values for Each Sentence: Min/Max Age QA Model

We approach the problem of extracting values of min/max age from a question-answering perspective. Specifically, our system first reads a sentence, then answers the questions "what is the min/max age of the participants?".

Various neural network models have been proposed for this task but these models trained on SQuAD do not work well in our scenario, because SQuAD does not contain this type of question-answer pairs. Therefore we create training data for max/min age value extraction by leveraging the massive structured clinical study records from *ClinicalTrials.gov* The training data are 10,000 <eligibility criteria–min age> pairs and 10,000 <eligibility criteria–max age> pairs described previously. Note that we use the whole eligibility criteria instead of choosing the specific sentence/clause which contain the min/max age value. We believe that with the additional min/max age information, the question-answering module can locate the position of the min/max age value and learn various patterns for the target question.

We train our min/max age question-answering module (*MinMaxAgeQA*) using the Bi-Directional Attention Flow (BiDAF) Network (Seo et al., 2017). BiDAF uses attention mechanisms in both directions (i.e., question-to-context and context-to-question) to find a sub-phrase from the input text to answer the question.

BiDAF includes both character-level and word-level embeddings. Most word tokenization models are not robust for numeric expressions in scientific literature. For instance, the Stanford CoreNLP tokenizer tokenizes the clause: *"aged 6-12 years old"* as "{*aged, 6-12, years, old*}" - it does not recognize 6 and 12 as two different tokens. The character-level embeddings in BiDAF can overcome this problem and the module correctly predicts 6 is the value of min age for this example.

3.5 Predicting Min/Max Age Values for Each Article

To predict min/max age values of the study samples for each article, we apply *MinMaxAgeQA* to each predicted sentence containing min/max age information from the *abstract*, *method*, and *result* sections on both questions (i.e., *what is the min age of the participants?* and *what is the max age of the participants?*). Answers that do not represent a valid integer number or answers whose confidence score are less than 0.5 are discarded. For each question, we keep the answer with the highest confidence score.

We do not include sentences from the *introduction* section because it may include other min/max age information which is not related to the study samples (see Example 5 and Example 6). We leave filtering out unrelated min/max age information from introductions as future work.

Finally, if both min and max age values are predicted for an article, we check whether the min age value is smaller than the max age value. Otherwise we keep the answer with the higher confidence score and discard the other one. For instance, as shown in Figure 3, the number 16 is predicted as both the min age value (with the probability of 0.956) and the max age value (with the probability of 0.624) for an article, we keep 16 as

Sent: the target sample comprised all cigarette smokers aged 16 or more who attended the surgeries to see a doctor between 4 and 27 November 1980.

Q: What is the min age of the participants?
A: 16 (confidence score: 0.956)

Q: What is the max age of the participants?
A: 16 (confidence score: 0.624) ⟶ **Null**

Figure 3: Conflicting min/max age values.

the prediction for the min age value and set the prediction of the max age to "Null".

3.6 Non-factual Age Expression Filter

In this component, we filter out a min/max age value prediction if it is expressed speculatively. We first extract the clause which contains the prediction, then check whether a speculation cue word/phrase is present in the clause using the speculation cues from (Light et al., 2004). These cue words are: {*if, at least, must, had to, has to, have to, need, needs*}.

4 Evaluation

4.1 Testing Dataset

The ground-truth dataset used for evaluation comprises a set of 50 published journal articles in PDF format on smoking cessation. The dataset contains around 432k tokens and 18k sentences. Table 1 shows some statistics about the testing dataset. Overall, we have 843 sentences containing the word "age/ages/aged" or "year/years" and these sentences contain 2,226 numeric tokens.

The articles were annotated by a team of four behaviour science domain experts in the context of a broader project focused on leveraging the scientific literature in behaviour change (Michie et al., 2017). Annotation for a particular document was performed by two human annotators using the EPPI tool[1]. The annotation process involved highlighting relevant pieces of text and then assigning them to the corresponding min/max age attribute. Additionally, in order to disambiguate the highlighted text, the annotators were asked to annotate the entire sentence containing the highlighted piece as the additional context. Conflicts in the annotation process were resolved through discussions. Note that not every document contains a min/max age annotation. This is because not every article reports the min/max age of the overall

[1]http://eppi.ioe.ac.uk/CMS/

Testing Dataset

# of articles	50
# of sentences	18,417
# of tokens (main text)	432,056
# of sentences containing "age/ages/aged" or "year/years"	843
# of numeric tokens in sentences containing "age/ages/aged" or "year/years"	2,226

Table 1: Statistics for the testing dataset.

study samples. In the testing dataset, 35 papers have min age annotations and 25 papers have max age annotations.

4.2 Evaluation Metric

We use recall, precision and F-score for evaluation. Recall is calculated as the number of articles where the min/max age values are correctly predicted divided by the number of articles where min/max age values are annotated. Precision is calculated as the number of articles where the min/max age values are correctly predicted divided by the number of articles where the system makes a min/max age value prediction. F-score is the harmonic average of the precision and recall.

4.3 Baseline 1: *PassageRetrievalBasedMin-MaxAgeExtractor*

We developed a passage retrieval based IE system to extract min/max age values (Ganguly et al., 2018). The first step is to retrieve the passages containing 10, 20, and 30 words using the query *"(age OR ages OR aged OR year OR years)"*. The intention of retrieving passages is to restrict extraction of factoid answers to potentially relevant small semantic units of text rather than the text of the whole document.

The next step is to use validation criteria to select the likely answer candidates. We use the min/max age patterns from (Summerscales, 2013) as the validation criteria to choose the likely answer candidates from each retrieved passage for min age and max age respectively. These patterns can be viewed as rules which are carefully designed by humans to extract min/max age values. For instance, a rule can be: *if a passage contains the phrase "greater than X" or "older than X" and X is an integer number between 10 to 100, then choose X as an answer candidate*. It is worth noting that (Summerscales, 2013) is the only pre-

vious work targeting the same task according to our best knowledge. We integrate all the heuristic rules for min/max age value extraction from (Summerscales, 2013) into our passage retrieval based IE system.

Finally, we score the answer candidates by a term proximity function that takes into account the differences in position between the query terms and the candidate answers (Zhao and Yun, 2009). The function is formally defined in the following Equation:

$$sim(c, Q) = \frac{1}{|Q|} \sum_{q \in Q} exp(-(p_c - p_q)^2/\sigma) \quad (1)$$

Equation 1 describes the proximity based ranking function between a candidate answer c and a query Q, denoted by $sim(c, Q)$. Practically, for each word in the passage that matches the query terms (q), the similarity function increases the score of that candidate by an amount that depends on the distance between that matched word and the candidate answer ($p_c - p_q$). Specifically, we use a Gaussian function centered at each query term to determine the increase in similarity score. The parameter σ controls the bandwidth of the Gaussians and is set to 1 in our experiments.

4.4 Baseline 2: *CRFBasedMinMaxAgeExtractor*

We also developed the second baseline using CRF (Sutton and McCallum, 2012). The training dataset contains the clauses/sentences which contains the annotated min/max age value(s) from the eligibility criteria of the clinical studies registered in *ClinicalTrials.gov*. For each clause/sentence, we use Stanford CoreNLP Toolkit (Manning et al., 2014) to obtain the tokens as well as the POS tags, then we create the corresponding training instance using BIO labels (i.e., Beginning/Inside/Outside

112

of a min/max age). Table 2 shows the training instance for the example illustrated in Figure 2.

Token	POS tag	MinAgeAnnotation
Women	NNS	O
and	CC	O
men	NNS	O
at	IN	O
least	JJS	O
21	CD	B
years	NNS	O
of	IN	O
age	NN	O
with	IN	O
suspected	VBN	O
NSCLC	NNP	O
…	…	…

Table 2: A training instance for the min age extraction CRF model.

We train two CRF models for min age and max age extraction respectively, using 10,000 training instances for each model. We use words as well as POS tags as features. More specifically, for the word type features, we consider the current word w_i, the surrounding words (w_{i-2}, w_{i-1}, w_{i+1}, w_{i+2}), as well as bi-grams ($w_{i-1} + w_i$, $w_i + w_{i+1}$) and tri-grams ($w_{i-2} + w_{i-1} + w_i$, $w_{i-1} + w_i + w_{i+1}$, $w_i + w_{i+1} + w_{i+2}$) created from words. We create similar unigram, bi-gram and tri-gram features using the automatically predicted POS tags as well. We also include the combinations of the previous prediction and the current prediction as bi-gram features.

At the inference stage, for each article, we first extract all sentences containing the word "age/ages/aged" or "year/years". We then apply the min/max age CRF model on these sentences and extract all tokens with the predicted label "B". In the end, among all predicted words, we choose the word which represents a valid integer number and has the highest confidence score as the predicted min/max age value for the article.

4.5 Results and Discussion

Table 3 shows the performance of the baselines (*PassageRetrievalBasedMinMaxAgeExtractor* and *CRFBasedMinMaxAgeExtractor*) as well as our system (*QABasedMinMaxAgeExtractor*, described in Section 3) for extracting min/max age values of the study samples.

For *MinAge*, the first baseline (*PassageRetrievalBasedMinMaxAgeExtractor*) achieves a very high precision score (90.9%) but suffers from low recall (28.6%). The second baseline (*CRFBasedMinMaxAgeExtractor*) improves the recall by 21.4 points but only achieves a precision score of 42.5%. Compared to the first baseline, our system manages to improve recall by 37.1 points and still achieves a reasonable level of precision (79.3%). Overall, our system improves the results over the two baselines by a large margin regarding F-score (71.9% vs. 43.5%, and 71.9% vs. 45.9%).

The similar pattern is also observed for *MaxAge*: Our system improves the results over the first baseline by a substantial margin on recall (60.0% vs. 32.0%) and F-score (66.7% vs. 44.4%) respectively.

It might seem surprising that *CRFBasedMinMaxAgeExtractor* performs much worse than *PassageRetrievalBasedMinMaxAgeExtractor* for *MaxAge*. This is because many max age values in scientific articles are not correctly recognized as a single token by Stanford CoreNLP Toolkit. For instance, the tokenization model predicts that "*18-60*" or "*<=60*" as single tokens. In contrast, our system is more robust for parsing such numeric expressions.

In addition, it seems that the carefully designed min/max age patterns in the first baseline only cover a few forms of min/max age expressions. On the contrary, our min/max age question-answering module (*MinMaxAgeQA*, Section 3.4) trained over a large-scale dataset can capture various linguistic expressions of min/max age in natural language, for instance, "$\geq$ 18 *years of age*" or "*age >= 18 years*".

4.6 Analysis

To better understand the roles of different components in our system, we carried out a few experiments:

- *—WO MinMaxAgeSentFinder*: instead of using *MinMaxAgeSentFinder* to find the sentences containing min/max age information, we pass all sentences containing the word "age/ages/aged" or "year/years" from the abstract, method, and result sections to the next component *MinMaxAgeQA*.

- *—WO MinMaxAgeQA*: we use the most common min/max age expression pattern in clini-

	MinAge			MaxAge		
	R	P	F	R	P	F
Baseline 1: PassageRetrievalBasedMinMaxAgeExtractor	28.6	90.9	43.5	32.0	72.7	44.4
Baseline 2: CRFBasedMinMaxAgeExtractor	50.0	42.5	45.9	25.0	18.2	21.1
This work: QABasedMinMaxAgeExtractor	65.7	79.3	**71.9**	60.0	75.0	**66.7**

Table 3: Experimental results. Bold indicates statistically significant differences over the baseline using randomization test ($p < 0.01$).

	MinAge			MaxAge		
	R	P	F	R	P	F
This work: QABasedMinMaxAgeExtractor	65.7	79.3	**71.9**	60.0	75.0	**66.7**
—WO MinMaxAgeSentFinder	68.6	68.6	**68.6**	52.0	56.5	54.2
—WO MinMaxAgeQA	31.4	84.6	45.8	40.0	71.4	51.3
—WO Non-factualSentFilter	68.6	70.6	**69.6**	60.0	71.4	**65.2**

Table 4: Contribution of each component to the overall system performance.

cal trial studies "*X-Y*" (e.g., *18-23 years old*) to predict min and max age values from the first sentence contain such a pattern.

- *—WO Non-factualSentFilter*: Non-factual age expression filter is not used.

The results of these experiments are shown in Table 4. It seems that *MinMaxAgeQA* has the most impact on the performance while *Non-factualSentFilter* has less of an impact. In addition, *MinMaxAgeSentFinder* has more impact on the results of *MaxAge* compared to *MinAge*.

We also performed some error analysis on our full system. We noticed that the noise introduced in the pre-processing step (e.g., missing some paragraphs) is the main reason to cause our system to predict "Null" for articles with min/max age annotation. For cases where a wrong min/max age value is predicted, they are often embedded in the speculative expressions which are not captured by our current *Non-factualSentFilter*. For instance, the system predicts **24** as the max age for one article in which **24** appears in a speculative sentence (see *speculative expression* in Example 7). For this article, the annotation for max age is **23** (see *factual expression* in Example 7).

(7) (*speculative expression*) Eligibility for this study included being a student (full or part time), smoking at least 1 cigarette/day in each of the past 7 days, being aged 18-**24** years, and being interested in quitting smoking in the next 6 months. (*factual expression*) Participants were 83 smok-

ers, who were 18-**23** years old and undergraduate students at a university.

5 Conclusions

This paper aims to extract factual min/max age values of the study samples from clinical research papers. We leverage the large-scale records from the *ClinicalTrials.gov* database to provide distant supervision for our system. We also explore "speculative cues" and the structure of the scientific papers to extract information from factual statements about the target study. We show that our approach outperforms a passage retrieval based IE system and a CRF-based model by a large margin on a testing dataset consisting of 50 journal articles and around 18,000 sentences.

In the future, we plan to extend our framework to extract other types of numeric values from the clinical research papers, such as the outcome values of the different intervention groups and the control group (e.g., *40% of PP abstinence rates*), as well as the time frame of the follow up (e.g., *52 weeks* or *6 months*).

Acknowledgments

This work was supported by a Wellcome Trust collaborative award as a part of the Human Behaviour-Change Project (HBCP): Building the science of behaviour change for complex intervention development (grant no. 201,524/Z/16/Z).

References

Berry de Bruijn, Simona Carini, Svetlana Kiritchenko, Joel Martin, and Ida Sim. 2008. Automated information extraction of key trial design elements from clinical trial publications. In *AMIA 2008 Annual Symposium, Washington DC, USA, November 8-12, 2008*, pages 141–145.

Richárd Farkas, Veronika Vincze, György Móra, János Csirik, and György Szarvas. 2010. The CoNLL-2010 shared task: Learning to detect hedges and their scope in natural language text. In *Proceedings of the Shared Task of the 14th Conference on Computational Natural Language Learning*, Uppsala, Sweden, 15–16 July 2010, pages 1–12.

Debasis Ganguly, Léa A Deleris, P Aonghusa Mac, Alison J Wright, Ailbhe N Finnerty, Emma Norris, Marta M Marques, and Susan Michie. 2018. Unsupervised information extraction from behaviour change literature. *Studies in health technology and informatics*, 247:680–684.

Marie J Hansen, Nana Ø Rasmussen, and Grace Chung. 2008. A method of extracting the number of trial participants from abstracts describing randomized controlled trials. *Journal of Telemedicine and Telecare*, 14(7):354–358. PMID: 18852316.

Hamed Hassanzadeh, Tudor Groza, and Jane Hunter. 2014. Identifying scientific artefacts in biomedical literature: The evidence based medicine use case. *Journal of Biomedical Informatics*, 49:159 – 170.

Ken Hyland. 1998. *Hedging in scientific research articles*. John Benjamins, Amsterdam, The Netherlands.

Halil Kilicoglu and Sabine Bergler. 2008. Recognizing speculative language in biomedical research articles: A linguistically motivated perspective. In *Proceedings of the Workshop on Current Trends in Biomedical Natural Language Processing*, Columbus, Ohio, 19 June 2008, pages 46–53.

Su Nam Kim, David Martinez, Lawrence Cavedon, and Lars Yencken. 2011. Automatic classification of sentences to support evidence based medicine. *BMC Bioinformatics*, 12(2):S5.

Svetlana Kiritchenko, Berry de Bruijn, Simona Carini, Joel Martin, and Ida Sim. 2010. ExaCT: automatic extraction of clinical trial characteristics from journal publications. *BMC Medical Informatics and Decision Making*, 10(1):56–73.

Marc Light, Xin Ying Qiu, and Padmini Srinivasan. 2004. The language of Bioscience: Facts, speculations, and statements in between. In *Proceedings of the HLT-NAACL 2004 Workshop: Biolink 2004, Linking Biological Literature, Ontologies and Databases*, Boston, Mass., 6 May 2004, pages 17–24.

Sein Lin, Jun-Ping Ng, Shreyasee Pradhan, Jatin Shah, Ricardo Pietrobon, and Min-Yen Kan. 2010. Extracting formulaic and free text clinical research articles metadata using conditional random fields. In *Proceedings of the NAACL HLT 2010 Second Louhi Workshop on Text and Data Mining of Health Documents*, Louhi '10, pages 90–95, Stroudsburg, PA, USA. Association for Computational Linguistics.

Patrice Lopez. 2009. GROBID: combining automatic bibliographic data recognition and term extraction for scholarship publications. In *The 13th European Conference on Digital Libraries (ECDL 2009), Corfu, Greece, September 27 - October 2, 2009*, pages 473–474.

Yi Luan, Mari Ostendorf, and Hannaneh Hajishirzi. 2017. Scientific information extraction with semi-supervised neural tagging. *CoRR*, abs/1708.06075.

Christopher Manning, Mihai Surdeanu, John Bauer, Jenny Finkel, Steven Bethard, and David McClosky. 2014. The stanford corenlp natural language processing toolkit. In *Proceedings of the ACL 2014 System Demonstrations*, Baltimore, USA, 22–27 June 2014, pages 55–50.

Ben Medlock and Ted Briscoe. 2007. Weakly supervised learning for hedge classification in scientific literature. In *Proceedings of the 45th Annual Meeting of the Association for Computational Linguistics*, Prague, Czech Republic, 23–30 June 2007, pages 992–999.

Susan Michie, James Thomas, Marie Johnston, Pol Mac Aonghusa, John Shawe-Taylor, Michael P Kelly, Léa A Deleris, Ailbhe N Finnerty, Marta M Marques, Emma Norris, et al. 2017. The human behaviour-change project: harnessing the power of artificial intelligence and machine learning for evidence synthesis and interpretation. *Implementation Science*, 12(1):121.

Roser Morante and Caroline Sporleder. 2012. Modality and negation: An introduction to the special issue. *Computational Linguistics*, 38(2):223–260.

Pranav Rajpurkar, Jian Zhang, Konstantin Lopyrev, and Percy Liang. 2016. Squad: 100, 000+ questions for machine comprehension of text. In *Proceedings of the 2016 Conference on Empirical Methods in Natural Language Processing*, Austin, Texas, USA, 1–4 November 2016, pages 2383–2392.

Min Joon Seo, Aniruddha Kembhavi, Ali Farhadi, and Hannaneh Hajishirzi. 2017. Bidirectional attention flow for machine comprehension. In *Proceedings of the 5th International Conference on Learning Representations*, Toulon, France, 2017.

Rodney L. Summerscales. 2013. *Automatic Summarization of clinical abstracts for evidence-based medicine*. Ph.D. thesis, Illinois Institute of Technology, Chicago, Illinois.

Charles Sutton and Andrew McCallum. 2012. An introduction to Conditional Random Fields. *Foundations and Trends in Machine Learning*, 4(4):267–373.

Simon Šuster and Walter Daelemans. 2018. Clicr: A dataset of clinical case reports for machine reading comprehension. In *Proceedings of the 2018 Conference of the North American Chapter of the Association for Computational Linguistics: Human Language Technologies,* New Orleans, Louisiana, 1–6 June 2018, pages 1551–1563.

Byron C. Wallace, Joël Kuiper, Aakash Sharma, Mingxi (Brian) Zhu, and Iain J. Marshall. 2016. Extracting PICO sentences from clinical trial reports using supervised distant supervision. *Journal of Machine Learning Research*, 17(132):1–25.

Jinglei Zhao and Yeogirl Yun. 2009. A proximity language model for information retrieval. In *Proceedings of the 32nd Annual International ACM SIGIR Conference on Research and Development in Information Retrieval* Boston, Mass., 19–23 July 2009, pages 291–298.

Distinguishing Clinical Sentiment: The Importance of Domain Adaptation in Psychiatric Patient Health Records

Eben Holderness[1,2], Philip Cawkwell[1], Kirsten Bolton[1],
James Pustejovsky[2] and Mei-Hua Hall[1]

[1]Psychosis Neurobiology Laboratory, McLean Hospital, Harvard Medical School
[2]Department of Computer Science, Brandeis University
{eholderness, mhall}@mclean.harvard.edu
{pcawkwell, kbolton}@partners.org
jamesp@cs.brandeis.edu

Abstract

Recently natural language processing (NLP) tools have been developed to identify and extract salient risk indicators in electronic health records (EHRs). Sentiment analysis, although widely used in non-medical areas for improving decision making, has been studied minimally in the clinical setting. In this study, we undertook, to our knowledge, the first domain adaptation of sentiment analysis to psychiatric EHRs by defining psychiatric clinical sentiment, performing an annotation project, and evaluating multiple sentence-level sentiment machine learning (ML) models. Results indicate that off-the-shelf sentiment analysis tools fail in identifying clinically positive or negative polarity, and that the definition of clinical sentiment that we provide is learnable with relatively small amounts of training data. This project is an initial step towards further refining sentiment analysis methods for clinical use. Our long-term objective is to incorporate the results of this project as part of a machine learning model that predicts inpatient readmission risk. We hope that this work will initiate a discussion concerning domain adaptation of sentiment analysis to the clinical setting.

1 Introduction

Psychotic disorders typically emerge in late adolescence or early adulthood (Kessler et al., 2007; Thomsen, 1996) and affect approximately 2.5-4% of the population (Perälä et al., 2007; Bogren et al., 2009), making them one of the leading causes of disability worldwide (Vos et al., 2015). A substantial proportion of psychiatric inpatients are readmitted after discharge (Wiersma et al., 1998). Readmissions are disruptive for both patients and families, and are a key driver of rising healthcare costs (Mangalore and Knapp, 2007; Wu et al., 2005). Reducing readmission risk is therefore a major unmet need of psychiatric care. Developing clinically implementable ML tools to enable accurate assessment of readmission risk factors offers opportunities to inform the selection of treatment interventions and to subsequently implement appropriate preventive measures.

Sentiment analysis (also known as opinion mining) has been used for capturing the subjective "feeling" (e.g. positive, negative, or neutral valence) of reviews and has recently been expanded to include other domains such as reactions to stock market prediction or political trends (Mäntylä et al., 2018). With the rise of social media and other user-generated web content, sentiment analysis has been adopted by many industries as a way of monitoring opinions towards their products, reputations, and for identifying opportunities for improvement. Traditionally, sentiment analysis has been approached with a lexicon-based majority vote approach, where a dictionary of terms and their associated sentiments (e.g. SentiWordnet, Pattern, SO-CAL, VADER) are queried to determine the sentiment of a given text (Taboada et al., 2011). However, this approach fails to account for many associated linguistic challenges such as negation handling, scope, sarcasm, qualified statements, and out-of-vocabulary terms. As such, research groups have moved towards approaching the problem from a corpus-based machine learning perspective. This approach has the added benefit of model flexibility depending on the training data and can capture more syntactic nuance. Most state-of-the-art performances on sentiment analysis benchmarks are currently achieved with deep learning sequence models that are trained on syntactically parsed corpora such as the Stanford Sentiment Treebank (Socher et al., 2013).

In clinical and medical domains, however, sentiment analysis has not yet been well studied. Yet retrieving subjective clinical attitudes (sentiment) from EHR narratives has the potential to facili-

117

Proceedings of the 2nd Clinical Natural Language Processing Workshop, pages 117–123
Minneapolis, Minnesota, June 7, 2019. ©2019 Association for Computational Linguistics

tate identification of a patient's symptomatological worsening or increased readmission risk.

The concept of medical sentiment is complex and vocabularies differ from general-domain sentiment. In the field of psychiatry, this is especially true. Therefore, there is a need for domain adaptation of sentiment analysis that includes a richer array of attributes than can typically be found in off-the-shelf tools. In this work, we established an annotation scheme to characterize sentiment-related features in EHRs, and used this to carry out, to our knowledge, the first psychiatry-specific sentiment annotation project on EHRs. The resulting datasets are used to train and evaluate a classifier to predict clinical sentiment at the sentence level. This classifier, which in future works will be integrated in a pipeline for predicting readmission risk, is clinically useful for targeting treatments and aiding in decision making.

2   Related Works

Although there has been some work on clinical adaptation of sentiment analysis using healthcare-related data extracted from web forums, biomedical texts, or social media postings (See for example (Smith and Lee, 2012; Niu et al., 2005; Salas-Zárate et al., 2017; Nguyen et al., 2014)), there has been minimal work on sentiment analysis when applied to actual EHR data.

McCoy et al. (2015) used a corpus of psychosis patient discharge summaries and the 3,000 word Pattern lexical opinion mining dictionary (Smedt and Daelemans, 2012) to classify the associated sentiment of documents using a majority vote classifier. Results of their Cox regression models showed that greater positive sentiment was associated with a reduction in inpatient readmission risk. Waudby-Smith et al. (2018) applied the same Pattern sentiment lexicon to a corpus of ICU nursing notes to predict 30-day mortality risk. They found that stronger negative sentiment polarity was associated with an increased 30-day mortality risk. One of the limitations in both studies is that Pattern is a general-domain sentiment lexicon that contains few informative medical or psychiatry-specific terminology. Also, the authors did not manually annotate the datasets they worked with. As a result, they were not able to confirm that the predicted sentiment aligned with the sentiment from a clinical perspective.

(Deng et al., 2014) and (Denecke and Deng, 2015) systematically compared word usage and sentiment distribution between clinical narratives (nurse letters, discharge summary, and radiology reports) and medical social media (MedBlog, drug reviews). They concluded that off-the-shelf sentiment tools were not ideal for analyzing sentiment in medical documents and that EHRs were significantly more difficult in predicting sentiment, in particular neutral sentiment (Neutral F1=0.216 and 0.080 for nurse letters and radiology reports, respectively). They developed annotation guidelines and undertook a span-level annotation task on 300 ICU nurse letters to identify words related to clinical sentiment (Deng et al., 2016). Results of applying ML algorithms to these data are not available yet.

3   Methods

In this work, we define psychiatric clinical sentiment as a clinician's attitudes (positive, negative, or neutral) towards a patient's prognosis with regards to seven readmission risk factor domains (appearance, mood, interpersonal relations, substance use, thought content, thought process, and occupation) that were identified in prior work (Holderness et al., 2018). The scope of our current definition is intentionally narrow such that the sentiment of a given sentence is considered in isolation without any prior knowledge.

Three clinicians participated in an annotation project that focused on identifying the clinical sentiment associated with psychiatric EHR texts at the sentence level. In total, two corpora of clinical narratives from institutional EHRs, one containing 3,500 sentences (training dataset) and the other 1,650 (test dataset) were annotated using the definition established in the annotation scheme.

The training dataset consisted exclusively of sentence-length sequences that involved only one risk factor domain in each example. The examples in the dataset were identified from a large corpus of unannotated psychosis patient EHR data sourced from the psychiatric units of several Boston-area hospitals in the Partners HealthCare network, including Massachusetts General Hospital and Brigham & Women's Hospital. We used our risk factor domain topic extraction model to automatically identify relevant sentences, which were then manually validated by one of the clinicians involved in this project to ensure they did not involve multiple domains in the same exam-

Domain	Positive Example	Neutral Example	Negative Example
Appearance	Presents on time, dressed and groomed nicely, good hygiene.	Casually dressed and wearing knit vest and belt.	Notes that he wears the same clothes 2-3 days at a time, he doesn't care for his appearance– which is atypical for him.
Mood	Her depression and anxiety have improved immensely.	Mood is largely euthymic although he stated he gets depressed occasionally.	Tearful, presented very depressed with sad affect.
Interpersonal	Continues to be happy in her relationship with her boyfriend and school friends are stable as well.	She voiced no complaints about her primary relationship or other social relationships.	Poor social supports, abusive relationship.
Substance Use	Denies substance use or alcohol other than an occasional glass of wine.	Remote history of cocaine (smoked), marijuana and mescaline use many years ago.	He reports daily k2 use in addition to using crack cocaine about once a week.
Occupation	Pt reports having taken further steps toward employment – applied for two jobs and has interview lined up for Saturday.	Discusses new job as part time substitute teacher.	Recently has a new job that she hates and took a paycut.
Thought Content	She never had auditory hallucinations or delusions of thought broadcasting and thought insertion.	No overt hallucinations or delusions but expansive thinking.	Delusions and hallucinations continue.
Thought Process	Stable, slow speech with fewer word finding difficulties today, linear thought process, cooperative,attentive.	Slightly pressured speech but not as bad as some past visits.	Speech spontaneous and decreased in volume, rate, and rhythm; hard to understand at times because she barely opens her mouth when she talks.

Table 1: Example EHR sentences reflecting sentiment polarity for each risk factor domain.

ple. See Table 1 for example sentences for each domain.

The test dataset is an extension of the corpus used previously to evaluate our risk factor domain topic extraction model and is non-overlapping with the training data, consisting of discharge summaries, admission notes, individual encounter notes, and other clinical notes from 220 patients in the OnTrack[TM] program at McLean Hospital. OnTrack[TM] is an outpatient program, focusing on treating adults ages 18 to 30 who are experiencing their first episodes of psychosis. Because we are interested in identifying the clinical sentiment associated with each risk factor domain individually, the test dataset consists of examples that were intentionally selected to be challenging for our model: they are variable in length, wide-ranging in vocabulary, and can involve multiple risk factor domains (e.g. "Work functioning is impaired, but pt has good relationship w/ his girlfriend and is not engaging in substance use.").

These corpora are available to other researchers upon request. Table 2 details the distribution of the training and test data. The imbalance of training examples across the three sentiment classes reflects the natural distribution of sentiment reflected in EHRs, as certain risk factor domains (e.g. substance use) will rarely be reflected in a neutral or

	Positive	Negative	Neutral
Appearance	290	69	141
Mood	100	322	77
Interpersonal	205	165	130
Substance Use	181	261	58
Occupation	250	143	150
Thought Process	150	266	84
Thought Content	183	253	64

Table 2: Distribution of training and test examples.

positive sense.

We evaluated three classification models. Our baseline model is a majority vote approach using the Pattern sentiment lexicon employed by McCoy (2015) and Waudby-Smith (2018). The second and third models use fully supervised and semi-supervised multilayer perceptron (MLP) architectures, respectively. Since positive and negative clinical sentiment can differ across each domain, we train a suite of seven models, one for each risk factor domain. The training and test data were vectorized at the sentence level using the pretrained Universal Sentence Encoder (USE) embedding module (Cer et al., 2018) that is available through TensorFlow Hub and is designed specifically for transfer learning tasks. Although USE is trained on a large volume of web-based, general-domain data, we have found in prior work that the embeddings lead to higher accuracy on down-

Model	Domain	Pos P	Pos R	Pos F1	Neg P	Neg R	Neg F1	Neu P	Neu R	Neu F1
Baseline (Pattern)	All	0.612	0.231	0.319	0.552	0.245	0.337	0.234	**0.736**	**0.348**
	Interpersonal	0.8	0.222	0.348	0.429	0.103	0.167	0.413	0.929	0.571
	Mood	0.511	0.233	0.32	0.558	0.352	0.432	0.266	0.672	0.381
	Occupation	0.75	0.129	0.22	0.328	0.188	0.265	0.329	0.917	0.484
	Substance Use	0.429	0.067	0.115	0.593	0.241	0.342	0.222	0.74	0.341
	Appearance	0.781	0.424	0.549	0.556	0.309	0.397	0.174	0.552	0.265
	Thought Content	0.556	0.19	0.283	0.723	0.29	0.414	0.055	0.6	0.101
	Thought Process	0.459	0.354	0.4	0.677	0.231	0.344	0.181	0.739	0.291
Fully Supervised MLP	All	**0.62**	0.416	**0.478**	**0.67**	0.652	**0.658**	**0.289**	0.437	0.329
	Interpersonal	0.632	0.667	0.649	0.731	0.656	0.691	0.567	0.607	0.558
	Mood	0.717	0.32	0.443	0.597	0.73	0.657	0.286	0.418	0.339
	Occupation	0.645	0.571	0.606	0.558	0.604	0.58	0.346	0.375	0.36
	Substance Use	0.423	0.244	0.31	0.674	0.714	0.693	0.344	0.42	0.378
	Appearance	0.705	0.525	0.602	0.69	0.605	0.645	0.241	0.448	0.313
	Thought Content	0.59	0.127	0.209	0.667	0.654	0.66	0.078	0.4	0.13
	Thought Process	0.629	0.458	0.53	0.775	0.604	0.679	0.161	0.391	0.228
Semi-Supervised MLP (Self-Training)	All	0.588	0.4	0.46	0.611	**0.733**	**0.658**	0.285	0.291	0.259
	Interpersonal	0.632	0.667	0.649	0.625	0.69	0.656	0.583	0.5	0.539
	Mood	0.645	0.301	0.411	0.502	0.885	0.641	0.233	0.105	0.144
	Occupation	0.671	0.671	0.671	0.539	0.583	0.56	0.364	0.333	0.348
	Substance Use	0.394	0.289	0.333	0.617	0.835	0.709	0.333	0.1	0.154
	Appearance	0.722	0.441	0.547	0.653	0.605	0.628	0.224	0.448	0.299
	Thought Content	0.5	0.139	0.218	0.689	0.753	0.72	0.088	0.333	0.139
	Thought Process	0.583	0.292	0.389	0.651	0.78	0.685	0.172	0.217	0.192

Table 3: Results of the clinical sentiment extraction task.

stream classification tasks than embedding models (e.g. ELMo, Doc2Vec, FastText) trained on smaller volumes of EHR data (Holderness et al., 2019).

Hyperparameters were tuned using grid search with 5-fold cross-validation on the training dataset and are specified in Table 4. Due to the relatively small amount of labeled training data, our proposed model architecture is designed to prevent overfitting by using a restricted view of the training data via a high rate of dropout in the hidden layers. Additionally, we use two hidden layers to extract a more abstracted form of the input. Additionally, because neutral sentiment is much broader in scope and has fewer training examples, resulting in covariate shift, we compute a threshold for classifying positive and negative sentiment using the formula min=avg(sim)+*(sim), where is standard deviation and is a constant, which we set to 0.2. If a given test sentence does not have positive or negative outputs that exceed this threshold, the sentence is classified as neutral even if neutral is not the maximal output.

We experimented with two semi-supervised learning configurations, Self-Training and K-Nearest Neighbors (KNN). The self-training approach involved first training our model on the labeled training data and then using this model to identify unlabeled examples from a large prepro-

Parameter	Value
Batch Size	28
Iterations	100
Hidden Units Per Layer	300
Dropout	0.75
Kernel Initializer	Uniform
Optimizer	Adam
Input/Hidden Layer Activations	ReLU
Output Layer Activations	Sigmoid

Table 4: Hyperparameters for sentiment model.

cessed corpus of unlabeled EHR data (2,100,000 sentences, 85,000,000 tokens). For the KNN approach, we projected all of the labeled and unlabeled examples into vector space and treated the labeled examples as centroids. For each centroid, we then used Euclidean distance to compute the five nearest unlabeled examples. Both models were trained using a 20:80 combination of the original labeled data and the additional unlabeled data.

4 Results and Discussion

Inter-annotator agreement (IAA) was substantial on the first corpus (Scott's Pi=0.691, Cohen's Kappa=0.693) and higher on the second (Pi=0.768, Kappa=0.768) (Fleiss, 1971; Davies and Fleiss, 1982). This is expected as the first corpus contains many sentences involving multiple readmission risk factor domains and annotators were instructed to provide clinical sentiment labels for each, whereas the second corpus consists entirely of single domain sentences. In both cases, IAA surpasses that reported by Denecke and Deng (2016), primarily because of the clinical expertise of the annotators involved in this project.

Results of the three classifiers are shown in Table 3, with the highest score on each performance metric in bold. The 'All' row for each model configuration was computed by averaging the scores of the sentiment models for each risk factor domain. Applying the Pattern sentiment lexicon to our test corpus showed a strong trend towards underclassification of positive and negative examples, which led to poor recall scores while maintaining moderate precision. Neutral examples, however, were correctly classified significantly more often. This confirms that many of the most informative words in terms of clinical sentiment (e.g. 'hallucination', 'depressed', 'employed', etc.) do not hold significance in general-domain sentiment and are therefore not part of the Pattern lexicon.

Despite the relatively small size of the training corpus, the EHR data used for training captured much of the domain-specific vocabulary related to clinical sentiment and our suite of models achieved F-measures on classifying positive and negative sentiment that exceed those reported in prior literature (Deng et al., 2014). Although direct comparison between our EHR dataset and the EHR datasets used by other researchers is limited due to HIPAA restrictions, our training EHR data is sourced from the same EHR database as McCoy (2015). Therefore, a better performance of our models indirectly supports that our model can better capture the underlying clinical sentiment embedded in EHRs.

Because clinical documents are written for a specific purpose such as assessing the outcome of treatment, they contain less neutral content and as a result sentiment distributions are intrinsically biased to either positive or negative polarity. Thus, identifying training examples with neutral sentiment was challenging and consequently both the fully and semi-supervised models were poor at identifying neutral sentiment across all seven domains. In addition, unless the patient is markedly improved, clinicians tend to document continuing unresolved symptoms. leading to a greater amount of negative content. We hypothesize that this may

be one reason for the lower overall F1 performance on positive versus negative sentiment.

We observed that per-domain performance of our models aligned with the natural distribution of positive vs. negative clinical sentiment in EHRs. Substance use, for example, had low positive F1 scores as the majority of references to substance use in EHRs involve negative sentiment unless the patient is noted to be abstaining from substance use. We also observed that sentiment distribution towards negative polarity is more evident in mood and thought content, which include, for example, delusions, depression, anxiety, and hallucinations.

When applying semi-supervised learning methods, we found self-training to marginally improve performance on negative clinical sentiment but the overall F1 score was not better than the fully supervised model due to lower precision. We observed minimal change in performance when using a k-nearest neighbors approach.

5 Conclusion and Future Work

We focused in this study on the clinical sentiment associated with readmission for seven risk factor domains identified in prior work by undertaking an annotation project and using the resultant gold standard to train semi-supervised ML algorithms to automatically infer this sentiment. Our results indicate that domain adaptation of sentiment analysis is necessary for aligning with clinician opinions.

We intend to improve our clinical sentiment classifier in future work by increasing the size of the annotated training corpus (in particular neutral examples) and by changing the model input to a sequence model as opposed to a full sentence vector representation. We also intend to modify our definition of clinical sentiment to include temporal linking of elements that involve clinical sentiment in an EHR to establish gradients of changes in patient status over time. Finally, we will incorporate our sentiment analysis model in a classifier that predicts inpatient readmission risk.

6 Acknowledgments

This work was supported by a grant from the National Institute of Mental Health (grant no. 5R01MH109687 to Mei-Hua Hall). We would also like to thank the Clinical NLP 2019 Workshop reviewers for their constructive and helpful comments.

References

Mats Bogren, Cecilia Mattisson, Per-Erik Isberg, and Per Nettelbladt. 2009. How common are psychotic and bipolar disorders? a 50-year follow-up of the lundby population. *Nordic journal of psychiatry*, 63(4):336–346.

Daniel Cer, Yinfei Yang, Sheng-yi Kong, Nan Hua, Nicole Limtiaco, Rhomni St John, Noah Constant, Mario Guajardo-Cespedes, Steve Yuan, Chris Tar, et al. 2018. Universal sentence encoder for english. In *Proceedings of the 2018 Conference on Empirical Methods in Natural Language Processing: System Demonstrations*, pages 169–174.

Mark Davies and Joseph L Fleiss. 1982. Measuring agreement for multinomial data. *Biometrics*, pages 1047–1051.

Kerstin Denecke and Yihan Deng. 2015. Sentiment analysis in medical settings: New opportunities and challenges. *Artificial intelligence in medicine*, 64(1):17–27.

Yihan Deng, Thierry Declerck, Piroska Lendvai, and Kerstin Denecke. 2016. The generation of a corpus for clinical sentiment analysis. In *European Semantic Web Conference*, pages 311–324. Springer.

Yihan Deng, Matthaeus Stoehr, and Kerstin Denecke. 2014. Retrieving attitudes: Sentiment analysis from clinical narratives. In *MedIR@ SIGIR*, pages 12–15.

Joseph L Fleiss. 1971. Measuring nominal scale agreement among many raters. *Psychological bulletin*, 76(5):378.

Eben Holderness, Marie Meteer, James Pustejovsky, and Mei-Hua Hall. 2019. Evaluating the role of pretraining in natural language processing of clinical narratives. Poster presented at McLean Research Day, Belmont, MA. Results are available upon request.

Eben Holderness, Nicholas Miller, Kirsten Bolton, Philip Cawkwell, Marie Meteer, James Pustejovsky, and Mei Hua-Hall. 2018. Analysis of risk factor domains in psychosis patient health records. In *Proceedings of the Ninth International Workshop on Health Text Mining and Information Analysis*, pages 129–138.

Ronald C Kessler, G Paul Amminger, Sergio Aguilar-Gaxiola, Jordi Alonso, Sing Lee, and T Bedirhan Ustun. 2007. Age of onset of mental disorders: a review of recent literature. *Current opinion in psychiatry*, 20(4):359.

Roshni Mangalore and Martin Knapp. 2007. Cost of schizophrenia in england. *The journal of mental health policy and economics*, 10(1):23–41.

Mika V Mäntylä, Daniel Graziotin, and Miikka Kuutila. 2018. The evolution of sentiment analysisa review of research topics, venues, and top cited papers. *Computer Science Review*, 27:16–32.

Thomas H McCoy, Victor M Castro, Andrew Cagan, Ashlee M Roberson, Isaac S Kohane, and Roy H Perlis. 2015. Sentiment measured in hospital discharge notes is associated with readmission and mortality risk: an electronic health record study. *PloS one*, 10(8):e0136341.

Thin Nguyen, Dinh Phung, Bo Dao, Svetha Venkatesh, and Michael Berk. 2014. Affective and content analysis of online depression communities. *IEEE Transactions on Affective Computing*, 5(3):217–226.

Yun Niu, Xiaodan Zhu, Jianhua Li, and Graeme Hirst. 2005. Analysis of polarity information in medical text. In *AMIA annual symposium proceedings*, volume 2005, page 570. American Medical Informatics Association.

Jonna Perälä, Jaana Suvisaari, Samuli I Saarni, Kimmo Kuoppasalmi, Erkki Isometsä, Sami Pirkola, Timo Partonen, Annamari Tuulio-Henriksson, Jukka Hintikka, Tuula Kieseppä, et al. 2007. Lifetime prevalence of psychotic and bipolar i disorders in a general population. *Archives of general psychiatry*, 64(1):19–28.

María del Pilar Salas-Zárate, Jose Medina-Moreira, Katty Lagos-Ortiz, Harry Luna-Aveiga, Miguel Angel Rodriguez-Garcia, and Rafael Valencia-Garcia. 2017. Sentiment analysis on tweets about diabetes: an aspect-level approach. *Computational and mathematical methods in medicine*, 2017.

Tom De Smedt and Walter Daelemans. 2012. Pattern for python. *Journal of Machine Learning Research*, 13(Jun):2063–2067.

Phillip Smith and Mark Lee. 2012. Cross-discourse development of supervised sentiment analysis in the clinical domain. In *Proceedings of the 3rd workshop in computational approaches to subjectivity and sentiment analysis*, pages 79–83. Association for Computational Linguistics.

Richard Socher, Alex Perelygin, Jean Wu, Jason Chuang, Christopher D Manning, Andrew Ng, and Christopher Potts. 2013. Recursive deep models for semantic compositionality over a sentiment treebank. In *Proceedings of the 2013 conference on empirical methods in natural language processing*, pages 1631–1642.

Maite Taboada, Julian Brooke, Milan Tofiloski, Kimberly Voll, and Manfred Stede. 2011. Lexicon-based methods for sentiment analysis. *Computational linguistics*, 37(2):267–307.

PH Thomsen. 1996. Schizophrenia with childhood and adolescent onseta nationwide register-based study. *Acta Psychiatrica Scandinavica*, 94(3):187–193.

Theo Vos, Ryan M Barber, Brad Bell, Amelia Bertozzi-Villa, Stan Biryukov, Ian Bolliger, Fiona Charlson, Adrian Davis, Louisa Degenhardt, Daniel Dicker, et al. 2015. Global, regional, and national incidence, prevalence, and years lived with disability for

301 acute and chronic diseases and injuries in 188 countries, 1990–2013: a systematic analysis for the global burden of disease study 2013. *The Lancet*, 386(9995):743–800.

Ian ER Waudby-Smith, Nam Tran, Joel A Dubin, and Joon Lee. 2018. Sentiment in nursing notes as an indicator of out-of-hospital mortality in intensive care patients. *PloS one*, 13(6):e0198687.

Durk Wiersma, Fokko J Nienhuis, Cees J Slooff, and Robert Giel. 1998. Natural course of schizophrenic disorders: a 15-year followup of a dutch incidence cohort. *Schizophrenia bulletin*, 24(1):75–85.

Eric Q Wu, Howard G Birnbaum, Lizheng Shi, Daniel E Ball, Ronald C Kessler, Matthew Moulis, and Jyoti Aggarwal. 2005. The economic burden of schizophrenia in the united states in 2002. *Journal of Clinical Psychiatry*, 66(9):1122–1129.

Medical Word Embeddings for Spanish: Development and Evaluation

Felipe Soares
Barcelona Supercomputing Center (BSC)
felipe.soares@bsc.es

Marta Villegas
Barcelona Supercomputing Center (BSC)
marta.villegas@bsc.es

Aitor Gonzalez-Agirre
Barcelona Supercomputing Center (BSC)
aitor.gonzalez@bsc.es

Martin Krallinger
Centro Nacional de Investigaciones Oncologicas (CNIO)
mkrallinger@cnio.es

Jordi Armengol-Estapé
Universitat Politècnica de Catalunya (UPC)
jordi.armengol.estape@gmail.com

Abstract

Word embeddings are representations of words in a dense vector space. Although they are not recent phenomena in Natural Language Processing (NLP), they have gained momentum after the recent developments of neural methods and Word2Vec. Regarding their applications in medical and clinical NLP, they are invaluable resources when training in-domain named entity recognition systems, classifiers or taggers, for instance. Thus, the development of tailored word embeddings for medical NLP is of great interest. However, we identified a gap in the literature which we aim to fill in this paper: the availability of embeddings for medical NLP in Spanish, as well as a standardized form of intrinsic evaluation. Since most work has been done for English, some established datasets for intrinsic evaluation are already available. In this paper, we show the steps we employed to adapt such datasets for the first time to Spanish, of particular relevance due to the considerable volume of EHRs in this language, as well as the creation of in-domain medical word embeddings for the Spanish using the state-of-the-art Fast-Text model. We performed intrinsic evaluation with our adapted datasets, as well as extrinsic evaluation with a named entity recognition systems using a baseline embedding of general-domain. Both experiments proved that our embeddings are suitable for use in medical NLP in the Spanish language, and are more accurate than general-domain ones.

1 Introduction

Representation of words in vector space, or word embedding, is not a new concept in Natural Language Processing (NLP) and are used in a several number of statistical and neural models (Ghannay et al., 2016). Word embeddings (WE) can include semantic information and are based on the general idea of an association of elements (words) with certain contexts and the similarity in word meanings. In more recent neural networks, embeddings are used to encode words in a space that is subsequently used as input for many possible models.

1.1 Background

In the work of Mikolov et al. (2013a), they introduced two new architectures for estimating continuous representations of words using log-linear models, called continuous bag-of-word (CBOW) and continuous skip-gram (skip-gram). CBOW calculates the projection for the current word given the context words in the particular sentence, while skip-gram, following its name, skip the word being processed and evaluates projections of the context words. Further works gave more insights about this method called Word2Vec (Mikolov et al., 2013b,c). Since its appearance, Word2Vec has been used and adapted for a wide range of applications, including sentiment analysis (Nakov et al., 2016; Yu et al., 2017), named entity recognition (Chiu and Nichols, 2016), clas-

124

Proceedings of the 2nd Clinical Natural Language Processing Workshop, pages 124–133
Minneapolis, Minnesota, June 7, 2019. ©2019 Association for Computational Linguistics

sification (Zhang et al., 2015), clustering (Kim et al., 2017), word sense disambiguation (Iacobacci et al., 2016) and many others. More recently, Mikolov et al. (2018) presented the combination of various "tricks" in training word embeddings that are rarely used together, but that outperforms the previous state-of-the-art vector representations.

1.2 Pre-trained embeddings

Pre-trained word embeddings are widely available for a plethora of languages and methods. Google, for instance, makes available Word2Vec models pre-trained on about 100 billion words from Google News corpus in English[1]. Regarding other languages, on FastText website[2] one can download pre-trained embeddings for 157 languages based on Common Crawl and Wikipedia. For the specific case of Spanish, the University of Chile NLP group makes available FasText and Word2Vec embeddings[3] using the Spanish Billion Word Corpus (SBWCE)[4].

1.3 Biomedical embeddings

As pointed out by Chiu et al. (2016), most of the studies and available embeddings are focused on general-domain texts and general evaluation datasets. Thus, their results not necessarily apply well to medical and biomedical text analysis. Their study, in English, demonstrates that bigger corpora do not necessarily produce better biomedical word embeddings. They also made their resulting embeddings available for download.

In another work, Chen et al. (2018) created sentence embeddings for clinical and biomedical texts, called BioSentVec trained on PubMed and clinical notes from the MIMIC-III Clinical Database(Johnson et al., 2016). Similarly, Sahu and Anand (2015) used the PubMed Central Open Access subset (PMC) and PubMed abstracts to train word embeddings for English using CBOW. They evaluate embeddings performance using similarity and relatedness datasets, which will be presented in Section 3.1. However, they do not compare the trained models with a general-domain one.

In a more fine-grained application, Zhang et al. (2018) adapted word embeddings to recognize symptoms in the target domain of psychiatry. As a source for their embeddings, they used four corpora: intensive care, biomedical literature, Wikipedia and Psychiatric Forum. Ling et al. (2017) developed a method to integrate extra knowledge into word embeddings for biomedical NLP tasks via graph regularization.

More related to our work, Santiso et al. (2018) developed word embeddings tailored for negation detection in health records written in Spanish. As corpora, they used both in-domain and general-domain data. For in-domain, they used unannotated Electronic Health Records (EHRs) from a hospital in Spain. For the general-domain, they used the SBWCE corpus. However, they did not perform any intrinsic evaluation of the generated embeddings; neither made them available for use or compared general-domain and in-domain performance.

Also regarding Spanish biomedical embeddings, the work of Segura-Bedmar and Martínez (2017) shows the use of pre-trained word embeddings with SBWCE for simplification of drug package leaflets so that they are more friendly to the patients. However, they do not use in-domain embeddings for such task. Also, Villegas et al. (2018) collected a census of Spanish texts that can be of use in text mining, however, they did not provide any sort of word embeddings.

1.4 Contributions and Structure

Given that very little attention has been given to producing and evaluating quality word embeddings in Spanish for the biomedical domain, we propose to develop embeddings based on the state-of-the-art FastText model with in-domain data. In addition, only works aiming the English language provide a comprehensive performance evaluation of in-domain embeddings when compared to general-domain ones. For that, we will adapt them to Spanish. We claim as relevant the following contributions:

- Development of Spanish embeddings for the Biomedical domain;

- Intrinsic and extrinsic evaluation of performance using established datasets and a Named Entity Recognition (NER) task;

---

[1] https://code.google.com/archive/p/word2vec/

[2] https://fasttext.cc/docs/en/crawl-vectors.html

[3] https://github.com/uchile-nlp/spanish-word-embeddings

[4] http://crscardellino.github.io/SBWCE/

- Comparison of in-domain and general-domain performance;

- Adaptation of established biomedical intrinsic evaluation datasets for the Spanish language;

- Embeddings are public available[5] and licensed under CC-BY 4.

We expect that the developed word embeddings will to be used in several clinical NLP applications, such as for the identification of sections in clinical documents since the embedddings can be used to create phrase and paragraph embeddings. Also, for text summarization based on neural networks, our embeddings can be used as a resource during training.

The rest of the paper is organized as follows. In Section 2, we explain the methods and the materials used in our experiments, including corpora and the training procedure. In Section 3, we detail the intrinsic and extrinsic evaluations, with the steps we employed to adapt English datasets to Spanish. In Section 4, we show the experiments and their results, while in Section 5 we perform a brief discussion and conclusion.

2 Material and Methods

In this Section, we present the corpora, the word embedding model used in our study and the training procedure.

2.1 FastText

The FastText model (Mikolov et al., 2018) uses the combination of various subcomponents to produce high-quality embeddings. It uses a standard CBOW or skip-gram models, with position-dependent weighting, phrase representations, and subword information in a combined manner. The CBOW and skip-gram models is the same as proposed in Mikolov et al. (2013a).

The position-dependent weighting introduces information regarding the position of the word being evaluated. As stated by the authors, the explicit encoding of the word and its position would lead to overfitting. The solution was to learn position representations and use them to reweight the word vectors at a minimum computational cost using linear combination of both representations.

The original Word2Vec is insensitive to word order, since it is only based on unigrams. To capture word order information in a phrase representation, the authors merge words with high mutual information in a single token. One example can be "brain" and "dead", which could be merged as "brain_dead". This process of merging tokens can be repeated several times to produce longer tokens.

To avoid the fact that standard word vectors ignore word-internal structure, which may contain useful information, the authors enrich the vectors with subword information. Each word is decomposed into its character n-grams which are then learned. After that, the final word vector is the simple sum of the word vector and their n-grams representations.

2.2 Corpora

To develop our in-domain embeddings, we used two sources of data: (i) the SciELO database, which contains full-text articles primarily in English, Spanish and Portuguese, and (ii) the Wikipedia, with a subset which we call Wikipedia Health, comprised by the categories of Pharmacology, Pharmacy, Medicine and Biology. This method of combining large corpora (i.e. SciELO) and smaller focused (i.e. Wikipedia) was shown to be an adequate approach to produce quality embeddings for clinical NLP (Roberts, 2016). The choice of SciELO is that this database is the most comprehensive in term of number of articles and abstracts available in Spanish. As for the Wikipedia, it can be a source of information for specific terms, which can benefit our models.

From Scielo.org, all documents in Spanish were downloaded, language checked and processed into sentences. For language check, we used the langdetect library[6] for Python. The scielo.org node contains all Spanish articles, regardless if they are from European or Latin American Spanish. In the database, articles from the health domain correspond to approximately 50% of the results.

Using the Wikipedia API for Python[7], we retrieved all articles that are from the aforementioned categories. We also performed language checking, to ensure that all sentences were in Spanish.

---

[5]http://doi.org/10.5281/zenodo.2542722

[6]https://github.com/fedelopez77/
langdetect
[7]https://pypi.org/project/wikipedia/

In Table 1, one can see the statistics regarding the gathered corpora. Sentences were produced using the sentence tokenizer from the NLTK package. The SciELO corpus is relatively smaller than the Wikipedia one regarding number of sentences. However, as for number of tokens, SciELO contains almost 22% more than Wikipedia. This is probably due to the fact that scientific article sentences are longer than the ones available in Wikipedia.

Table 1: Statistics for the gathered corpora

Corpus	Sentences	Tokens
SciELO Full-Text	3.3M	100M
Wikipedia Health	4M	82M

2.3 Training

We used the FastText implementation available in `https://fasttext.cc` to train our word embeddings. The following setup was used:

- Minimum number of word occurrences: 5

- Phrase representation: No (i.e. length of word n-gram = 1)

- Minimum length of character n-gram: 3

- Maximum length of character n-gram: 6

- Size of word vectors: 300

- Epochs: 20

3 Evaluation

For the evaluation of our embeddings, we use both intrinsic and extrinsic evaluation, which are now detailed, as well as the baseline word embedding.

3.1 Intrinsic

In the intrinsic evaluation, the performances are measured regarding specific tasks that are only related to the embedding itself, such as syntactic of semantic relationships between words. The most common examples are similarity, relatedness and analogy evaluations (Schnabel et al., 2015).

For the biomedical domain, some standard datasets are available for the evaluation of semantic similarity and relatedness. The UMNSRS similarity (UMNSRS-sim) and UMNSRS relatedness (UMNSRS-rel) are datasets consisting of pairs of UMLS (Unified Medical Language System) concepts manually annotated for similarity and relatedness. Details about the original datasets can be found in Pakhomov et al. (2010). The UMNSRS-sim contains 566 pairs of concepts, while the UMNSRS-rel contains 587 pairs.

Another well-known dataset for intrinsic evaluation in biomedical embeddings is the MayoSRS (Pakhomov et al., 2011), which is used for similarity evaluation and is comprised of 101 UMLS pairs and their respective manual scores.

The aforementioned datasets, however, are only available in English. For the best of our knowledge, no standard Spanish dataset is available for the biomedical domain. Thus, in order to be able to evaluate our embeddings, we adapted the aforementioned datasets for Spanish.

In Figure 1, we depict the steps employed to adapt the datasets. In step 1, the datasets are translated to Spanish using Google Translate[8]. However, due to the possible polysemy and translation errors, we employed additional checking steps.

In step 2, the translated terms are queried against the already available translations for that specific CUI (Concept Unique Identifier) in UMLS. If the translated term is already in the UMLS translations, we assign such term as a valid translation.

In step 3, if the translated term is not found in UMLS, we perform manual evaluation of possible translations using UMLS browser. The assigned translations were then revised by a medical doctor and corrected when needed. Also, at this point all other assignd terms were also revised.

We must notice that we did not include the concepts that were originally referring to commercial drug names (which are not in the UMLS, just their pharmacological substance), since this may vary depending on the country and also depending on regional medical protocols. The final number of pairs of terms for UMNSRS-rel is 384, that is, 65.41% of the original in English. As for UMNSRS-sim, the final number is 380, or 67.14% of the original dataset in English. For the MayoSRS, all 101 pairs are included in the final dataset in Spanish, since no drug is included in the original data.

---

[8]`https://translate.google.com/`

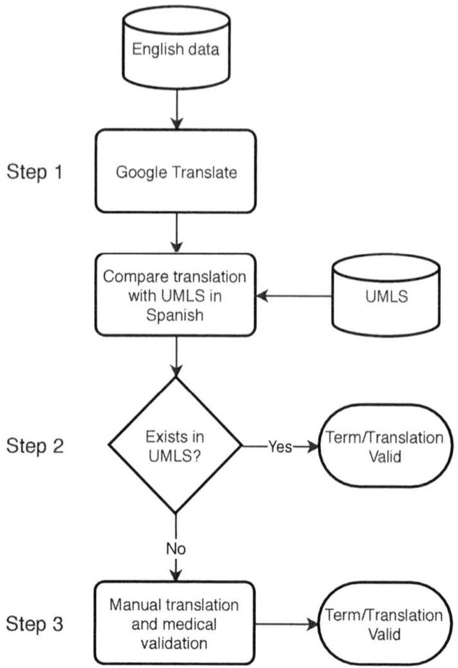

Figure 1: Steps performed to translate the UMNSRS-sim, UMNSRS-rel and MayoSRS datasets to Spanish

3.2 Extrinsic

As for the extrinsic evaluation, we employed our embeddings in an NER task to identify pharmacological substances, compounds and proteins in clinical texts.

3.2.1 Data

The data for this experiment comprehends manually classified collection of clinical case sections derived from Open access Spanish medical publications, named the Spanish Clinical Case Corpus (SPACCC). All clinical case records derived from various databases were gathered in a first step, preprocessed and the actual clinical case section was extracted removing embedded figure references or citations. These records where classified manually using the MyMiner[9] file labeling online application by a practicing oncologist and revised by a clinical documentalist in order to assure that these records were related to the medical domain and they resembled the kind of structure and content that is relevant to process clinical content.

The final collection of 1000 clinical cases that make up the corpus had a total of 16504 sentences, with an average of 16.5 sentences per clinical case.

The SPACCC corpus contains a total of 396,988 words, with an average of 396.2 words per clinical case. It is noteworthy to say that this kind of narrative shows properties of both, the biomedical and medical literature as well as clinical records. Moreover, the clinical cases were not restricted to a single medical discipline, and thus cover a variety of medical topics, including oncology, urology, cardiology, pneumology or infectious diseases, which is key in order to cover a diverse collection of chemicals and drugs.

We must notice that this corpus will not be available at this point since it is currently being used as evaluation in a shared task track. However, in the future, users will be able to access the corpus from the same link to the word embeddings.

3.2.2 Software

As for the NER system, we employed an off-the-shelf framework called NeuroNER(Dernoncourt et al., 2017)[10]. The engine is based on artificial neural networks, relying on long short-term memory (LSTM) to predict the label of a sequence of tokens. The network contains three main layers: (i) the character-enhanced token-embedding layer, (ii) the label prediction layer, and (iii) the label sequence optimization layer. The word embeddings are fed to the first layer (i.e token-embedding).

3.2.3 Baseline Word Embedding

As a baseline for our comparisons, we decided to use the embeddings available from the University of Chile NLP Group[11]. The embeddings are trained based on the SBWC corpus and the training settings are the same we have shown in Section 2.3, thus making our comparisons fair.

One big difference between our training process is related to the corpora used. SBWC is a general-domain corpus, comprised of approximately 1.4 billion words, while our combined corpora contain roughly 1.2 million words. Thus, the general-domain corpus is approximately one order of magnitude larger than ours.

4 Experiments and Results

In this section, we detail how the experiments were carried out and the results we obtained for both intrinsic and extrinsic evaluation methods, as

---

[9]http://myminer.armi.monash.edu.au

[10]http://neuroner.com/
[11]https://github.com/uchile-nlp/spanish-word-embeddings

well as the comparisons with the baseline embedding presented in Section 3.2.3 and our embeddings, which we now call Spanish Health Embedding (SHE).

4.1 Intrinsic

In the intrinsic experiment, for the sake of a fair comparison between our proposed embedding and the baseline, we made sure that all the pairs being compared were available both in SHE and in the SBWC. For this, we checked for each pair of translated CUIs (explained in Section 3.1) if the words were present in both embeddings vocabularies. For multi-word terms, we averaged individual word vectors to compose the final term vector. The final number of compared pairs for each translated dataset are: UMNSRS-sim(322), UMNSRS-rel(252) and MayoSRS(101).

Regarding the evaluation, we calculated the cosine distance for each pair of terms and later compared those values with the human annotated ones in the datasets by means of Pearson correlation coefficient (ρ).

In Table 2, we depict the results for the comparison for each dataset regarding the Pearson correlation coefficient. One can notice that SHE presented the highest coefficient for the three used datasets by a large margin, being such statistically significant for all of them, except to SBWC with the MayoSRS dataset. Thus, as for intrinsic evaluation, we can assume that our embeddings are better than the general-domain embedding trained on SBWC.

Table 2: Comparison of the intrinsic evaluation between the proposed embeddings (SHE) and the general-domain ones (SBWC). Bold numbers represent the best results for each dataset, while asterisc means that such coefficient was statistically significant.

	SHE (our)	SBWC
Dataset	ρ	ρ
UMNSRS-sim	**0.5826***	0.4319*
UMNSRS-rel	**0.5239***	0.3947*
MayoSRS	**0.3174***	0.1237

4.2 Extrinsic

For the extrinsic evaluation, we used the NeuroNER framework, which was described in Section 3.2.2, with a biomedical corpus of clinical notes described in Section 3.2.1. The corpus has 4 entity labels: Proteins, Normalizable Chemicals, No-Normalizable Chemicals, and Unclear mentions. The reason for such lables is that they can be normalized to a fixed ontology, in the case of Proteins and Chemicals, while some chemicals cannot be normalzied or are unclear. Since the number of "No-Normalizable" mentions is very low compared to all labels, we did not include them in our evaluation.

We trained NeuroNER with the following standard parameters using our embeddings and the SBWC one:

- Data splitting: 80% training, 10% validation, 10% test. Stratified and fixed for both embeddings;

- Character-embedding dimension: 25

- Charater LSTM hidden state dimension : 25

- Token LSTM hidden state dimension: 300

- Patience: 10

- Maximum number of epochs: 100

- Optimizer: SGD

- Learning rate: 0.005

- Dropout rate: 0.5

In Table 3 we show the results of our embeddings compared to the SBWC trained with the same parameters as detailed in Section 2.3. One can notice that our proposed embedding achieved the best results in the validation set for all the named entity labels. As for the test set, we achieved the best scores in 8 out of 13 possible evaluations. But we must notice that as overall performance, our system achieved an F1 score of 88.18%, while the baseline achieved only 87.76%. Thus, our embeddings showed to be superior to general-domain one in this extrinsic evaluation.

4.3 Visual Evaluation

In Figures 2 and 3, we show the PCA (Principal Component Analysis) projections of our embeddings and the SBWC, respectively. We tried to follow the standards of Pakhomov et al. (2010) to categorize the terms using UMLS semantic types in the following categories: symptoms, diseases and drugs. Better quality and larger figures can be accessed online[12]

---

[12]http://doi.org/10.5281/zenodo.2542722

Table 3: Comparison of the extrinsic evaluation between the proposed embeddings (SHE) and the general-domain ones (SBWC). Bold numbers represent the best results for each metric and data parition, with Val meaning validation set.

	SHE (our)		SBWC	
	Val	Test	Val	Test
Overall				
Accuracy	**99.51**	**99.62**	99.45	99.57
Precision	**90.63**	90.42	90.30	**90.87**
Recall	**88.25**	**86.03**	86.12	84.45
F1	**89.42**	**88.17**	88.16	87.76
Normalizables				
Precision	**92.82**	93.18	91.87	**93.93**
Recall	**89.81**	88.09	88.89	88.34
F1	**91.29**	90.56	90.35	**91.05**
Proteins				
Precision	87.86	**86.94**	88.22	86.19
Recall	**87.86**	84.52	84.39	81.75
F1	**87.86**	85.71	86.26	83.91
Unclear				
Precision	**100**	84.21	92.86	88.24
Recall	**81.25**	**84.21**	81.25	78.95
F1	**89.66**	84.21	86.67	83.33

One can notice that in Figure 2, there is some overlapping between the disease and symptoms categories, but they are not as much overlapped as shown in Figure 3. In addition, in our embeddings, on the top of the drugs cluster, one can see that most of the antibiotics are clustered together (e.g. *penicilina, eritromicina, cefazolina, doxiciclina*). However, in the SBWC projection, such drugs are spread inside the cluster. Interestingly, for both embeddings, the words *hierro, calamina, ajo, alcohol* are the ones that are more closer to the other two clusters.

5 Discussion and Conclusion

By the intrinsic and extrinsic experiments performed in Sections 4.1 and 4.2 we were able to show that our proposed embeddings can provide better performance than a general-domain one, even being trained in a corpus one order of magnitude smaller. We made our embeddings available in `http://doi.org/10.5281/zenodo.2542722`.

By performing a visual evaluation of the PCA projections of our embeddings and a general-domain one, we also provided strong evidence that the ones trained in a in-domain corpus can provide better-defined clusters of words.

We oversee that the embeddings we provide can be used in many different applications that require them as a resource, especially the ones which employ artificial neural networks. For instance, we studied the application in a named entity recognition example, but they can be used for sentence similarity evaluation, text classification, machine translation, clustering, relation extraction, for instance.

6 Acknowledgements

This work was supported by the Encargo de Gestion SEAD-CNIO and SEAD-BSC of the Spanish National Plan for the Advancement of Language technologies, the ICTUSnet INTERREG Sudoe programme and the Amazon AWS Cloud Credits for Research.

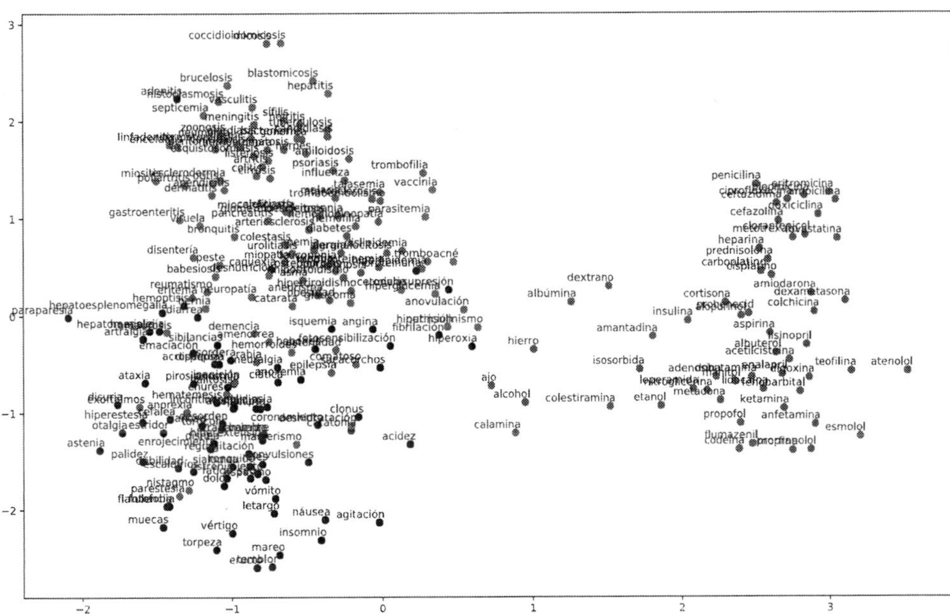

Figure 2: PCA projection of the UMNSRS concepts using our embeddings. Black means symptoms-related terms, red means disease-related terms, while green means drug-related terms.

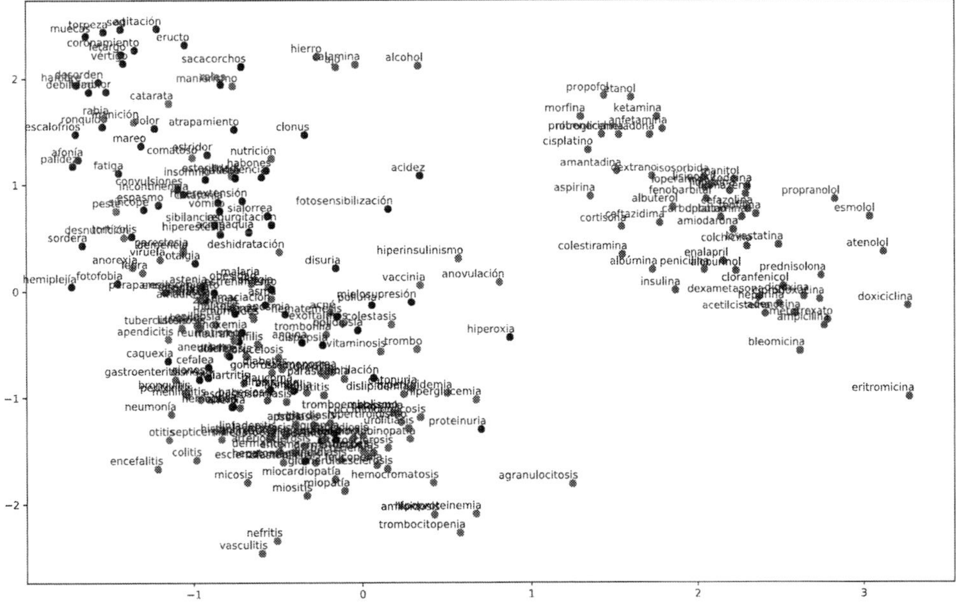

Figure 3: PCA projection of the UMNSRS concepts using the SBWC embeddings. Black means symptoms-related terms, red means disease-related terms, while green means drug-related terms.

References

Qingyu Chen, Yifan Peng, and Zhiyong Lu. 2018. Biosentvec: creating sentence embeddings for biomedical texts. *arXiv preprint arXiv:1810.09302*.

Billy Chiu, Gamal Crichton, Anna Korhonen, and Sampo Pyysalo. 2016. How to train good word embeddings for biomedical nlp. In *Proceedings of the 15th workshop on biomedical natural language processing*, pages 166–174.

Jason PC Chiu and Eric Nichols. 2016. Named entity recognition with bidirectional lstm-cnns. *Transactions of the Association for Computational Linguistics*, 4:357–370.

Franck Dernoncourt, Ji Young Lee, and Peter Szolovits. 2017. Neuroner: an easy-to-use program for named-entity recognition based on neural networks. *arXiv preprint arXiv:1705.05487*.

Sahar Ghannay, Benoit Favre, Yannick Esteve, and Nathalie Camelin. 2016. Word embedding evaluation and combination. In *LREC*, pages 300–305.

Ignacio Iacobacci, Mohammad Taher Pilehvar, and Roberto Navigli. 2016. Embeddings for word sense disambiguation: An evaluation study. In *Proceedings of the 54th Annual Meeting of the Association for Computational Linguistics (Volume 1: Long Papers)*, volume 1, pages 897–907.

Alistair EW Johnson, Tom J Pollard, Lu Shen, H Lehman Li-wei, Mengling Feng, Mohammad Ghassemi, Benjamin Moody, Peter Szolovits, Leo Anthony Celi, and Roger G Mark. 2016. Mimic-iii, a freely accessible critical care database. *Scientific data*, 3:160035.

Han Kyul Kim, Hyunjoong Kim, and Sungzoon Cho. 2017. Bag-of-concepts: Comprehending document representation through clustering words in distributed representation. *Neurocomputing*, 266:336–352.

Yuan Ling, Yuan An, Mengwen Liu, Sadid A Hasan, Yetian Fan, and Xiaohua Hu. 2017. Integrating extra knowledge into word embedding models for biomedical nlp tasks. In *2017 International Joint Conference on Neural Networks (IJCNN)*, pages 968–975. IEEE.

Tomas Mikolov, Kai Chen, Greg Corrado, and Jeffrey Dean. 2013a. Efficient estimation of word representations in vector space. *arXiv preprint arXiv:1301.3781*.

Tomas Mikolov, Edouard Grave, Piotr Bojanowski, Christian Puhrsch, and Armand Joulin. 2018. Advances in pre-training distributed word representations. In *Proceedings of the International Conference on Language Resources and Evaluation (LREC 2018)*.

Tomas Mikolov, Ilya Sutskever, Kai Chen, Greg S Corrado, and Jeff Dean. 2013b. Distributed representations of words and phrases and their compositionality. In *Advances in neural information processing systems*, pages 3111–3119.

Tomas Mikolov, Wen-tau Yih, and Geoffrey Zweig. 2013c. Linguistic regularities in continuous space word representations. In *Proceedings of the 2013 Conference of the North American Chapter of the Association for Computational Linguistics: Human Language Technologies*, pages 746–751.

Preslav Nakov, Alan Ritter, Sara Rosenthal, Fabrizio Sebastiani, and Veselin Stoyanov. 2016. Semeval-2016 task 4: Sentiment analysis in twitter. In *Proceedings of the 10th international workshop on semantic evaluation (semeval-2016)*, pages 1–18.

Serguei Pakhomov, Bridget McInnes, Terrence Adam, Ying Liu, Ted Pedersen, and Genevieve B Melton. 2010. Semantic similarity and relatedness between clinical terms: an experimental study. In *AMIA annual symposium proceedings*, volume 2010, page 572. American Medical Informatics Association.

Serguei VS Pakhomov, Ted Pedersen, Bridget McInnes, Genevieve B Melton, Alexander Ruggieri, and Christopher G Chute. 2011. Towards a framework for developing semantic relatedness reference standards. *Journal of biomedical informatics*, 44(2):251–265.

Kirk Roberts. 2016. Assessing the corpus size vs. similarity trade-off for word embeddings in clinical nlp. In *Proceedings of the Clinical Natural Language Processing Workshop (ClinicalNLP)*, pages 54–63.

Sunil Sahu and Ashish Anand. 2015. Evaluating distributed word representations for capturing semantics of biomedical concepts. *Proceedings of BioNLP 15*, pages 158–163.

Sara Santiso, Arantza Casillas, Alicia Pérez, and Maite Oronoz. 2018. Word embeddings for negation detection in health records written in spanish. *Soft Computing*, pages 1–7.

Tobias Schnabel, Igor Labutov, David Mimno, and Thorsten Joachims. 2015. Evaluation methods for unsupervised word embeddings. In *Proceedings of the 2015 Conference on Empirical Methods in Natural Language Processing*, pages 298–307.

Isabel Segura-Bedmar and Paloma Martínez. 2017. Simplifying drug package leaflets written in spanish by using word embedding. *Journal of biomedical semantics*, 8(1):45.

Marta Villegas, Ander Intxaurrondo, Aitor Gonzalez-Agirre, Montserrat Marimón, and Martin Krallinger. 2018. The mespen resource for english-spanish medical machine translation and terminologies: Census of parallel corpora, glossaries and term translations. In *Proceedings of the LREC 2018 Workshop "MultilingualBIO: Multilingual Biomedical Text Processing"*, Paris, France. European Language Resources Association (ELRA).

Liang-Chih Yu, Jin Wang, K Robert Lai, and Xuejie Zhang. 2017. Refining word embeddings for sentiment analysis. In *Proceedings of the 2017 Conference on Empirical Methods in Natural Language Processing*, pages 534–539.

Dongwen Zhang, Hua Xu, Zengcai Su, and Yunfeng Xu. 2015. Chinese comments sentiment classification based on word2vec and svmperf. *Expert Systems with Applications*, 42(4):1857–1863.

Yaoyun Zhang, Hee-Jin Li, Jingqi Wang, Trevor Cohen, Kirk Roberts, and Hua Xu. 2018. Adapting word embeddings from multiple domains to symptom recognition from psychiatric notes. *AMIA Summits on Translational Science Proceedings*, 2017:281.

Attention Neural Model for Temporal Relation Extraction

Sijia Liu[1,2], Liwei Wang[1], Vipin Chaudhary[2], Hongfang Liu[1]
[1]Department of Health Sciences Research, Mayo Clinic
{lastname.firstname}@mayo.edu
[2]Department of Computer Science and Engineering, University at Buffalo
vipin@buffalo.edu

Abstract

Neural network models have shown promise in the temporal relation extraction task. In this paper, we present the attention based neural network model to extract the containment relations within sentences from clinical narratives. The attention mechanism used on top of GRU model outperforms the existing state-of-the-art neural network models on THYME corpus in intra-sentence temporal relation extraction.

1 Introduction

A well-known challenge in leveraging electronic health records (EHRs) for research is to extract the information embedded in clinical texts. The recent progress in Natural Language Processing (NLP) techniques has facilitated the use of information in text for various clinical applications (Wang et al., 2017). One important NLP task in the clinical domain is to extract temporal relations between events and time expressions from clinical text for various EHR-based applications, such as clinical decision support and predictive modeling.

Along with studies in modeling clinical temporal events using structured EHR data (Zhao et al., 2017; Che et al., 2018), a series of temporal information extraction share tasks have been organized to encourage community efforts on the temporal relation extraction on unstructured clinical texts from EHR, such as i2b2 (Informatics for Integrating Biology and the Bedside) 2012 challenge (Sun et al., 2013) and Clinical TempEval shared tasks (Bethard et al., 2014, 2015, 2016). While both corpora are based on de-identified clinical notes, the major differences between i2b2 and TempEval are the evaluation and temporal event modeling. The i2b2 challenge evaluation enumerates all possible entity pairs from a clinical document into the evaluation, while the TempEval tasks leverage the concept of narrative containers which

will enhance conventional temporal relations. In this study, we focus on the containment information extraction in TempEval.

In addition to the feature-based machine learning approaches such as Support Vector Machines (SVM) and conditional random field from top-performing TempEval 2016 systems (Lee et al., 2016; Abdulsalam et al., 2016; Tourille et al., 2016), there are several machine learning systems proposed after the shared task. Leeuwenberg and Moens (2017) used a structured learning method to predict temporal relations: Dligach et al. (2017) proposed an XML tag representation neural models such as Convolutional Neural Network (CNN) and Long Short Term Memory (LSTM) (Hochreiter and Schmidhuber, 1997) to mark the positions of the entities and achieved better performance compared to token position embeddings. They also evaluated the contains relations solely on medical events. Lin et al. (2016) experimented on different representations of XML tags proposed in (Dligach et al., 2017), and the results indicated that the input representation is an importance factor for the performance of neural models. A bidirectional LSTM (BiLSTM) approach has also been proposed in (Tourille et al., 2017). Their model utilized character embeddings to create a hierarchical LSTM model with corpus entities attributes as input into the embedding layer of their neural architecture. Recent related works using self-training (Lin et al., 2018) and human-like temporal reasoning via tree-based LSTM-RNN (Galvan et al., 2018) also achieved good performance in various evaluation scenarios, but direct comparisons are challenging due to differences in evaluation.

Inspired by visual attention models for object recognition in computer vision (Xu et al., 2015; Mnih et al., 2014), attention mechanism has also been successfully applied in several NLP tasks

Proceedings of the 2nd Clinical Natural Language Processing Workshop, pages 134–139
Minneapolis, Minnesota, June 7, 2019. ©2019 Association for Computational Linguistics

such as machine translation (Luong et al., 2015), machine reading (Cheng et al., 2016), document classification (Yang et al., 2016) and relation extraction (Lin et al., 2016), to obtain state-of-the-art performance. The attention layer oversees the entire sequence of recurrent neural network (RNN) units and is trained to pay more "attention" to salient units.

In this paper, we present an attention neural model to identify containment relations from clinical narratives with annotated medical events and temporal information. The model achieves state-of-the-art performance in intra-sentence temporal relation extraction while using minimal entity features and external knowledge.

2 Materials

We use the THYME (Temporal Histories of Your Medical Event) corpus (Styler IV et al., 2014) to evaluate our proposed models. THYME corpus is extracted from Mayo Clinic colon cancer data, which contains clinical notes from 200 patients. The corpus is manually de-identified to remove patient identification, and is fully annotated into two types of entities: Timex3 and Event. Timex3 contains temporal information like event dates and timestamps. The definition of event is a broad concept of patient health related conditions and mentions.

All the Event entities contain 5 attributes, "Modality", "Degree", "Polarity", "Type" and "DocTimeRel". The Document Time Relations (DocTimeRel) specifies the temporal relation of the event to the time of service. In this study, we focused on the temporal relations between two different entities within one sentence, namely intra-sentence relations as referred in (Tourille et al., 2017). Therefore, we did not include DocTimeRel, which is an event attribute, into our model and evaluation.

3 Methods

We define the temporal relation extraction problem as a relation classification problem among relation candidates generated from annotated entities. Specifically, for all the events within one sentence, we enumerate all possible entity pairs as relation candidates. Then, we assign relation labels based on the gold standard annotations provided with the corpora. In THYME corpus, the gold standard annotations consist of relation between two entities and its relation type. When we prepare the dataset for relation classification, for each combination of entities, we have three potential labels: 1) the first entity "CONTAINS" the second entity in temporal; 2) the first entity is "CONTAINED" by the second entity; 3) the two entities do not have a containment temporal relation, i.e. "NA".

3.1 Input Representation

Given clinical narratives with annotated entities, we first use the Punkt sentence tokenizer[1] to separate the sectionized raw text into section titles and sentences. Then an associated encoding of entities into XML tags are constructed, following the work of Lin et al (Lin et al., 2017). The event entities are surrounded by "<e>" and "</e>". The temporal entities are replaced by the special XML tags from time class provided with the entity annotations, e.g. "<time>", "<date>", "<duration>" and "<prepostexp>", and surrounded by "<t>" and "</t>". In our preliminary experiments, this entity representation also leads to better results than position embeddings, which use relative distances between two entities as index to compute the high-dimensional embeddings of each word (Zeng et al., 2014).

3.2 Attention Neural Models

To improve the system performance of neural network models, we would like to leverage the emerging attention mechanism. Attention based RNN uses an attention layer to capture the salient units of a sequence by maintaining a context vector for the sequence models. Word-level attention weights can be interpreted as importance measure in given contexts, i.e. temporal relation indicators for each relation instance of a sentence. The architecture of our proposed model is shown in Figure 1. In the example, the entities "monitored" and "three months" are surrounded by the XML tags introduced above. The Timex3 entity "three months" is replaced by the entity type "<duration>" when feeding into the word embedding layer. Ideally, a high attention weight will be given to the preposition "in", as it is the word expressing the containment relations between the event and the time. Besides, the entity and the tags may also need to contribute to the discrimination of different relation types.

---

[1] `https://www.nltk.org/_modules/nltk/tokenize/punkt.html`

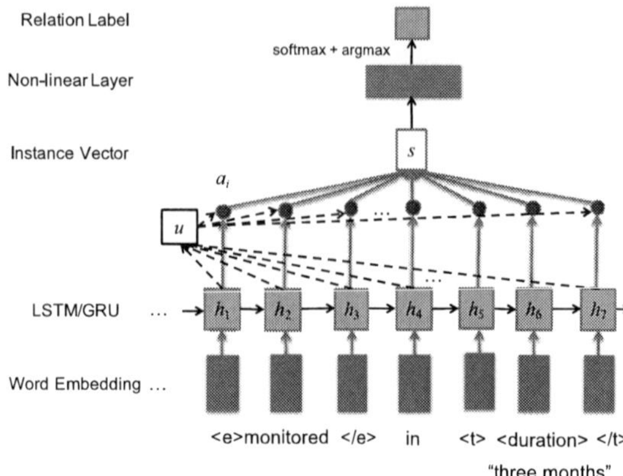

Figure 1: The architecture of attention based RNN for temporal relation extraction.

The vectors of RNN units are denoted as h_i, where i is the index of the input tokens in the generated relation instances. Similar to (Yang et al., 2016), we would like to obtain a word-level attention weights a_i for each entity pair, which is calculated based on the sequence of RNN outputs, either LSTM or Gated Recurrent Unit (GRU) proposed in (Cho et al., 2014). To reward the salient units for relation classification, a trainable context vector u_v is used to retrieve the attention weights a_i, and it is computed from trainable parameters W_v and b_v from the attention layer. The word-level attention weight a_i is calculated using a softmax function. Afterwards, the sentence vector s is computed as the weighted sum of a_i. Specifically, the sentence vector can be computed as:

$$u_i = \tanh(W_v h_i + b_v),$$

$$a_i = \frac{\exp(u_i^T u_v)}{\sum_i \exp(u_i^T u_v)},$$

$$s = \sum_i a_i h_i.$$

The word embedding, RNN and attention layers combined can be regarded as an instance encoder. For each relation instance generated as described in Section 3.1, those layers together encode the instance into a multi-dimensional vector s. The encoded relation instance vector s is then fed into a fully connected layer. The output dimension of the fully connected layer is set to the number of potential labels, which is 3 in this study.

Then, a softmax function normalizes the outputs into a predicted probability of 3 labels, where the sparse cross entropy loss is calculated and minimized during training. We take the maximum probability as the relation label for the evaluation of closure-enhanced precision, recall and F1-score.

3.3 Evaluation

The official evaluation scripts of TempEval[2] use the concept of "narrative containers" (Miller et al., 2013) to validate the results. Narrative containers is a set of events that contains multiple temporal relations. The official evaluation uses narrative container to evaluate the system performance, instead of evaluating directly from the relation classification results by instances. The usage of closure is intended to reduce the penalty caused by extracting the implicit relations that can be inferred between events but are not included in the annotation.

Following the shared task of TempEval 2016 and recent related work on the THYME corpus, we focus on the extraction of temporal containment relations. This is because the prevalence of contains relations is much higher than other temporal relations.

4 Experiments and Discussion

We ran our experiments on similar settings as (Dligach et al., 2017). The cross sentence relations are excluded in our evaluation.

The models are implemented in Keras with Tensorflow backend. The experiments are done on a computing server with NVIDIA Tesla P40 GPU. Each epoch of attention based LSTM took approximately 300 seconds while GRU will take approximately 250 seconds, due to fewer trainable parameters needed for each unit.

The 300-dimension word embeddings from Glove-6B[3] are selected as the input based on our preliminary experiments on trained embeddings from biomedical domain (Wang et al., 2018) as well as the THYME corpus. The embedding of out-of-vocabulary words, including special XML tags, are determined by random sampling from unit distribution in [-0.1, 0.1]. The hyperparameters are selected based on the optimal combination from the development set when training on

---

[2] https://github.com/bethard/anaforatools

[3] https://nlp.stanford.edu/projects/glove/

Model	Event-Time			Event-Event		
	P	R	F1	P	R	F1
THYME (Dligach et al., 2017)	0.577	0.845	0.685	0.595	0.572	**0.584**
CNN tokens (Dligach et al., 2017)	0.683	0.717	0.700	0.688	0.412	0.515
ATT-LSTM	0.770	0.722	0.744	0.535	0.582	0.558
ATT-GRU	0.765	0.737	**0.750**	0.617	0.550	0.579

Table 1: Performance comparison in Event-Time and Event-Event containment relations on test set

Model	P	R	F1
BiLSTM (Tourille et al., 2017)	0.670	0.681	0.675
BiLSTM + cTAKES (Tourille et al., 2017)	0.663	0.704	0.683
ATT-LSTM	0.687	0.666	0.676
ATT-GRU	0.698	0.684	**0.690**

Table 2: Performance comparison in intra-sentence containment relations on test set

the training set. To avoid potential overfitting during the training phase, we apply drop out technique (Srivastava et al., 2014) with the drop out rate of 0.5. Adam optimizer (Kingma and Ba, 2014) is used with learning rate 0.001 to train the model and sparse categorical cross entropy as the loss function. We apply early stopping during training to avoid overfitting by terminating the training process if there is no validation accuracy increase in consecutive 4 epochs. Then the training and development set are combined to train the model while tested on the testing set. The batch size of training is 64, and the unit size for RNN units is set 128 based on hyperparameter tuning.

The evaluation results on Event-Time and Event-Event relation extraction in closure-enhanced precision (P), recall (R) and F1-score are shown in Table 1. "ATT-" denotes our attention based RNN models. The results in Table 1 are directly comparable with the work in (Dligach et al., 2017), since the models of Event-Time Event-Event relations are trained separately. The most significant improvement is from the Event-Time relation extraction, where the ATT-GRU (0.750) outperforms the CNN model by 0.050. In the Event-Event relations, ATT-GRU model outperforms the CNN model, but is not as good as the feature based SVM model in the THYME system (-0.05). One potential reason for the performance gain is that the ATT models oversee all units from the RNN layer rather than focusing on the max pooling of local features as CNN.

When we combined both Event-Time and Event-Event relations together, Table 2 shows the results for all temporal relations within each sentence. Compared to other neural network models, our proposed ATT-GRU (0.690 F1) is favorably comparable to the BiLSTM model incorporating cTAKES outputs[4] (BiLSTM+cTAKES) and character embeddings (+0.007). We only use the raw text and annotated entity types, while BiLSTM+cTAKES requires finer granularity of the UMLS[5] entity types and semantic types as inputs. It is our future perspective to utilize character-level information and entity attributes as the input to further improve our system. ATT-GRU performs better than LSTM in all the three evaluation scenarios. One potential reason is that GRU has less trainable parameters compared to LSTM, thus it may converge better in a corpus with relatively limited positive relational instances.

One challenge for neural models in the temporal relation extraction task is class imbalance. The majority of the errors are caused by the confusion between negative ("NA") and positive ("CONTAINS"+"CONTAINED") instances, while very few of the errors are from the confusion of "CONTAINS" and "CONTAINED" relations. The ratios between positive and negative relations of Event-Event, Event-Time and those combined are 1:3.4, 1:12.7 and 1:8.4, respectively. The class weights are tuned in the feature-based THYME system to improve the balance of precision and recall, but there is no such effort on other neural models in both our work and (Dligach et al., 2017).

---

[4]https://ctakes.apache.org/

[5]Unified Medical Language System: https://www.nlm.nih.gov/research/umls/

Lin et al. (2017) analyzed the impact of different XML tags for the temporal entities as inputs. The one-token tag representation for multi-word temporal repressions (e.g. replacing the Timex3 mention "March 11, 2014" by "<date>") shows improvements on the classification, which is also used in our study. Compared to Lin's method, our model is a single neural model instead of a combined model of CNN and SVM for Event-Event and Event-Time relations, respectively. Leeuwenberg and Moens (Leeuwenberg and Moens, 2017) used structured learning on all relations within token distance of 30. The framework can also be extended to model inter-sentence relations by adding such relation instances into the training and testing, but fine-tuned down-sampling needs to be done to optimize its performance.

5 Conclusion and Future Work

In this paper, we presented the attention-based neural networks on temporal relation extraction. The proposed attention based GRU model achieved state-of-the-art performance in intra-sentence containment temporal relation extraction on THYME corpus.

In future, we would like to adopt the hierarchical model with character embeddings in the word-level representation into our attention based neural networks. We would also like to explore the comparison between different variations of the attention mechanisms such as multi-head attention (Vaswani et al., 2017) and self-attention (Cheng et al., 2016; Verga et al., 2018).

Acknowledgment

We thank anonymous reviewers for their constructive feedbacks to this manuscript. The work is supported by National Library of Medicine grant R01LM011829 and National Science Foundation IPA grant. Opinions, findings and conclusions or recommendations expressed in this material are those of the authors and do not necessarily reflect the views of the National Institutes of Health or National Science Foundation.

References

Abdulrahman AAl Abdulsalam, Sumithra Velupillai, and Stephane Meystre. 2016. Utahbmi at semeval-2016 task 12: Extracting temporal information from clinical text. In *Proceedings of the 10th International Workshop on Semantic Evaluation (SemEval-2016)*, pages 1256–1262.

Steven Bethard, Leon Derczynski, James Pustejovsky, and Marc Verhagen. 2014. Clinical tempeval. *arXiv preprint arXiv:1403.4928*.

Steven Bethard, Leon Derczynski, Guergana Savova, James Pustejovsky, and Marc Verhagen. 2015. Semeval-2015 task 6: Clinical tempeval. In *SemEval@ NAACL-HLT*, pages 806–814.

Steven Bethard, Guergana Savova, Wei-Te Chen, Leon Derczynski, James Pustejovsky, and Marc Verhagen. 2016. Semeval-2016 task 12: Clinical tempeval. *Proceedings of SemEval*, pages 1052–1062.

Zhengping Che, Sanjay Purushotham, Kyunghyun Cho, David Sontag, and Yan Liu. 2018. Recurrent neural networks for multivariate time series with missing values. *Scientific reports*, 8(1):6085.

Jianpeng Cheng, Li Dong, and Mirella Lapata. 2016. Long short-term memory-networks for machine reading. *arXiv preprint arXiv:1601.06733*.

Kyunghyun Cho, Bart Van Merriënboer, Caglar Gulcehre, Dzmitry Bahdanau, Fethi Bougares, Holger Schwenk, and Yoshua Bengio. 2014. Learning phrase representations using rnn encoder-decoder for statistical machine translation. *arXiv preprint arXiv:1406.1078*.

Dmitriy Dligach, Timothy A. Miller, , Chen Lin, Steven Bethard, and Guergana Savova. 2017. Neural temporal relation extraction. In *Proceedings of the 15th Conference of the European Chapter of the Association for Computational Linguistics, EACL 2017, Valencia, Spain, April 3-7, 2017, Volume 2: Short Papers*, pages 746–751. Association for Computational Linguistics.

Diana Galvan, Naoaki Okazaki, Koji Matsuda, and Kentaro Inui. 2018. Investigating the challenges of temporal relation extraction from clinical text. In *Proceedings of the Ninth International Workshop on Health Text Mining and Information Analysis*, pages 55–64, Brussels, Belgium. Association for Computational Linguistics.

Sepp Hochreiter and Jürgen Schmidhuber. 1997. Long short-term memory. *Neural computation*, 9(8):1735–1780.

Diederik P. Kingma and Jimmy Ba. 2014. Adam: A method for stochastic optimization. *CoRR*, abs/1412.6980.

Hee-Jin Lee, Hua Xu, Jingqi Wang, Yaoyun Zhang, Sungrim Moon, Jun Xu, and Yonghui Wu. 2016. Uthealth at semeval-2016 task 12: an end-to-end system for temporal information extraction from clinical notes. In *Proceedings of the 10th International Workshop on Semantic Evaluation, SemEval@NAACL-HLT 2016, San Diego, CA, USA, June 16-17, 2016*, pages 1292–1297. The Association for Computer Linguistics.

Tuur Leeuwenberg and Marie-Francine Moens. 2017. Structured learning for temporal relation extraction from clinical records. In *Proceedings of the 15th Conference of the European Chapter of the Association for Computational Linguistics*.

Chen Lin, T. Miller, Dmitriy Dligach, Steven Bethard, and Guergana Savova. 2017. Representations of time expressions for temporal relation extraction with convolutional neural networks. In *BioNLP*.

Chen Lin, Timothy Miller, Dmitriy Dligach, Hadi Amiri, Steven Bethard, and Guergana Savova. 2018. Self-training improves recurrent neural networks performance for temporal relation extraction. In *Proceedings of the Ninth International Workshop on Health Text Mining and Information Analysis*, pages 165–176, Brussels, Belgium. Association for Computational Linguistics.

Yankai Lin, Shiqi Shen, Zhiyuan Liu, Huanbo Luan, and Maosong Sun. 2016. Neural relation extraction with selective attention over instances. In *ACL*.

Minh-Thang Luong, Hieu Pham, and Christopher D Manning. 2015. Effective approaches to attention-based neural machine translation. *arXiv preprint arXiv:1508.04025*.

Timothy A Miller, Steven Bethard, Dmitriy Dligach, Sameer Pradhan, Chen Lin, and Guergana K Savova. 2013. Discovering narrative containers in clinical text. *ACL 2013*, page 18.

Volodymyr Mnih, Nicolas Heess, Alex Graves, et al. 2014. Recurrent models of visual attention. In *Advances in Neural Information Processing Systems*, pages 2204–2212.

Nitish Srivastava, Geoffrey E. Hinton, Alex Krizhevsky, Ilya Sutskever, and Ruslan Salakhutdinov. 2014. Dropout: a simple way to prevent neural networks from overfitting. *Journal of Machine Learning Research*, 15(1):1929–1958.

William F Styler IV, Steven Bethard, Sean Finan, Martha Palmer, Sameer Pradhan, Piet C de Groen, Brad Erickson, Timothy Miller, Chen Lin, Guergana Savova, and James Pustejovsky. 2014. Temporal annotation in the clinical domain. *Transactions of the Association for Computational Linguistics*, 2:143–154.

Weiyi Sun, Anna Rumshisky, and Ozlem Uzuner. 2013. Evaluating temporal relations in clinical text: 2012 i2b2 challenge. *Journal of the American Medical Informatics Association*, 20(5):806–813.

Julien Tourille, Olivier Ferret, Aurélie Névéol, and Xavier Tannier. 2016. Limsi-cot at semeval-2016 task 12: Temporal relation identification using a pipeline of classifiers. In *Proceedings of the 10th International Workshop on Semantic Evaluation (SemEval-2016)*, pages 1136–1142.

Julien Tourille, Olivier Ferret, Aurélie Névéol, and Xavier Tannier. 2017. Neural architecture for temporal relation extraction: A bi-lstm approach for detecting narrative containers. In *Proceedings of the 55th Annual Meeting of the Association for Computational Linguistics, ACL 2017, Vancouver, Canada, July 30 - August 4, Volume 2: Short Papers*, pages 224–230. Association for Computational Linguistics.

Ashish Vaswani, Noam Shazeer, Niki Parmar, Jakob Uszkoreit, Llion Jones, Aidan N Gomez, Łukasz Kaiser, and Illia Polosukhin. 2017. Attention is all you need. In *Advances in Neural Information Processing Systems*, pages 5998–6008.

Patrick Verga, Emma Strubell, and Andrew McCallum. 2018. Simultaneously self-attending to all mentions for full-abstract biological relation extraction. In *Proceedings of the 2018 Conference of the North American Chapter of the Association for Computational Linguistics: Human Language Technologies, Volume 1 (Long Papers)*, pages 872–884. Association for Computational Linguistics.

Yanshan Wang, Sijia Liu, Naveed Afzal, Majid Rastegar-Mojarad, Liwei Wang, Feichen Shen, Paul Kingsbury, and Hongfang Liu. 2018. A comparison of word embeddings for the biomedical natural language processing. *Journal of biomedical informatics*, 87:12–20.

Yanshan Wang, Liwei Wang, Majid Rastegar-Mojarad, Sungrim Moon, Feichen Shen, Naveed Afzal, Sijia Liu, Yuqun Zeng, Saeed Mehrabi, Sunghwan Sohn, et al. 2017. Clinical information extraction applications: a literature review. *Journal of biomedical informatics*.

Kelvin Xu, Jimmy Ba, Ryan Kiros, Kyunghyun Cho, Aaron Courville, Ruslan Salakhudinov, Rich Zemel, and Yoshua Bengio. 2015. Show, attend and tell: Neural image caption generation with visual attention. In *International Conference on Machine Learning*, pages 2048–2057.

Zichao Yang, Diyi Yang, Chris Dyer, Xiaodong He, Alexander J Smola, and Eduard H Hovy. 2016. Hierarchical attention networks for document classification. In *HLT-NAACL*, pages 1480–1489.

Daojian Zeng, Kang Liu, Siwei Lai, Guangyou Zhou, Jun Zhao, et al. 2014. Relation classification via convolutional deep neural network. In *COLING*, pages 2335–2344.

Jing Zhao, Panagiotis Papapetrou, Lars Asker, and Henrik Boström. 2017. Learning from heterogeneous temporal data in electronic health records. *Journal of Biomedical Informatics*, 65:105–119.

Automatically Generating Psychiatric Case Notes From Digital Transcripts of Doctor-Patient Conversations

Nazmul Kazi
Gianforte School of Computing
Montana State University
Bozeman, MT, USA
kazinazmul.hasan@montana.edu

Indika Kahanda
Gianforte School of Computing
Montana State University
Bozeman, MT, USA
indika.kahanda@montana.edu

Abstract

Electronic health records (EHRs) are notorious for reducing the face-to-face time with patients while increasing the screen-time for clinicians leading to burnout. This is especially problematic for psychiatry care in which maintaining consistent eye-contact and non-verbal cues are just as important as the spoken words. In this ongoing work, we explore the feasibility of automatically generating psychiatric EHR case notes from digital transcripts of doctor-patient conversation using a two-step approach: (1) predicting semantic topics for segments of transcripts using supervised machine learning, and (2) generating formal text of those segments using natural language processing. Through a series of preliminary experimental results obtained through a collection of synthetic and real-life transcripts, we demonstrate the viability of this approach.

1 Introduction

An electronic health record (EHR) is a digital version of a patient's health record. EHRs were introduced as a means to improve the health care system. EHRs are real-time and store patient's records in one place and can be shared with other clinicians, researchers and authorized personals instantly and securely. The use and implementation of EHRs were spurred by the 2009 US Health Information Technology for Economic and Clinical Health (HITECH) Act and 78% office-based clinicians reported using some form of EHR by 2013 (Hsiao and Hing, 2014).

Presently, all clinicians are required to digitally document their interactions with their patients using EHRs. These digital documents are called case notes. Manually typing case notes is time consuming (Payne et al., 2015) and limits the face-to-face time with their patients, which leads to both patient dis-satisfaction and clinician burnout.

Limited face-to-face time is especially disadvantageous for working with mental health patients where the psychiatrist could easily miss a non-verbal cue highly important for the correct diagnosis. Moreover, EHR's usability related problems lead to unstructured and incomplete case notes (Kaufman et al., 2016) which are difficult to search and access.

Due to the above-mentioned downsides of EHRs, there have been recent attempts for developing novel methods for incorporating various techniques and technologies such as natural language processing (NLP) for improving the EHR documentation process. In 2015, American Medical Informatics Association reported time-consuming data entry is one of the major problems in EHRs and recommended to improve EHRs by allowing multiple modes of data entry such as audio recording and handwritten notes (Payne et al., 2015). Nagy et al. (2008) developed a voice-controlled EHR system for dentists, called *DentVoice*, that enables dentists to control the EHR and take notes over voice and without taking off their gloves while working with their patients. Kaufman et al. (2016) also developed an NLP-enabled dictation-based data entry where clinicians can write case notes over voice and able to reduce the time by more than 60%.

Psychiatrists mostly collect information from their patients through conversations and these conversations are the primary source of their case notes. In a long-term project in collaboration with National Alliance of Mental illness (NAMI) Montana and the Center for Mental Health Research and Recovery (CMHRR) at Montana State University, we envision a pipeline that automatically records a doctor-patient conversation, generates the corresponding digital transcript of the conversation using speech-to-text API and uses natural language processing and machine learning tech-

Proceedings of the 2nd Clinical Natural Language Processing Workshop, pages 140–148
Minneapolis, Minnesota, June 7, 2019. ©2019 Association for Computational Linguistics

niques to predict and/ or extract important pieces of information from the text. This relevant text is then converted to a more formal written version of the text and are used for auto-populating the different sections of the EHR form.

In this work, we focus on the back-end of the above mentioned pipeline, i.e. we explore the feasibility of populating sections of EHR form using the information extracted from a digital transcript of a doctor-patient conversation. In order to gather gold-standard data, we develop a human powered digital transcript annotator and acquire annotated versions of digital transcripts of doctor-patient conversations with the help domain experts. As the first step in our two-step approach, we develop a machine learning model that can predict the semantic topics of segments of conversations. Then we develop natural language processing techniques to generate a formal written text using the corresponding segments. In this paper, we present our preliminary findings from these two tasks; Figure 1 depicts the high-level overview of our two-step approach.

Previous studies most related to our work are (1) Lacson et al. (2006) predicting semantic topics for medical dialogue turns in the home hemodialysis, and (2) Wallace et al. (2014) automatically annotating topics in transcripts of patient-provider interactions regarding antiretroviral adherence. While both studies successfully use machine learning for predicting semantic topics (albeit different topics to ours) they do not focus on the development of NLP models for text summarization (i.e. formal text generation).

The rest of the paper is structured as follows. We describe our two-step approach, data collection and processing, machine learning models and natural language processing methods in chapter 2. In chapter 3, we report and discuss the performance of our methods. We summarize our findings, discuss limitations and potential future work in chapter 4.

2 Methods

2.1 Approach

As depicted in Figure 1, we divide the task of generating case notes from digital transcripts of doctor-patient conversations into two sub tasks: (1) using supervised learning models to predict semantic topics for segments of the transcripts and then (2) using natural language processing models

to generate a more formal (i.e. written) version of the text which goes in to the corresponding section of the EHR form.

These semantic topics are suggested by the domain experts from NAMI Montana and correspond to the main sections of a typical EHR form. They are (1) Client details: personal information of a patient, such as name, age, birth date etc., (2) Chief complaint: refers to the information regarding a patient's primary problem for which the patient is seeking medical attention., (3) Medical history: any past medical condition(s), treatment(s) and record(s), (4) Family history: indicates medical history of a family member of the patient, and (5) Social history: refers to information about patient's social interactions, e.g. friends, work, family dinner etc. We call these semantic categories "EHR categories" interchangeably. The *formal text* is essentially the summary text that the clinician would write or type into the EHR form based on the interaction with the patient.

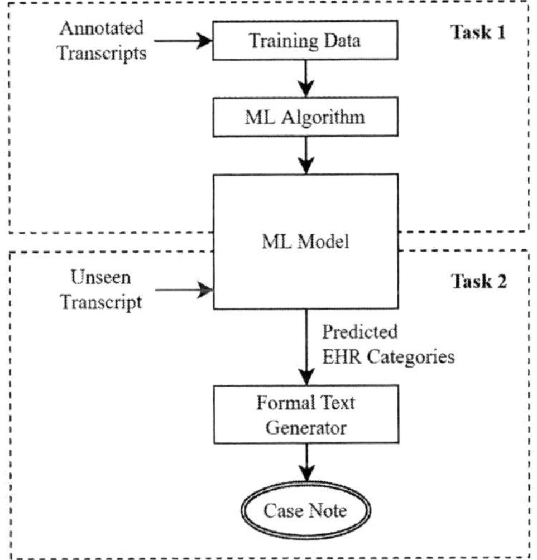

Figure 1: High-level overview of our approach. Task1: Predicting EHR categories. Task 2: Formal text generation. ML: Machine Learning. EHR: Electronic Heallth Record.

2.2 Transcripts of doctor-patient dialogue

Our raw dataset is composed of 18 digital transcripts of doctor-patient conversations and covers 11 presenting conditions. The presenting conditions are Attention-deficit/ hyperactivity disorder (ADHD), Alzheimer's disease, Anger, Anorexia, Anxiety, Bipolar, Borderline Personality Disorder (BPD), Depression, Obsessive Compulsive Disorder (OCD), Post Traumatic Stress Disorder (PTSD) and Schizophrenia. All transcripts are labeled with speaker tags "Doctor:" and "Patient:" to indicate the words uttered by each individual.

Thirteen of these transcripts are *synthetic* in that they are handwritten (i.e. typed) by a domain expert from NAMI Montana who has years of experience working with mental illness patients. Hence, each synthetic transcript represents a real case scenario of conversation between a patient (suffering from one of the presenting conditions mentioned above) and a psychiatric doctor/ clinician who verbally interviews the patient in a 2-person dialogue set up. Table 1 reports summary statistics.

Rest of the five transcripts are part of *Counseling & Therapy* database[1] from the Alexander Street website. Hence, we refer to them as AS transcripts for the rest of the paper. Each of these AS transcripts is generated from a real-life conversation between a patient and a clinician. Majority of these transcripts cover multiple mental conditions.

In order to annotate transcripts using semantic topics mentioned above, we develop a human-powered transcript annotator as shown in Figure 2, a responsive web application, that takes digital transcripts as input, breaks down each transcript into segments where each segment starts with a speaker tag (Doctor: or Patient:) and generates samples by pairing each doctor segment with the followed by patient segment. The application displays the generated samples, from one transcript at a time, in the same order as they appear in the transcript and allows the user to annotate them with one of the six semantic topics.

A group of three annotators including two domain-experts from NAMI Montana use the above annotator tool to single-annotate (through collaboration) all 18 transcripts. As highlighted in Figure 2, annotations are added at the *conversation pair* level. We define the conversation pair as the entire text associated with a consecutive pair of "Doctor:" and "Patient:" speaker tags. Each conversation pair is annotated with one of the five topics (i.e. EHR categories). These labels are based on the main focus/ subject/ topic of the corresponding conversation pair as judged by

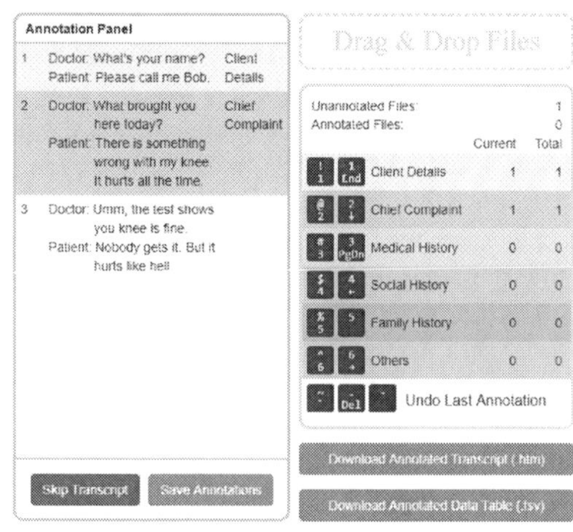

Figure 2: Screen shot of the human-powered transcript annotator. Left panel displays an example transcript while the semantic concepts are shown on the right.

the expert annotators. Any conversation pair that was found to be irrelevant to the five categories is annotated with a new category called "Others". Conversation pair level annotations eliminated the challenges in annotating a question or an answer on their own without the proper context provided by the preceding/ following sentences.

2.3 Task 1: Predicting EHR categories

In this task, we use the annotated digital transcripts to generate the training data to train supervised classification models using two different approaches. These two approaches mainly differ in how the transcripts were segmented into examples (i.e. training instances) for generating the training datasets as described in the sections 2.3.1 and 2.3.2. Regardless of the approach, we label the examples with one of the six class labels analogs to the semantic topics (EHR categories): Client Details, Chief Complaint, Family History, Social History, Medical History and Others.

2.3.1 Training data - Model 1

In this approach, we build a training dataset by taking a conversation pair as a single example (i.e. instance). Each example contains at least two sentences where the first sentence is spoken by the doctor and the second sentence is spoken by the patient. The class label for each example is the corresponding annotation from the original transcript; this results in six class labels. A short examples of the training dataset and distribution of class labels are reported in Tables 2 and 3.

---

[1]https://search.alexanderstreet.com/health-sciences/counseling-therapy

Property	Synthetic Transcripts			AS Transcripts		
	Total	Mean	STDEV	Total	Mean	STDEV
No. Sentences	1930	148.4	55.6	1390	278.0	74.9
No. Questions	513	39.4	19.8	188	37.6	7.1
No. Dialogue turns	861	66.2	40.0	684	136.8	55.0
No. Sentences spoken by the Doctor	751	57.7	30.0	581	116.2	44.3
No. Sentences spoken by the Patient	1179	90.6	33.2	809	161.8	60.5

Table 1: Summary statistics on 13 synthetic transcripts vs. 5 (AS) Alexander Street transcripts.

No.	Example		Class Label
1	Doctor:	How many voices do you hear?	Chief Complaint
	Patient:	Two. They talk all the time.	
2	Doctor:	Your record shows that you take antidepressants pills regularly. Do you hang out with your parents, co-workers or friends? Do you talk to them?	Social History
	Patient:	Sometimes I hang out with my mom. Yes, I talk to my co-workers but only for work. I used to have a friend who moved couple months ago and we don't talk anymore.	

Table 2: Examples in Model 1 training data.

Class Label	Synthetic		All
	Model 1	Model 2	
Chief Complaint	309	870	1746
Client Details	32	88	198
Family History	28	101	149
Medical History	34	74	85
Others	12	174	264
Social History	19	51	110
Total	434	1358	2552

Table 3: Distribution of class labels in training data. All: represents Model 2 training data with all 18 transcripts.

Segmenting the transcripts into training examples in this fashion is convenient because there is a one-to-one mapping between the semantic topics in the original annotated transcripts and the class labels of the examples; additional reconciliation is not needed. However, sometimes, the doctor or the patient talks about more than one topic (inside the same conversation pair). For example, although example 2 in Table 2 is labeled with Social History, the conversation pair is composed of information relevant to both the medical history and social history. Therefore, segmenting the transcript to smaller pieces could be more beneficial for improved overall performance. This is the motivation for the second approach mentioned in the next sec-tion.

2.3.2 Training data - Model 2

In this approach, we use a finer-level granularity (than conversation pairs) for segmenting the transcripts for generating training examples. We start with the Model 1 training data and tokenize the text of each example at the sentence level by identifying the sentence boundaries using sentence tokenizer in NLTK[2]. We first assign labels to each sentence based on the class label of the original source (i.e. conversation pair). Then, one of the human annotators manually reviewed the class labels and makes corrections if needed.

However, labeling at the sentence-level is also challenging because the information that defines the topic (class label) lies in the question and is sometimes followed by a short answer, e.g. Table 4 example 1. We also observe the opposite scenario where the answer holds the context, e.g. Table 4 example 2, and scenarios where the information lies in both the question and the answer, e.g. Table 4 example 3. So, it is understood that without pairing the questions with their corresponding answers (or being aware of the context provided by the question or the answer), it is challenging even for human annotators to label these sentences individually. However, We also observe that a

[2]https://www.nltk.org/

question is commonly followed by its corresponding answer in the form of a non-interrogative sentence. Therefore, we use the following approach to overcome the above challenge.

We first combine the grammatical rules of the English language in forming a question (British Council, 2019) and spaCy[3], an industrial-strength natural language processing API, to identify the questions in the transcript. Then, to preserve the context, we pair each question with the following non-interrogative sentence and combine them into a single example. In other words, Model 2 training instances can be single sentences or a conversation pair or anything in between. Several examples of Model 2 dataset is shown in Table 5. These examples correspond to the Model 1 examples depicted in Table 2.

#	Question-answer pair	Class Label
1	Doctor: How old are you? Patient: 23.	Client Details
2	Doctor: Who do you take? Patient: I take Ibuprofen.	Medical History
3	Doctor: What is your name? Patient: Name is a game.	Chief Compliant

Table 4: Question-answer pair dependency.

2.3.3 Machine learning models

To explore the feasibility of classifying information from digital transcripts, we train separate supervised learning classifiers using both training datasets (i.e. Model 1 and Model 2). Specifically, since each instance is annotated with exactly one class label (out of six), we model this as a multi-class problem and use the one-vs-rest (Bishop, 2006) classification strategy.

We apply Support Vector Machines (SVMs) as our machine learning algorithm (which was found to be the best performer in an initial study in comparison with a few other popular machine learning algorithms: k-Nearest Neighbors, Naïve Bayes, Decision Tree, Neural Networks – data not shown). We use stop word removal and lemmatization for pre-processing and Bag-of-Words model for feature extraction. We use sci-kit learn (Pedregosa et al., 2011) python machine learning library for implementing these models. For our preliminary experiments reported in this

paper, we do not use any model checking or parameter tuning and use default settings.

2.3.4 Task 2: Formal text generation

Due to the error-prone nature of Model 1 training data described above, we exclusively use Model 2 training data for the formal text generation. The high-level idea is that in order to generate a case note for an unseen transcript, we first segment the transcript at the Model 2 granularity and predict the EHR categories using the Model 2 classifier. Then instances are grouped based on their predicted EHR categories. Generating case notes with sentences as they appear in the transcripts (i.e. verbatim) will result in redundant case notes that will be difficult to search for important information. An assertive sentence generated by gathering information from a question-answer pair will be easier to read and concise. Therefore, for each category, a formal written version of the text is generated using the method described below. We ignore 'Others' category in our current setup because they represent irrelevant information and any information under this class is likely not important for case note.

In order to generate formal text from an instance, the entire text needs to be rewritten using an assertive sentence, subject in third person singular form, correct tense, verb form and sentence structure. We concatenate each piece of formal text within the category to form a paragraph. Thus, our method results in generating a case note composed of five paragraphs corresponding to the first five EHR categories.

As illustrated in Figure 3, our method generates formal text in several steps. As mentioned above, a sample can be either a sentence or a question-answer pair (as depicted in Table 5). First, we identify the number of sentences in the example text. Examples composed of a single sentence (e.g. Table 7, examples 1-3) requires minimal processing to generate formal text. We use part-of-speech tagging from python module spaCy to identify the subject, main verb and the auxiliary verb(s) of the sentences. If the subject is a first (I) or second person (you), the subject is replaced with the third person singular form (he/she). Clinicians typically collect personal information, such as name, gender and contact information, prior to their conversation or appointment and so they can be fed into our model as input to generate accurate case notes.

[3]https://spacy.io/

No.	Example	Class Label
1	How many voices do you hear? Two.	Chief Complaint
2	They talk all the time.	Chief Complaint
3	Your record shows that you take antidepressants pills regularly.	Medical History
4	Do you hang out with your parents, co-workers or friends? Do you talk to them? Sometimes I hang out with my mom.	Social History
5	Yes, I talk to my co-workers but only for work.	Social History
6	I used to have a friend who moved couple months ago and we don't talk anymore.	Social History

Table 5: Examples in Model 2 training data.

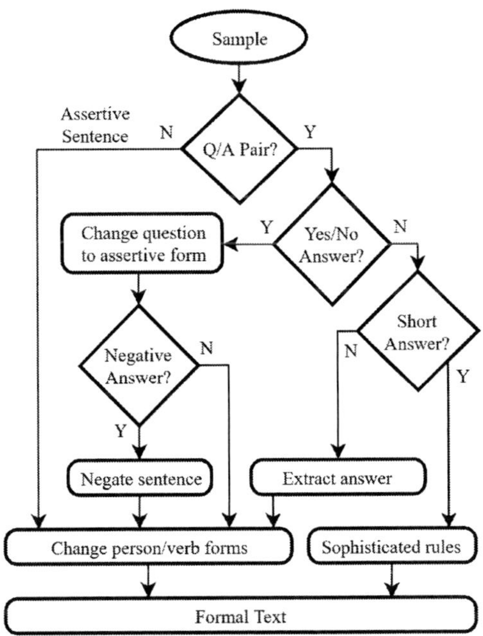

Figure 3: An overview of formal text generation steps.

If the sentence contains auxiliary verb(s), the first auxiliary verb is replaced with its third person singular form, e.g. *am* with *is*, and the second auxiliary verb, if any, and the main verb are kept as they are. If the sentence does not contain any auxiliary verbs, the proper form of the main verb depends on the tense of the sentence. If the sentence is in the present tense, the main verb is replaced with its third person singular form, e.g. *run* with *runs*. For sentences in the past tense, the main verb is kept unchanged since the form of the verb is the same for all persons, e.g. *took*. A sentence in future tense contains at least one auxiliary verb, *shall* or *will*, and therefore our method processes the sentence as a sentence in the present tense; there is no need to add any additional func-

tionality to cover this tense.

If an instance is composed of multiple sentences, the last sentence is always a non-interrogative sentence and is the answer to the question posed in the very first sentence. In this case, the formal text depends on both the question and the answer. If the answer starts with an affirmation or negation word (e.g. yes, no, yeah, never), the question is changed to an affirmative or negative sentence, respectively, and the assertive sentence is added as a separate sentence after removing the leading affirmation or negation word (e.g. Table 7, examples 4-5). If the answer does not start with any affirmation or negation word, the answer is further analyzed to see whether it is a short answer. If not, the question text is ignored and the answer text is returned as the formal text (e.g. Table 7, example 6).

In the case of short answers, an answer alone does not provide the full context to construct the formal text and we need to rely on both the question and the answer. For e.g. the wh- questions (e.g. when, who) are usually followed by a relatively short answer that requires context from the question text as well. This required more sophisticated rules and we are presently working on generating formal text for this scenario. Examples and the intended "ideal" formal text for them are given in Table 8.

While generating formal text, all first and second person pronouns, regardless their position, are replaced with their third person singular form and the verbs are also replaced with its third person singular form, where applicable. Regular expressions are used to remove leading words (e.g. ok, right, yes, and, but, hmm) from the assertive sentences that have no importance to be included in the formal texts. This functionality was implemented using NodeBox[4] Python library.

2.4 Experimental setup and metrics

In terms of Task 1, we evaluate our supervised machine learning models using 5 fold stratified cross-validation and the performance is reported using the AUROC (Area Under the ROC Curve) scale (Bewick et al., 2004). A score of 1 corresponds to the performance of an ideal classifier whereas a score of 0.5 relates to the performance of a random classifier. Because Task 2 (formal text generation aspect) of the project is a work-in-progress, we highlight the scenarios that our model is able to handle and mention the more challenging scenarios in future work.

3 Results and Discussion

In an initial experiment, we assessed the performance of Model 1 and Model 2 training data using the 13 synthetic transcripts. According to our preliminary results, SVMs with linear kernel performs the best with a macro-average AUROC score of 79% for Model 1. For Model 2, the SVMs classifier achieves a macro-average AUROC score of 81%. However, note that these numbers are not directly comparable because Model 1 training instances are different from that of Model 2. Still, this suggested that Model 2 is superior in performance. This is intuitive because Model 2 training data is a more refined dataset as described previously. This observation, coupled with the fact that Model 2 data are more conducive to formal text generation, we used Model 2 training data for the rest of the experiments.

Next, we assessed the performance of Model 2 using all the transcripts (i.e. 13 synthetic and 5 AS transcripts). There is a clear performance dip (0.81 vs. 0.76) when the AS transcripts are added to the training data. This is intuitive because we believe the AS transcripts may have lead to data that is harder to generalize for the classifiers. The reason is that the majority of them is associated with multiple presenting conditions and hence the content of the questions and answers may be broader than synthetic transcripts. Also, the language characteristics between the synthetic and AS transcripts have a noticeable difference according to Table 1. However, this provides valuable insight into the importance of the robustness of the classifier. In

other words, caution must be exercised when synthetic data are used for training machine learning models. Note that we did not conduct a separate experiment with only the AS transcripts because the number of examples for some of the ill-represented classes were deemed inadequate.

Class Label	AUROC	STDEV
Chief Complaint	0.74	0.02
Client Details	0.73	0.04
Family History	0.77	0.04
Medical History	0.78	0.07
Others	0.84	0.03
Social History	0.67	0.06
Macro-average	0.76	

Table 6: Performance of Model 2 training data using all transcripts (13 artificial and 5 AS). Performance collected through 5-fold cross validation, repeated 10 times.

We observe that the performance for the individual semantic topics (EHR categories) fall in the range of 0.67 (Social History) and 0.84 (Others) as depicted in Table 6. But there is no correlation between the class distribution and the performance as evident from Table 3. Overall, these numbers suggest that the words of the transcript are reasonably informative for differentiating EHR categories but there is definitely room for improvement. One such improvement may come from focusing on the *type* of the words in addition to their lexical value. This view is supported by the top 5 tokens identified by the classifier as the most important tokens for each category (Table 9). For example, many of the top words for Family History are names of family members. We also emphasize that the performance reported is from models that work with BoW features and default parameter values, suggesting that the use of a comprehensive feature/ model selection procedure would likely yield better results.

As mentioned above, our formal text generation module is able to handle the scenarios listed in Table 7. However, instances in which the context lies in both the question and the answer (e.g. Table 4 example 3) are clearly more challenging and hence would require sophisticated rules. In such cases, the challenge is to extract information from both the question as well as the answer and to form an assertive sentence using the combined information. We are currently working on this scenario.

---

[4]https://www.nodebox.net/code/index.php/Linguistics

No.	Example	Generated Formal Text
1	I do not seem to be coping with things.	He does not seem to be coping with things.
2	I woke up about 4 am last night.	He woke up about 4 am last night.
3	My sister said I should come.	His sister said he should come.
4	Do you have any sort of hallucination and delusion? No.	He does not have any sort of hallucination and delusion.
5	Has this been going on for some time? Yeah, a few months really.	This has been going on for some time. A few months really.
6	Ok, so what is brought you here today? My sister's noticed, I am just a bit fed up really with some mood swings.	His sister's noticed, he is just a bit fed up really with some mood swings.

Table 7: Formal Text Generation: example inputs and the generated text.

No.	Example	Ideal Formal Text
1	Where do you work? A shop near the mall.	He works in a shop near the mall.
2	When did you wake up last night? It was before 4.	He woke up before 4 last night.
3	When did that happen? Then I was 10.	That happened when he was 10.
4	How often do you exercise? Not that much, I play basketball on Mondays and go for a run on Wednesdays and Saturdays.	He does not exercises much. He plays basketball on Mondays and goes for a run on Wednesdays and Saturdays.
5	Which color shall we use? Red, use red.	We shall use red.
6	In what way does he push her? Not like with hands, just ignores her to make her mad.	He does not push her with hands, just ignores her to make her mad.

Table 8: Formal Text Generation: challenging examples (requiring sophisticated rules) and their *ideal* formal text.

Class Label	Top five features
Chief Complaint	percent, stuff, feeling, number, feel
Client Details	meet, learned, write, pack, style
Family History	cousin, supportive, dad, married, family
Medical History	teen, asthma, dr., prozac, advair
Others	lab, ok, let, right, thank
Social History	comment, wellbutrin, racist, share, friend

Table 9: List of top five features per category used by the machine learning classifier.

Table 8 depicts examples from this scenario and the ideal formal text that must be generated.

4 Conclusion and Future Work

In this work, we focus on the problem of automatically generating case notes from digital transcripts of doctor-patient conversations, using a two-step approach: (1) predicting EHR categories and (2) generating formal text. On the task of predicting semantic topics for segments of the transcripts, we develop a supervised learning model while for the subsequent task of generating a formal version of the text from those segments, we develop a natural language processing model. According to preliminary experimental results obtained using a set of annotated synthetic and real-life transcripts, we demonstrate that our two-step approach is a viable option for automatically generating case notes from digital transcripts of doctor-patient conversations.

However, as noted previously, this is an ongoing project. The immediate attention is paid to handling the case of generating case notes for examples related to short answers given in Table 8. Due to the complexity of this scenario, sophisticated rules that make use for entities identified in the text must be utilized. We plan to transcribe authentic doctor-patient interactions and train a new classification model using these transcripts. We also intend to build a prototype and send it to clinicians for testing using PDQI-9 (Stetson et al., 2012) to check the quality of our generated case notes.

5 Acknowledgements

We like to thank Matt Kuntz from NAMI Montana and CMHRR at Montana State University for his valuable contributions in bringing forth the vision, providing insight as well as assisting with gold standard data. We would also like to thank Cheryl Bristow from NAMI Montana for generating the synthetic transcripts and assistance in annotating transcripts.

References

Viv Bewick, Liz Cheek, and Jonathan Ball. 2004. Statistics review 13: receiver operating characteristic curves. *Critical care*, 8(6):508.

Christopher M Bishop. 2006. *Pattern recognition and machine learning*. springer.

British Council. 2019. Questions and negatives. *Learn English British Council, retrived from: https://learnenglish.britishcouncil.org/en/english-grammar/questions-and-negatives*.

Hsiao and Hing. 2014. Use and characteristics of electronic health record systems among office-based physician practices: United states, 20012013. *NCHS Data Brief, No 143. Hyattsville, MD: National Center for Health Statistics*.

David R Kaufman, Barbara Sheehan, Peter Stetson, Ashish R Bhatt, Adele I Field, Chirag Patel, and James Mark Maisel. 2016. Natural language processing-enabled and conventional data capture methods for input to electronic health records: a comparative usability study. *JMIR medical informatics*, 4(4).

Ronilda C Lacson, Regina Barzilay, and William J Long. 2006. Automatic analysis of medical dialogue in the home hemodialysis domain: structure induction and summarization. *Journal of biomedical informatics*, 39(5):541–555.

Miroslav Nagy, Petr Hanzlicek, Jana Zvarova, Tatjana Dostalova, Michaela Seydlova, Radim Hippman, Lubos Smidl, Jan Trmal, and Josef Psutka. 2008. Voice-controlled data entry in dental electronic health record. *Studies in health technology and informatics*, 136:529.

Thomas H Payne, Sarah Corley, Theresa A Cullen, Tejal K Gandhi, Linda Harrington, Gilad J Kuperman, John E Mattison, David P McCallie, Clement J McDonald, Paul C Tang, et al. 2015. Report of the amia ehr-2020 task force on the status and future direction of ehrs. *Journal of the American Medical Informatics Association*, 22(5):1102–1110.

Fabian Pedregosa, Gaël Varoquaux, Alexandre Gramfort, Vincent Michel, Bertrand Thirion, Olivier Grisel, Mathieu Blondel, Peter Prettenhofer, Ron Weiss, Vincent Dubourg, et al. 2011. Scikit-learn: Machine learning in python. *Journal of machine learning research*, 12(Oct):2825–2830.

Peter D Stetson, Suzanne Bakken, Jesse O Wrenn, and Eugenia L Siegler. 2012. Assessing electronic note quality using the physician documentation quality instrument (pdqi-9). *Applied clinical informatics*, 3(2):164.

Byron C Wallace, M Barton Laws, Kevin Small, Ira B Wilson, and Thomas A Trikalinos. 2014. Automatically annotating topics in transcripts of patient-provider interactions via machine learning. *Medical Decision Making*, 34(4):503–512.

Clinical Data Classification using Conditional Random Fields and Neural Parsing for Morphologically Rich Languages

Razieh Ehsani, Tyko Niemi, Gaurav Khullar and Tiina Leivo
Digital Workforce Services Oy, Helsinki, Finland
`{name.lastname}@digitalworkforce.fi`

Abstract

Past prescriptions constitute a central element in patient records. These are often written in an unstructured and brief form. Extracting information from such prescriptions enables the development of automated processes in the medical data mining field. This paper presents a Conditional Random Fields (CRFs) based approach to extract relevant information from prescriptions. We focus on Finnish language prescriptions and make use of Finnish language specific features. Our labeling accuracy is 95%, which compares favorably to the current state-of-the-art in English language prescriptions. This, to the best of our knowledge, is the first such work for the Finnish language.

1 Introduction

Processing and mining unstructured data is a major contemporary challenge. Automated methods reduce human labor and increase accuracy and proficiency. Application of such methods revolutionized many processes in the healthcare sector by eliminating huge amounts of manual work needed to process archive files. Automated processing of past patient data, such as prescriptions, allows easy digital access to patient records and allows healthcare practitioners to quickly inquire about family history, past medication usage, and other important data.

A large number of medical archives are in text format. Prescriptions, clinical reports, and other clinical texts are widely available but the problem with most of these texts is that they are unstructured and cannot be processed into a structured database directly. Extracting information from these is an important data mining problem called clinical text analysis.

In this paper, we will introduce an approach to extract entities from prescriptions. These entities are dosage, dosage unit and frequency. All prescriptions are in the Finnish language. Finnish is an agglutinative language with rich derivational and inflectional morphology. Morphemes mostly come afterword stem as suffixes and phonetics may also change depending on the morphemes. Finnish has complex vowel harmony and consonant gradation processes which causes large variations in each word stem.

This paper is organized as follows: In Section 2 we briefly introduce some important works as related works. Section 3 is about data that we used for training and also is about prepossessing step. In Section 4 we give information about the model and approach that we used in the paper. In Section 5 we present experimental results and we discuss over different tests. In Section 6 we describe postprocessing step for mapping extracted information from prescriptions to the standardized master table data. Finally in Section 7 we conclude this paper.

2 Related work

CRFs are widely used in agglutinative language processing and have good accuracy when linguistic features are used (Yıldız et al., 2015), (Ehsani et al., 2012).

Here we list some of the existing tools in medication extraction. MedLEE (Friedman, 2000) is one which uses handwritten rules for extracting and encoding and structuring clinical information using free-form texts like patient reports. MetaMap (Aronson and Lang, 2010) also is a rule-based tool which extracts medication names by querying in the Unified Medical Language System (UMLS) Metathesaurus (Bodenreider, 2004).

Patrik et.al. (Patrick and Li, 2009) uses CRFs and also rule based approach to extract information form i2b2 data (Uzuner et al., 2011). Halgrim et.al. (Li et al., 2010) uses CRFs with simple fea-

Proceedings of the 2nd Clinical Natural Language Processing Workshop, pages 149–155
Minneapolis, Minnesota, June 7, 2019. ©2019 Association for Computational Linguistics

tures like n-grams and length of words over a small dataset from i2b2 task. They use a rule-based algorithm to improve the accuracy of CRF classification.

Another work (Tao et al., 2017) is also related to the same i2b2 shared task. They use CRFs to extract dosage unit, dosage and frequency. They show that CRFs performs better than other classifiers. They also try adding word embedding to their model but there is no significant improvement in dosage, dosage unit and frequency labeling. They employ POS tags of tokens besides some categorical features.

3 Data and preprocessing

Our training data contains 9692 prescriptions. We annotate these prescriptions to 4 categories: i) Dosage, which shows the amount of dosage of medication ii) Dosage unit gives the unit of medication, like "tablet" iii) Frequency of using dosage can be more than one token and iv) Comments category is for all other tokens in prescription. We annotated data manually by Finnish native speakers and with the supervision of healthcare professionals.

As mentioned before, working with the Finnish language brings its own challenges, we now discuss these in more detail. Beside compound words, rich morphology and phonology of Finnish language means that the same root word can appear in vastly different forms in texts. In addition to that, the colloquial patient-friendly language of the prescriptions means that they don't perfectly follow grammatical rules or spelling.

For example, the word "tabletti", (tablet in English), can appear like "tbl", "tabl", "tablettia" or "tb" and word "annos" (dose in English) can appear in different compound words like "annospussi" (dosage bag in English), "annosruisku" (syringe in English) ,"annossuihke" (dosage spray in English), "annosmitta" (measurement cup) when word "annosmitta" itself can appear in different grammatical forms like : "annosmitallinen" (a measuring cup's worth in English), "annosmitallista" (partitive form of "annosmitallinen"), "annosmittaa" (partitive from), "annospussillista" (partitive form of annospussi) and "annostelumitallinen" (portioning measurement unit in English). In many cases, we also have "dosage" and "unit name" joined together without space character in between. For example, most doctors write

"1 tabletti" as "1tabletti". All these listed difficulties necessitate a robust prepossessing step before the actual labeling.

4 Model and feature extraction

This section is about model creation using CRFs and feature extraction steps.

4.1 Model

Conditional random fields (CRFs) (Lafferty et al., 2001) is a powerful method to solve labeling problem in a sequence of input word tokens. CRF models the conditional probability of a sequence of labels with respect to the input sequence. It takes into account the sequential relations between labels as well as the relations between a label and its corresponding input token. The inference is done by finding the most probable label sequence given input features, this holistic nature implies consistency, as opposed to the case where one would label each word (or n-gram) individually and separately. Here we use it to model prescription entities (dosage, dosage unit, frequency) using various linguistic and categorical features. We use Crfsuite C++ library for the implementation of our method (Okazaki, 2007). Crfsuite provides fast training and labeling and uses the standard feature templates.

4.2 Features

We make use of both linguistic as well as categorical features for the modeling problem. Table 1 lists defined feature templates that we use. Categorical features are created using two lists, first is the list of dosage unit while second is the list of frequency identifier names. Both lists are taken from a predefined list in the health care system for regular prescriptions. Naturally, these lists do not contain all possible form of dosage unit or frequencies, as we mentioned in previous section, dosages and frequencies can appear in different grammatical forms or as abbreviations or even typos.

Due to the rich morphology of the Finnish language, there is a relation between morphological categories and label output. We need the morphological analysis of prescription text to make use of this relation. In order to obtain this morphological analysis, we used Turku dependency parser (Kanerva et al., 2018). Turku dependency parser is a neural parsing pipeline for segmenta-

Identifier	Feature	Definition
F0	p_i	Current POS
F1	p_{i+1}	Next POS
F2	p_{i-1}	Previous POS
F3	c_i	Current case
F6	g_i	Current is a number, binary
F7	g_{i+1}	Next is a number, binary
F8	s_i	Current is in dosage unit list, binary
F9	s_{i+1}	Next is in dosage unit list, binary
F10	s_i	Current is in frequency list, binary
F11	r_{i+1}	Next is in frequency list
F12	r_i	Current root
F13	r_{i+1}	Next root
F14	r_{i-1}	Previous root
F15	r_{i+2}	Second next root

Table 1: List of features templates

tion, morphological tagging, dependency parsing and lemmatization for the Finnish language. We use morphological tagging outputs of Turku dependency parser in this work. There is a relation between output labels and morphemes. For example, dosage are numbers and POS tag "NUM" (number) refers to being number. Feature IsNumber is a binary feature in cases that POS tag is not "NUM" but token includes numbers like ranges. The Finnish language has very rich noun cases. Often there is a relation between the case of a token in prescription and its output label. Table 2 shows the percentage of tokens in prescriptions that have a specific case for each label. In Finnish, cases indicate the syntactic function of a noun in the sentence. The case markings are suffixed to the end of the token. Thus, the presence of a case marking in the token can give information about the label like frequency. Because frequency is mostly related to time or duration, when the token has "Adessive" case. Adessive case corresponds to prepositions "on" or "at" in English. Second informative feature for label frequency is "Inessive" which corresponds to "in" in English. Case "Allative" ("onto") has very small relation with being frequency.

5 Experimental Results

In this section, we show the experimental results for our proposed CRFs based tagging method. We tested the model using 10-fold cross-validation. In order to assess the importance of different elements of our proposed model, we train a sequence of classifiers of increasing complexity. We start with a memorization classifier, where each token is labeled individually by looking up the most frequent label it is associated with in the training data. This baseline method corresponds to a 0-order CRF with the word surface forms as the only feature. The results of this baseline classifier are shown in Table 3. Next, we try a CRF with order 1 and surface forms as features. This allows us to measure the effect of enforcing label order consistency. As seen in Table 4, the effect varies for each label, e.g. dosage labeling shows the biggest improvement over the simple memorization method. In particular, numeric tokens are hard to distinguish individually since they can be a frequency or a dosage, but when taken in the context of the token sequence they are much easier to classify. Without other more complicated features, F1 measure is over 90%, this shows that CRFs are very powerful in sequential tagging just by enforcing labeling consistency.

	Precision	recall	F1
Dosage	0.6677	0.8460	0.7464
Dosage unit	0.9562	0.9707	0.9634
Frequency	0.8361	0.9006	0.8672
Comments	0.9541	0.8337	0.8898
Macro-average	0.8535	0.8877	0.8667

Table 3: Baseline results

Case	Dosage	Dosage unit	Frequency	Comments
Adessive	0	0	84.4	15.3
Inessive	0	0	81.7	18.2
Instructive	0	0	78.5	21.4
Partitive	0	21.5	62.3	16.1
Translative	0	0	55.8	44.1
Essive	0	0.8	8.8	90.35
Genitive	0	0.7	8.5	90.63
Nominative	0	20.5	5.9	72.85
Elative	0	1.1	5.8	89.53
Illative	0	0	19	98.0
Allative	0	0	12	97.4

Table 2: Percentage of cases in labels

	Precision	recall	F1
Dosage	0.9686	0.9546	0.9616
Dosage unit	0.9642	0.9601	0.9622
Frequency	0.8909	0.9071	0.8989
Comments	0.9350	0.9303	0.9326
Macro-average	0.9396	0.9380	0.9388

Table 4: CRFs Baseline results

	Precision	recall	F1
Dosage	0.9677	0.9588	0.9632
Dosage unit	0.9733	0.9849	0.9791
Frequency	0.8951	0.9128	0.903
Comments	0.9453	0.9341	0.9397
Macro-average	0.9453	0.9476	0.9464

Table 5: Categorical features results

In Table 5 we show results of tagging for each label when we use just categorical features and the surface form of current token. As before, dosage unit benefits the most from the inclusion of categorical features.

Table 6 shows the result for tagging when we use linguistic features and surface form of the current token. F1 measure of label frequency compared to baseline and categorical feature exhibits a clear improvement. The relation between linguistic features and the tags can be observed simply by counting the associated cases. In Table 2 we show the percentage of certain grammatical cases being labeled with a given tag. It is immediately observed that most of the cases are highly informative for the labels, for example "Adessive" case strongly suggests the label frequency while eliminating the possibilities of dosage and dosage unit. On the other hand, "Translative" case is much less informative in distinguishing between a frequency and a comment; hence we require additional features and the label sequence consistency provided by CRFs to correctly identify them. It is also seen that these cases only provide negative information about the dosage label, instead, the POS tag value of "NUM" is positively associated with that label (not shown in the table).

	Precision	recall	F1
Dosage	0.9780	0.9619	0.9699
Dosage unit	0.9764	0.9806	0.9785
Frequency	0.9219	0.9444	0.9331
Comments	0.9609	0.9510	0.9559
Macro-average	0.9593	0.9594	0.9593

Table 6: Linguistic features results

In Table 7 we show results for the final model with all features. Using previous and next token information has a positive impact on F1 measure.

	Precision	recall	F1
Dosage	0.9822	0.9680	0.9751
Dosage unit	0.9819	0.9924	0.9871
Frequency	0.9253	0.9460	0.9356
Comments	0.9653	0.9542	0.9597
Macro-average	0.9636	0.9651	0.9643

Table 7: All features results

Table 8 show the accuracy for different tests. Item accuracy refers to accuracy of each token's label in prescriptions. Adding more linguistic features clearly improves the accuracy. Instance accuracy is accuracy of all tokens in one prescription that are labeled correctly, i.e. even a single labeling error is counted as an error for the whole prescription. In instance accuracy we observe a remarkable improvement when we add linguistic features.

6 Post processing

In attaining this preferred state of data quality, we would be required to further classify our model results into a set of known categories found in this target information system that are defined as the subsets of natural classes of "dosage frequency" and "dosage unit", an action which we would be calling as conducting the database mapping.

For testing the accuracy of database mapping we developed an automated testing solution that would perform full end-to-end integration testing of the complete solution and simulate possible natural world usage such as concurrent and batch processing of unstructured prescriptions. The automated testing solution would use a set of 3694 hand-labeled prescriptions provided by a third-party actor as the ground-truth with guaranteed labeling accuracy of over 98% if the prescription in question had all classes labeled.

This sequential classification event creates a compound probability problem where the actual model performance can be considered as a priori probability for conducting the database mapping as its performance directly affects the results of database mapping. As a result, post-processing encounters two primary challenges: model labeling error and variance in language-specific syntax as well as semantics.

Language variance was solved by a combination of three different solutions: First we introduced internal orthography for the system by implementing robust rule-based heuristics in preprocessing that would perform spell-correction on input strings by transforming them into a more standardized language e.g. prescription string "tarv 1 1/2 -2 3/4x3 -5 pv:ssä" would be transformed into "1.5-2.75 tablettia 3-5 kertaa päivässä tarvittaessa" (In English, 1.5-2.75 tablets 3-5 times per day if required), thus reducing language complexity with negligible data loss (less than 0.5% in all categories combined). Improvement is seen in Figure 1 as iteration 2 from baseline iteration of 1.

Second, we analyzed results for string frequencies and created stemmed versions of object-relational-mapping (ORM) pair dictionaries, where the key was a stemmed class name e.g. "3 kerta päivä" and the value was in a code representation e.g. "100056" based on string occurrences. Stemming was performed on the same Turku neural parsing pipeline that is used for model generation. By matching stemmed versions of classes and model results we were able to further reduce complexity as demonstrated in Figure 1 as iteration 3.

The third solution was the implementation of approximate string matching, colloquially known as fuzzy matching, based on Levenshtein distance (Yujian and Bo, 2007) between the stemmed input string and stemmed class name. As we can see from Figure 1 iteration 4 this improved our results in "frequency" substantially. This solution had outstanding performance when the class names are relatively short e.g. unit "ml" (in English, ml, abbreviation of milliliter) compared to frequency "3 kertaa päivässä tarvittaessa" (In English, 3 times per day if required). In longer class names we experienced challenges in Hamming distance (Xu and Xia, 2011) conditions, where strings had equal length, but semantically different, class names. For example "2 times per day" and "8 times per day" have a Hamming distance of 1, but this difference has a high risk of the detrimental outcome in a clinical setting from potential under or overdose. Separability of classes was increased by writing out numbers, thus increasing their Levenshtein distance and minimizing the possible occurrences of equal length strings i.e. Hamming distance conditions.

Further on we implemented rule-based heuristics based on observed standard errors from model inference and database mapping functionality to increase our overall accuracy. This was implemented in a form of stepped funnel process, where the incorrectly mapped code representations were gathered in a list that would be processed by a set of heuristics. As a step result average of the system error would be reduced and a new list of incorrectly mapped code representations would be gathered and the process would be repeated recursively until required levels of accuracy would be attained.

For future work we will try semantic based search to solve frequency mapping problem. This can be an ontology based semantic search.

	Baseline	Categorical features	Linguistic features	All features
Item accuracy	0.9312	0.9383	0.9545	0.9588
Instance accuracy	0.6863	0.7100	0.78740	0.7998

Table 8: Item and instance accuracy for different feature sets

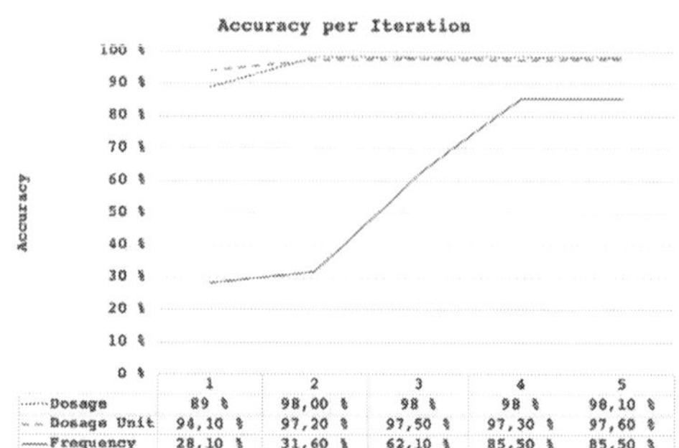

Figure 1: Mapping accuracy

7 Conclusion

In this paper, we used CRFs to model conditional probability between tokens in prescriptions and output labels, dosage, dosage unit, frequency, and comments. This model is for Finnish prescriptions. Since Finnish is an agglutinative language and has rich morphology we define two types of features. First, are categorical features which are binary features of belonging to a certain list of tokens. Second features are linguistic features which are based on the morphological analysis. In previous works, linguistic features were under-utilized. We show that linguistic features are more informative than categorical features. This model is the state of art for prescription extraction problem in the Finnish language. We are using 9692 prescriptions and our reported results are based on 10-fold cross-validation. We show that a robust pre-processing step followed by a CRF based classifier using a combination of linguistic and categorical features yield an excellent labeling accuracy. Finally by implementing heuristics in postprocessing based on observed standard errors in the system we were able to reach clinical standard in classification results.

References

Alan R Aronson and François-Michel Lang. 2010. An overview of metamap: historical perspective and recent advances. *Journal of the American Medical Informatics Association*, 17(3):229–236.

Olivier Bodenreider. 2004. The unified medical language system (umls): integrating biomedical terminology. *Nucleic acids research*, 32(suppl_1):D267–D270.

Razieh Ehsani, Muzaffer Ege Alper, Gulsen Eryigit, and Esref Adali. 2012. Disambiguating main pos tags for turkish. In *Proceedings of the 24th Conference on Computational Linguistics and Speech Processing (ROCLING 2012)*, pages 202–213.

Carol Friedman. 2000. A broad-coverage natural language processing system. In *Proceedings of the AMIA Symposium*, page 270. American Medical Informatics Association.

Jenna Kanerva, Filip Ginter, Niko Miekka, Akseli Leino, and Tapio Salakoski. 2018. Turku neural parser pipeline: An end-to-end system for the conll 2018 shared task. In *Proceedings of the CoNLL 2018 Shared Task: Multilingual Parsing from Raw Text to Universal Dependencies*. Association for Computational Linguistics.

John Lafferty, Andrew McCallum, and Fernando CN Pereira. 2001. Conditional random fields: Probabilistic models for segmenting and labeling sequence data.

Zuofeng Li, Feifan Liu, Lamont Antieau, Yonggang Cao, and Hong Yu. 2010. Lancet: a high precision medication event extraction system for clinical text. *Journal of the American Medical Informatics Association*, 17(5):563–567.

Naoaki Okazaki. 2007. Crfsuite: a fast implementation of conditional random fields (crfs).

Jon Patrick and Min Li. 2009. A cascade approach to extracting medication events. In *Proceedings of the Australasian Language Technology Association Workshop 2009*, pages 99–103.

Carson Tao, Michele Filannino, and Özlem Uzuner. 2017. Prescription extraction using crfs and word embeddings. *Journal of biomedical informatics*, 72:60–66.

Özlem Uzuner, Brett R South, Shuying Shen, and Scott L DuVall. 2011. 2010 i2b2/va challenge on concepts, assertions, and relations in clinical text. *Journal of the American Medical Informatics Association*, 18(5):552–556.

Zeshui Xu and Meimei Xia. 2011. Distance and similarity measures for hesitant fuzzy sets. *Information Sciences*, 181(11):2128–2138.

Olcay Taner Yıldız, Ercan Solak, Razieh Ehsani, and Onur Görgün. 2015. Chunking in turkish with conditional random fields. In *International Conference on Intelligent Text Processing and Computational Linguistics*, pages 173–184. Springer.

Li Yujian and Liu Bo. 2007. A normalized levenshtein distance metric. *IEEE transactions on pattern analysis and machine intelligence*, 29(6):1091–1095.

Author Index